HOW TO CLEAN EVERYTHING

HOW TO CLEAN **everything**

Alma Chesnut Moore

Edited and adapted by Honor Wyatt

Drawings by Glan Williams

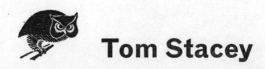

Tom Stacey

First published in U.S.A. in 1952

This edition published in 1972
by Tom Stacey Ltd., 28–29 Maiden Lane, London WC2E 7JP England
Second impression 1973

ISBN 0 85468 189 2

Printed in Great Britain by
C. Tinling & Co. Ltd, London and Prescot

CONTENTS

Introduction

This book is for women who dislike housework but like nice homes. Though obviously it will be useful for brides, it was not written especially for them, but for those of us with growing families who must be efficient or go under.

Cleaning is just one aspect of the role we play, and we want to finish it fast. We get more of a kick out of discovering the world with our children, playing umpire, psychologist, interior decorator, gardener, and in being a companion to our husbands.

When we are reminded that we live in an era of labour-saving devices and packaged products that have practically eliminated housework, we tend to smile rather sourly. Naturally things are not the same as they were in our grandmother's day. But, with due respect to her, we have more interests and duties outside the home and less help in it. We know, too, that each new material and gadget brings its special problem and if we do not know how to treat the new textiles and special cloth finishes, how to handle plastics and coddle the dishwasher, it will be cash out of a hard-pressed budget. Housekeeping has become scientific.

In the wake of the confusing array of new materials we face a flood of 'super' cleaners which are supposed to clean everything 'like magic'. They go by trade names and some of them are wonderful, but we don't know what they really are and not always what they do best.

Every woman knows that there is no one cleaner for everything and that what is good for one material may destroy another. And every woman also knows that there is no 'magic' in cleaning anything ... just knowledge of what to use and how to use it.

This knowledge has never been obtainable in a single volume. Furthermore, it is not easy to get. Experts in different fields are often reluctant to part with information which they consider part of their stock in trade, but not reluctant to disparage our ability to follow instructions. They say we don't know one material from another and that we 'wreck the stuff'. To these charges I am obliged to answer that they are often right. It is not easy to tell one kind of rayon from another, Orlon from silk, some synthetics from leather. As for following directions, I must add that the directions are often at fault, and that if we are going to 'wreck the stuff' by our ineptitude, we might as well wreck it following directions that are correct.

It is true, as charged by one authority, that we have attempted to boil our own linseed oil, to clean oil paintings with sliced potato and cut onion and to give sparkle to platinum by soaking it in bleach. But this is the kind of misinformation that is sometimes given out in the Press and on the air by inexpert advisers, and how are we to know?

Manufacturers' directions should be read carefully and followed exactly, but often they are buried so deep among laudatory paragraphs that we have difficulty in finding them. Sometimes the print is so small that we skip it rather than hunt for a magnifying glass. And what about those wavy directions on the insides of bottle labels? Directions tend to get lost too no matter how carefully we file them.

I doubt if any expert could do much better than we do if he received as little training. Women contemplating marriage and a family should perhaps take courses in plumbing, electrical engineering and household chemistry, among other things. But this is an ideal, difficult to achieve. So most of us sail into the world's most difficult job on a rosy cloud, to the accompaniment of soft music and flowers, absolutely ignorant of all the problems soon to face us. How close upon the wedding ring, very often, come not only the dirty dishes but the nappies. Just thinking about it all is what makes older women cry at weddings.

This book supplies concise information about different articles and materials and their care. It has been checked and counterchecked with multiple sources for accuracy and completeness and, finally, by a qualified chemist.

The alphabetical arrangement is intended to make it easy and quick to use, and the type was selected to avoid eyestrain. Special sections give directions for treating stains, controlling pests and using cleaning agents.

HOW TO CLEAN EVERYTHING is not intended to convert women into demon housewives. Consult it as you would your cookery book, when in doubt or faced with a special problem.

Happily, the best cleaning method is usually the easiest and safest. But please *do* take time to read the directions carefully and follow them exactly.

ALMA CHESNUT MOORE

Avoid home accidents

The number of domestic tragedies reported almost daily indicates the danger that lurks in the modern home. An ever increasing array of special cleaners, insecticides and household remedies accumulates on shelves and in cabinets. They make life easier and most of them are harmless when properly used and stored safely. However, each year they take their toll – mostly of toddlers and young children who use their sense of taste as a means of learning.

We can avoid accidents to ourselves and our children by being extremely careful in our use of commercial products and by storing them where inquisitive little hands cannot reach them (or little legs either: even a toddler knows how to pull up a chair in order to gain access to a shelf or cupboard).

1 Keep all medicines in a safe place. Be especially careful with bright colourful tablets, pills and capsules that look rather like sweets.

2 Weed out all unlabelled bottles from your medicine cabinet and discard old prescriptions when the illness is over. (Some chemicals deteriorate with age; some, like iodine, become stronger through evaporation.) Flush the contents of containers down the toilet, then rinse the bottles or crush the boxes and put them in the dustbin. Keep poisonous mixtures in a separate place, preferably locked, and the key removed.

3 Detergents, bleaches, drain cleaners, cleaning fluids, insecticides and polishes – labels intact – should be kept out of reach of small children. Do not store them under the sink or on a shelf con-

taining food. If you buy a 'giant size' do not, for convenience, put small amounts in an old soft drink or other attractive looking bottle. Small children 'read' pictures, and so will not know that a bottle with a pretty picture of oranges in fact contains bleach – until it's too late.

4   Before using any special cleaner, read or re-read the directions on the container and follow them exactly. And do not EVER make the mistake of thinking that because they do a good job separately a mixture will be even better; combinations can be lethal. For example if chlorine bleach is combined with a lavatory bowl cleanser, ammonia, lye, rust remover or oven cleaner, toxic gases are released which can cause severe illness or death. (Many scouring powders now contain chlorine bleach.)

5   Wear rubber gloves when using detergents, strong cleaners, steel wool. Wear canvas gloves when doing rough clean-up work.

6   Paints, solvents, all preparations containing spirit, pesticides, garden sprays and weed killers are dangerous to pets as well as people. Some are both flammable and poisonous. Store them carefully in a cool place and take time to read or re-read the directions before using them.

7   Never keep large amounts of petrol, paraffin or spirit in your home or garage. Keep small amounts only in metal safety containers with tight lids. (Heat expansion can cause a glass container to explode.)

8   Think twice before you make electrical repairs. There are tricks to re-wiring a lamp, splicing a cord or flex, or adjusting an outlet. Unless you know what you are doing, get competent help. Correctly handled electricity is a docile helper. Abused, it can be a malevolent genie.

9   As a precaution against fire, keep your home free of junk. Oily or paint-stained rags are a particular hazard; they can ignite spontaneously. Don't keep unnecessary accumulations of old magazines and papers.

10 KEEP MATCHES, CIGARETTE LIGHTERS and ALL SHARP INSTRUMENTS AWAY FROM CHILDREN.

How to clean and what to use

Acetate Acetate fibres are produced from cellulose and found in nearly all plants. One of the main sources is wood pulp. Purified cellulose is treated with acetic acid to produce cellulose acetate. The cellulose acetate is dissolved in acetone and forced through a spinneret into a shaft containing warm air, where the acetone evaporates, leaving the yarn. Here is the test for identifying acetates. A drop of acetone on a snipping will dissolve an acetate and make blends sticky. But ordinary dry cleaning fluids and bleaches do not harm it.

Acetate combines many of rayon's qualities with lustre and draping quality. It is water absorbent, non-static and colourfast. It can be dyed in a wide range of colours and woven as satin, taffeta, tricot, sharkskin and twill. In blends it appears as brocades, crepes, cords, gabardines and flannels. Acetate fabrics are less absorbent than rayon and therefore dry faster. They are sensitive to heat but some can stand higher heat than others. They resist shrinking and swelling, mildew (discolour only), insects, sunlight, radiator heat, bleaches.

Acetate fabrics can be hand washed or dry-cleaned, depending on their construction, finish and dyes. Some are machine washable. Be guided by the label. If instructions are not provided for washable acetates, follow these directions from a leading manufacturer:

Dissolve a fairly powerful detergent completely in warm (never hot) water and then place the garment in it. Squeeze the water through the garment gently, avoiding any rough handling. Rinse thoroughly in clear lukewarm water. Do not wring or twist it. Roll it in a Turkish towel to absorb excess water, then hang it to dry. (No clothes pegs.) Acetates are best ironed when they are nearly dry. (Like silk they sometimes look spotty if they are sprinkled and ironed.) Set your iron for rayon and press on the wrong side. (On the right side touch it up through a cloth.) A steam iron is best. It is not necessary to remove all the moisture. Let them finish drying on hangers.

Acetate Plastics See *Cellulosics*.

Acoustic Tile A porous material used for ceilings. If painted, treat it like any other painted surface. If unpainted, clean it with a brush or use a standard wallpaper cleaner or rubber sponge. See *Walls and Ceilings (Painted)*.

Acrilan Acrilan is the trade name for a versatile acrylic fibre which is chemically similar to Orlon. To produce it, air and natural gas are combined and polymerized (converted to long-chain giant molecules). A liquid solution is then made and spun into fibre, which is crimped and cut into staple lengths for processing into yarn.

Acrilan is used alone and in blends, in a wide range of colours, for all types of knitted and woven clothing fabrics, for blankets, carpets and rugs, deep-pile fabrics, draperies and upholstery. Acrilan fabrics are soft and warm to the touch and feel like silk or wool, depending on their type. They are completely washable, dry rapidly, retain pleats, keep their shape during wear, and do not shrink.

They resist soil, mildew, insects, and damage from sunlight, and are not harmed by common solvents and a wide range of chemicals. Shrinkage in boiling water is less than one per cent.

Wash or dry-clean Acrilan clothing according to the label. If adequate washing directions are not given, follow those outlined under *Drip Dry*. See also *Sweaters, Blanket (Synthetic)*, *Acrylic Textiles*.

Acrylic Plastics One of ten main branches of the plastics family. Acrylics are sold under the trade names 'Lucite' and 'Plexiglas'. Although light in weight and delicate in appearance, they are resistant to sharp blows and temperature changes. Acrylics can be tinted in a full range of transparent, translucent and opaque colours. Their surface textures too can be varied. Clear acrylics are so absolutely transparent that they can be used for camera viewing lenses and television image magnifiers. Acrylics weather well and can be used outdoors indefinitely. Their water resistance is good.

A decorative advantage is the ability of these plastics to pick up light at an edge and transmit it invisibly around curves and bends to the opposite side or until it reaches a groove. Acrylics are odourless, tasteless and non-toxic. Their burning rate is low.

Lucite and Plexiglas are used for hairbrushes, lamps, clock cases, salad bowls, small tables, decorative shelves, trays, partitions, roofing, handbags, spectacles, bookends, light fixtures, window glazing and picture frames, and other things as well. They should be cleaned with warm water and soap or detergent, rinsed, wiped dry. If the water is too hot the article may soften. Protect acrylic surfaces from lighted cigarettes and all high heat. Ink and many household chemicals will not affect acrylics, but keep cleaning fluids, nail polish and nail polish remover, hair tonics and spirit away.

Do not use abrasives in cleaning acrylics; they scratch the surface. If accidentally scratched, a little wax will help hide the blemish.

Acrylic Textiles The man-made fibres which compose the textile group known as acrylics are made from a versatile chemical compound called acrylonitrile. Sources of this compound are such basic raw materials as air, water, natural gas, coal, petroleum, and limestone. To qualify as an acrylic a fabric must be 85 per cent acrylonitrile. Acrylonitrile is important in the manufacture of synthetic rubber. The commercial processes used to produce it were developed during World War II when sources of natural rubber were cut off and a substitute was crucially important. After the war, acrylonitrile found many additional uses: one was the creation of textile fibres.

To produce textile fibres, acrylonitrile is dissolved in a solvent. It is then extruded (spun into fibre) and the solvent removed.

Acrylic fibres are very strong yet soft and silky to the touch. They have natural warmth and resilience as well as resistance to sunlight and weathering. Acrylic fabrics hang well, wash easily, dry rapidly, and require little ironing. They are more easily dyed than nylon, more absorbent, and of higher bulk. They can be used alone or in blends.

Acrylics are almost shrinkproof. They are resistant to most chemicals, including bleaches and cleaning fluids, and to damage from insects, sunlight, and atmospheric gases. They are sensitive to heat, becoming sticky at temperatures ranging from 300°F to 400°F.

Acrylics are sold under such trade names as Orlon and Acrilan. These are listed separately. For washing instructions (in lieu of a label) see *Drip Dry*, *Blanket (Synthetic)* and *Pile Coats*.

Air-cooled Finish A finish applied to fabrics at the textile factory to keep the spaces between the threads open. Such a finish increases the comfort of summer fabrics. There are no special washing instructions for air-cooled fabrics.

Alabaster A material similar to marble, it is found in various colours, but is most valued when of purest white. Alabaster is soft and can be carved and ground easily to make lamp bases, statuettes and other decorative articles. The finest stone comes from Florence, Italy.

Cleaning instructions are the same as for marble. See *Marble*.

Alloy Instead of being a pure metal, an alloy is a combination of two or more metals. About two thousand seven hundred alloys are now listed. Metallurgists cook them up as we do pies. See *Bronze, Pewter*, etc.

Alpaca Cloth made from the wool of the domesticated South American llama. See *Woollens*.

Aluminium Aluminium is derived from the chemical, alumina, a kind of earth. One-twelfth of the earth's crust is alumina in various compounds, which makes it seem plentiful; but many intricate processes are involved in extracting it for use.

New aluminium utensils can be kept bright and shining for a long time by using mild soap or a detergent and water alone, if care is taken not to burn food in them. Rinse with scalding water and polish with a soft tea towel.

To remove burned or scorched food from the bottom of an aluminium vessel, fill it with water, allow it to boil, then remove the softened food with a wooden spoon or pan scraper. Finish the job with steel wool. Steel wool pads with soap are the best and least damaging for aluminium. Although steel wool scratches the surface to some extent the filaments are so fine that no damage is caused. Coloured aluminium should not go into washing-up machines.

Certain alkaline foods, such as spinach and potatoes, tend to darken aluminium; acid foods, like apples and rhubarb, brighten it without injury to the food.

Lime scale, which forms in kettles in hard water areas, can be loosened with boiling water and vinegar (half and half). Let this stand in the kettle for several hours, or overnight, then scrape out the deposit with steel wool. If necessary repeat the process.

CAUTION: Never use aluminium containers for storing food because chemicals in the food may cause pitting of the metal. There is no danger of food poisoning involved, but badly pitted or dented aluminium is unsanitary and should be discarded. See also *Duralumin, Coffee Maker*.

Amber See *Jewellery*.

Amethyst See *Quartz, Jewellery*.

Andirons Andirons (fire-dogs) and FIRE TOOLS are usually made either of brass or of iron. If iron, clean with a brush or duster and rub occasionally with a cloth moistened with paraffin. This blackens the iron and prevents rusting. If desired, iron fireplace equipment can be finished with special, heat resistant paint, dull or glossy finish, obtainable from household stores.

Brass fittings are cleaned and

cared for like any other articles of this metal. Portions that have become fire-blackened and encrusted with resins from wood will be difficult to restore to their proper lustre, but it can be done. Steel wool is sometimes recommended but is tricky to handle and takes hours of scrubbing. Try fine emery cloth which you can buy at a household store. Rub in one direction. Polish brass afterwards.

Lacquered brass should only be dusted. If the lacquer starts to crack and peel you may want to remove it and, possibly, renew the lacquer. Directions for this are given under *Brass*. Fire screens should be kept dusted. If gummy and soiled, clean them with paraffin (but not in front of the fire!) or wash them with soap or detergent and water, using a brush. See *Brass* and *Iron*.

Angora Angora is a fine yarn or fabric made from the wool of the silky Angora goat. In washing follow the rules for wool. Use lukewarm suds made with mild soapflakes or a synthetic detergent. Rinse carefully, handle lightly. Before shaping it to dry on a Turkish towel, shake it out gently to fluff up the yarn. See *Woollens* and *Sweaters*.

Antiques The routine care of fine antiques is the same as for other objects of similar materials. However, if repairs are required or special cleaning indicated, take a valuable piece to a professional rather than attempt it yourself. Your nearest museum may be able to advise you.

Antistatic Plastics, and fabrics made of silk, wool, and synthetic fibres especially, tend to accumulate static electricity, particularly in dry cold weather. The static charge attracts dust to plastic objects and makes garments cling.

To counteract static build-up in washable clothing add a little liquid detergent fabric softener (for example 'Comfort', 'Stergene').

Clothing provided with an anti-static finish at the factory should be washed with soap or soap flakes because detergents remove the finish.

Artificial Leather See *Leather, Artificial*.

Artificial Rubber See *Rubber* (gloves), and *Spandex*.

Asbestos Asbestos is an indestructible mineral substance of fibrous construction. It is valued in commerce because it cannot be destroyed by fire. Several different minerals are mined as asbestos. It is as heavy as rock. However, it can be separated into delicate silky fibres, some of which are capable of being woven into cloth.

Asbestos is used as a covering for stove and furnace pipes, as a fireproofing material for buildings, for lamp wicks and gas logs, glassworkers' gloves and firemen's clothing. Theatres are safeguarded against fire spreading by asbestos curtains and even rugs. The housewife uses it for mats on the stove, ironing board covers and sometimes mixed with cotton in dishcloths. Wash it with soap and water, rinse and replace it on the board to dry; or wash it on the board with soapsuds and a soft brush. Light scorch stains may be removed by adding household bleach to the washing water. Rinse and allow to dry.

Asbestos on pipes and gas logs can be brushed with a soft brush or vacuum cleaner attachment.

Ash Trays Wash in soapy water, unless made of unglazed pottery (in which case they should be dusted). Polish metal ash trays according to the metal of which they are made.

For a quick clean-up, empty the trays and wipe them with a damp cloth. Very useful at parties is a little device known as a 'silent butler'. It is a very small dustpan with a spring lid.

Asphalt Tile A tile made of asphalt, a kind of mineral pitch, used as flooring especially in basements as it withstands moisture.

Dust asphalt with a dry mop, or with a wet mop wrung out in cool water. Do not use harsh abrasives or strong cleaning powders. Use no oil or wax polishes either liquid or paste. About once a month wash the floor with mild, warm suds, rinse and dry.

Automatic Dryer Clean the exterior of your dryer occasionally by wiping it with a cloth or sponge dipped in warm suds and squeezed out. Rinse with a clean damp cloth or sponge.

If the basket is spotted after drying starched articles, or stained from tinted items, wipe it with a cloth moistened with a chlorine bleach solution and rinse with a clean damp cloth.

After drying a few loads (some manufacturers say after each load), pull out the lint tray and remove the layers of lint. Occasionally clean out the opening below the lint collector (air intake) with a long-handled brush or with your vacuum cleaner.

Do not store clothing in your dryer.

Automatic dryers are permanently lubricated at the factory and never need oiling. In using your dryer, follow the directions provided by the manufacturer. If you have lost these, write for new ones, giving the number of your model.

Automatic Washer See *Washing Machine*.

Avicron Avicron is the trade name for a crimped rayon filament yarn produced for carpets and bedspreads. The crimp cannot be removed by wetting.

Awnings Duck and canvas awnings cannot be cleaned but stains and mildew can be prevented by drying them properly after rain. Do not put them away till they are thoroughly dry. Lower them so as to drain off water which has collected in the folds. Many awnings are treated for mildew resistance.

Awnings should be stored during the winter in a cool dry place. If they are badly damaged the frames can be re-covered. Awnings of the newer synthetic textiles do not weather or mildew.

Baby Clothes For the first five or six months do not include the baby's cotton clothing in the family wash. Launder it separately; also his bed and linen and, separately again, his nappies. Use hot water and a mild detergent or laundry soap. Rinse several times if the water is soft to medium, four times if it is hard. In a washing machine the usual cycle is adequate, but provide an extra rinse. Do not use starch. It is likely to irritate a baby's delicate skin and the clothes are obviously softer without it.

Wash woollens, rayons, silks, and synthetics according to directions given under these headings. Woollen clothing and blankets that have been mothproofed should be washed or dry cleaned before they are used again.

See also *Nappies*.

Bamboo Giant grass. See *Furniture*.

Basement As a precaution against accidents and fire for your own satisfaction, your basement should be kept uncluttered, reasonably clean and orderly. Accumulations of old paper, rags and shavings are an acute fire hazard. Untidy, badly lit stairs may cause a broken leg or hip. So, whether yours is a slick modern basement or an old-fashioned cellar, keep it neat and air it properly.

Air your basement when the air outside is cooler than inside. Keep the window closed during wet or humid weather. Avoid storing things on the floor, where it is likely to be damp. Slatted shelves are best for storage because they allow air to circulate on all sides of articles placed on them. Store paints and painting equipment at a safe distance from any source of heat. They are a fire hazard.

Excessive dampness in a basement can be due to several factors. One is condensation of moisture contained in the air on cool surfaces such as walls, floors, and cold-water pipes. Look for leaking pipes and have them mended. Have the cold-water pipes insulated, and prune any heavy shrubbery that may be impeding the circulation of air in the basement. The most common cause of excess humidity is laundering. Use of an air conditioner can correct this. For a discussion of these, see *Mildew*, p. 147.

Basket A good wetting now and then will prevent basketware from becoming brittle.

Bath The job of cleaning the bath is easier if you use a long-handled brush, made especially for the purpose, and water containing washing soda or other softener, or a synthetic detergent. For a thorough cleaning use a mild scouring powder. Coarse cleaning powders scratch the porcelain enamel finish and make it increasingly difficult to clean.

Clean the fixtures according to the metal of which they are made. See *Chromium, Nickel*, etc.

Light iron rust stains can often be removed by rubbing them with a cut lemon. For more stubborn stains use a 5 per cent solution of oxalic acid (poison) or a 10 per cent hydrochloric acid solution (poison). After applying the acid with a cloth or paper towelling, rinse bath enamel. Copper stains (green) sometimes yield to soapsuds containing ammonia. If stubborn, use oxalic acid as described for iron rust stains. (Dripping taps cause these stains: so install new washers.)

To improve the appearance of an extremely stained or discoloured bath use a mixture of cream of tartar and peroxide. Stir in enough peroxide to make a paste and scrub the bath vigorously, using a small stiff brush. The result will surprise you. Even dark brown stains caused by potassium permanganate baths prescribed for skin infections, disappear quickly and easily under this treatment.

And now for a few don'ts. Don't use the bath for washing venetian blinds or sharp-edged articles which could scratch it. Don't stand in it or place a stepladder in it to wash walls or a window without first protecting the surface with a rug or non-slip mat. Don't use the bath or lavatory as a home photography accessory: photo solutions damage porcelain enamel. Don't let strong solutions of household bleaches, hair bleaches, vinegar or lemon stand for any length of time in a lavatory. Some of these will etch even acid-resistant enamel. Don't fail to rinse the lavatory thoroughly after cosmetic solutions, hair tints, or medicines have been put in it; they can cause discolouration. And don't leave non-slip mats in the bath to dry; some cause permanent stains.

Bedspreads Machine-wash cotton bedspreads and hang them outdoors to dry or put them in a dryer. If you use a clothesline, shake out candlewick and chenille spreads now and then while they are drying to fluff them up. If you double them over the line with the tufts inside, stray breezes will help fluff the tufts by rubbing them gently together. When dry, brush up the tufts with a clean dry stiff handbrush. Do not iron.

If your spread is fringed, you will find it easier to comb out the strands while they are still wet. Crochetted spreads should be stretched gently to their proportions while drying.

Silk and rayon spreads should be dry-cleaned unless the manufacturer's instructions stipulate that they are washable. See *Silk, Rayon.* Launder spreads of synthetic textiles according to fibre. See *Orlon.* For cotton spreads with non-iron finishes see *Permanent Press.*

Bedsprings Box springs are cleaned with a stiff brush, or with upholstery attachments of vacuum cleaners. Metal should be cleaned with a hand brush, duster, or the dusting brush of the vacuum cleaner. If necessary box springs can be scrubbed like upholstered furniture. See *Furniture – Upholstered.*

Bemberg Trade-mark for cuprammonium rayon. See *Rayon.*

B

Blanket (Electric) Don't wash an electric blanket unless the manufacturer's instructions say that it can be done. If so, it can be washed by hand or in a machine by the soak-wash method. It should never be dry-cleaned because solvents used in dry cleaning might damage the insulation on the wires inside. Some laundries specialize in handling such blankets. Ask your laundry about this service and give them the blanket separately. If you want to wash the blanket yourself and instructions are lacking, the following instructions from a leading manufacturer, should be safe for all fabrics.

HAND WASHING: Shake out loose dust gently and soak the blanket for 10–15 minutes in lukewarm suds (100°F), made with a mild synthetic detergent. Occasionally, press the suds through the fabric. Rinse three times in the same way. Squeeze out excess water by hand. Do not wring or twist the blanket.

TUMBLER WASHER: Fill the machine with lukewarm water, add a mild detergent, and run the machine a minute or two to mix it in. Stop the washer. Immerse the blanket and let it soak, *without tumbling,* for 15–20 minutes. Advance the dial and spin off the wash water. Allow the machine to fill with lukewarm water for a deep rinse. Stop the machine and soak the blanket, *without tumbling,* for 2–3 minutes. Spin off the water and repeat the rinse. Advance the dial to the final spin, and spin for 2–3 minutes.

TOP-LOADING WASHER: Fill the machine with lukewarm water, add a mild synthetic detergent, and let the machine agitate briefly to mix it in. Use a delicate fabric setting, if available. Stop the washer, immerse the blanket and let it soak for 15–20 minutes. *Do not agitate.* Advance the dial, spin off the wash water, and allow the machine to fill with lukewarm rinse water. Let the blanket soak for 2–3 minutes. Spin off the rinse water. Repeat the soak rinse. Advance the dial to the final spin. Stop the washer after 2–3 minutes. DRYING: Pull and stretch the blanket gently into shape and hang it over two parallel lines to dry – in the shade. Only use an automatic dryer if the directions for your blanket say it is safe. In any case, such a dryer should be used only if it can be operated without heat. The directions are: Put three or four bath towels in the dryer and heat at the regular setting for five minutes. Turn off the heat. Put the blanket in the dryer and tuck the towels into its folds. Tumble for 10–15 minutes. Remove the blanket (still damp), ease it into shape, and hang it over parallel clotheslines. If clotheslines are not available, spread it over a protected flat surface to dry completely.

CAUTION: Mothproofing agents should not be used on an electric blanket because of possible damage to the wiring. Wrap your clean blanket in a cloth or plastic sheeting and store it in the box it came in.

For complete safety it is a good idea to return the blanket to the manufacturer for a check up periodically, when not in use, either direct or through your dealer. NOTE: Be sure never to buy a secondhand electric blanket. See that your new one is approved by the British Electrical Approvals Board (look for a blue and yellow label).

Blanket (Synthetic) If you do not have instructions for washing your synthetic blanket, follow these directions for 100 per cent Orlon acrylic blankets and for other acrylics such as Acrilan.

Prior to either hand or machine washing, pretreat spots or soiled bindings with a detergent or soap solution. If desired, the bindings can be pressed after the blanket has been laundered. Use a steam iron or a dry iron at a rayon or synthetic setting. Do not iron the blanket itself. The nap can be fluffed with a soft brush.

Machine-wash acrylics in lukewarm suds (100°F) of a synthetic detergent, or soap plus a water softener, for five minutes. Stop the machine after two or three minutes of the final spin-dry cycle. (Use the complete special fabric cycle if it is available.) Remove the blanket and air dry it by hanging it evenly over a clean clothesline. Straighten the blanket and smooth the bindings. If desired, a home dryer may be used. Preheat the dryer for ten minutes at 180°F – 190°F. Tumble the blanket for ten minutes. Remove the blanket from the dryer promptly when it is dry.

If the blanket is washed by hand, work it up and down in the suds until the dirt is removed. Rinse in as many warm rinses as are necessary to remove the suds. Squeeze out or drain away excess water without vigorous wringing or twisting. Dry as described for machine washing.

Union Carbide provides these instructions for all-Dynel blankets. Soak them for ten minutes in warm water (not over 170°F) with soap or detergent. Agitate them in your washer for 1½ minutes (no more). Use a dryer only if the temperature can be kept at 'low' and then to 'damp dry'. If hung when quite damp the wrinkles will fall out. If acetate bindings are pressed do not let the hot iron touch the nap of the blanket.

Synthetic blankets can also be dry-cleaned.

Blanket (Treated Woollen) Some woollen blankets have been treated with finishes that make them completely machine washable. Because the treatment method varies, the safest advice is to follow the manufacturer's instructions. See *Woollens* (*Treated*).

Blanket (Untreated Woollen) Blankets made of wool or wool blends can be washed or dry-cleaned, according to personal preference. If you send them to the laundry be sure you have selected a reliable one and that the blankets are marked for special attention.

If you are washing blankets at home, choose a fine warm day with a light breeze blowing. Wash one blanket at a time. First shake it out lightly to remove loose dust, then pay special attention to spots and bindings. Using a soft brush and lukewarm water, work a mild synthetic detergent into especially soiled portions.

For washing the blanket use the same mild detergent and lukewarm water (95°F – 105°F). Water that is too hot shrinks wool. Do not use a water softener: they are not needed when synthetic detergents are used. Furthermore they are alkaline and harmful to wool fibres. Do not use soap; even the gentlest is mildly alkaline.

Too much handling, rubbing, twisting or agitating in water makes wool mat, pill and roughen. Recommended today for both hand and machine washing of woollen blankets is the 'easy soak' method – better for blankets, easier for you.

Fill your bowl or machine with lukewarm water, remembering

that wool absorbs a great deal. Dissolve in the water enough synthetic detergent to make good suds. Place the blanket in the water and let it soak for fifteen to twenty minutes. Turn the blanket once or twice by hand, then drain away, or spin off the water. Refill bowl of machine for the first rinse. This will also be a soak operation. (Do not operate the machine.) Soak the blanket for about five minutes in the lukewarm rinse water, then repeat.

If a light froth of bubbles remains after the second rinse, do not feel that you must rinse a third time. The bubbles are due to the chemical nature of the detergent, which froths even in the hardest water if the merest trace is present. Actually, the detergent rinses out better than soap.

Spin or drain away the last rinse. It is not important to extract a great deal of water from a blanket before hanging it because woollens drip dry quickly. An automatic dryer can be used with caution to hasten the drying. Put five or six bath towels in the dryer as a buffer load and preheat the dryer for five minutes at a high setting. Add the blanket and tuck the towels into the folds. Let the dryer operate on high heat for ten minutes, then check the blanket. Remove it when it is about three-quarters dry and hang it for complete drying.

Blankets should be hung in the shade on a good tight line, preferably over an old sheet for perfect cleanliness. For maximum drying efficiency hang the blankets lengthwise over parallel lines, placed a foot or two apart. Shake them lightly to fluff the nap. When partially dry, turn them over and shake them out again.

When the blanket is thoroughly

dry, brush up the nap with a clean brush. The warmth of a blanket as well as its appearance, depends to a great extent upon the amount of nap. Press the bindings gently with a warm iron.

Blanket Cover If you use blanket covers on your beds, your blankets won't have to be washed very often. A sheet will do if you don't feel like going to the expense of a special cover.

Bluestone See *Stone Floors*.

Bonded Fabrics Bonded fabrics consist of two or more layers of material, at least one of which is a textile. The purpose of bonding is to give fabrics, especially knitted ones, bulk without weight, and help them to keep their shape. Manufacturing processes vary.

At the time of writing, two methods of bonding are used. The first involves melting one surface of polyurethane (plastic) foam and, while it is molten and sticky, pressing it into a fabric.

Books Don't let your books slump on partly filled shelves if you want to preserve their bindings. Use book ends or brackets. Books should be arranged upright and loosely enough to allow them to be taken out easily without damaging the delicate spines. Place them near the edge of the shelf so the air can circulate behind them. Oversized books, such as atlases, art books and music, may be stacked flat. A library should be neither too dry nor too damp. Too much dry heat will damage leather-backed books and make the pages and bindings of clothbound books brittle. Dampness will cause mildew and other moulds. Bright sunlight will fade the colours of the bindings.

Books can be best dusted with the dusting brush of a vacuum cleaner or with a clean soft paint-brush. Dust outwards from the binding. You may flip the pages to get dust out but don't bang them together.

Leather bookbindings deteriorate from two causes, acidity and lack of oil. Both conditions have been attributed to manufacturing processes but may be due to natural causes – the absorption of acidic gases in polluted air and the gradual destruction of the oil in the leather.

Damage to leather books in good condition can be minimized by replacing the oils lost with use. The treatment *should* begin when the books are new and be repeated every year or two. Emulsions containing four or five ingredients are sometimes used, but the following simple preparations are all effective: saddle soap, a commercial preparation (from shoe repair shops); neat's-foot oil (also from the shoe repair shop) for dull leather: petroleum jelly (from chemists); a mixture of neat's-foot oil and castor oil in equal parts; four parts of lanolin oil (from chemists) to six of neat's-foot oil. To prepare this last dressing warm the lanolin oil slowly in a double boiler until it liquefies and then stir in the neat's-foot oil.

These dressings are best applied with the fingers or palm of the hand, or you can use a small swab of felt, cheesecloth or chamois. Spread the dressing quickly and sparingly over the leather, being careful not to stain the cloth or paper portions of the covers. Rub it in gently until it has been absorbed. Wait several hours, then repeat. Oiling leather usually darkens it slightly, and almost inevitably there are areas where the colour is of unequal depth.

Leatherbound books that have

begun to powder are sometimes improved by lacquering. First smooth the leather very gently, using very fine emery cloth. Pay special attention to where it is powdery or scuffed. Oil can be applied next if desired (it cannot, of course, be applied after lacquering). Light-coloured patches can be touched up with a spirit solution of a suitable leather dye. Prepared lacquers in aerosol-type sprayers are next applied. Select a thin lacquer recommended for leather (cellulose nitrate, acrylic) and spray a thin even coating on the bindings. When the lacquer has dried, apply a second coating. (Do not work near an open flame, lacquers are inflammable.)

Torn pages can be mended with gum tissue, or with strips cut from rice paper or thin onion skin. Many people use transparent sticky tape ('Sellotape' etc.) but, being shiny, one can hardly call such repair 'invisible mending'. Rice paper is not so obvious. Loose pages can be replaced by pasting with a folded strip of paper. After repairs have been done it is a good idea to flank the mended pages with waxed paper before closing the book. This will prevent the pages from sticking together. Press rumpled pages with a warm iron, using a sheet of paper between the page and iron as a precaution against scorching. Valuable books, in bad repair, should be handled by an expert. Your local library can probably recommend one.

Mildew and other moulds are caused by excessive dampness. When moulds begin to form your first step is to dry out the room with some form of heater (electric is dry), with the windows closed. Fresh moulds can be wiped off the bindings with a clean soft cloth.

Mildew on pages can sometimes be wiped off in the same way. Or use a cloth very slightly dampened with white spirit and spread the pages fanwise to dry (but don't do this near your heater). Another method is to dust the stained pages with cornflour (sometimes known as maire starch) or with French chalk. Let the powder remain in the closed book for several days then brush it off. It is sometimes impossible to remove mildew stains from the pages of books. See *Mildew*, p. 147, for ways to *prevent* mildew.

WARNING : Think twice before you have a rare book rebound. If it is a first edition, its value will be considerably reduced.

Bottle Use a detergent, or soap and water and a bottle brush. To remove mineral stains or cloudiness from the bottom of an ornamental bottle (or flower vase), fill it partially with water, add ammonia, and let it stand for several hours or overnight. Then rinse it out.

FEEDING BOTTLES: Milton's cleansing and sterilizing liquid for feeding bottles is well known. Boots also make a special bottle sterilizer. These are used not only for the bottles (bottle brushes are useful for getting inside these) but also for the teats and covers.

Bouclé Knitted or woven fabrics made from looped yarns. Wash as for wool.

Brass Brass is an alloy of copper and zinc. Usually two parts of copper are used to one part of zinc. Formerly the copper was also combined with tin and other base metals.

Tarnished brass is sometimes easier to polish if it is first washed in hot soapsuds. After drying it, remove the tarnish and spots of corrosion by rubbing it thoroughly with a good polish made specially for brass. When it is clean, polish it with a soft flannel cloth or chamois. This will give the brass a bright finish. If a dull finish is desired, substitute for the polish a thin paste made by mixing rotten-stone powder and linseed oil. Wipe off the excess oil and polish with a clean cloth. Rub antique brass with lemon (mineral) oil and polish it softly.

A piece of lemon dipped in salt, or hot vinegar and salt, will remove corrosion from brass. This is an old-fashioned method but one that can be adapted profitably to small ornaments or miniatures that are difficult to clean. Provided they are not decorated with materials that hot water will damage, they can be boiled in water containing salt and vinegar. Or you can use washing soda in the same way. Most of the corrosion will be loosened or removed. You can then finish with brass polish or the impregnated pad with the trade name of 'Duraglit'.

Lacquered brass only needs dusting and, occasionally, washing with light mild suds made with lukewarm water. Rinse and dry. If the lacquer becomes damaged it can be removed with acetone or amyl acetate. Small articles can be covered with boiling water which soaks off the lacquer. To relacquer, polish it to the desired lustre, wipe it with acetone to remove every trace of film, then brush or spray on transparent metal lacquer. This is not an easy job and unless you are skilled in crafts it is better to have your brass redone professionally.

Brass andirons and fire tools that have been long neglected may prove a tough job, owing to burned-in resins from the fire. Fine steel wool (page 188) may be

required for a clean job but will take plenty of time and elbow grease. Easier to handle and very effective is fine emery cloth of the sort used by metalworkers. You can buy it at a hardware, and sometimes at a household store. In using it rub the metal in one direction, not round and round, and when it is clean polish it with brass polish.

After polishing, wash brass thoroughly with soapsuds to remove traces of acid polish and avoid rapid retarnishing.

Brassière If you are fussy about the fit of your 'bra' don't iron it. Replace tired elastic and broken fasteners. Do not use chlorine bleach on brassières with spandex elastic.

Brick Floors, Glazed Dust them with a broom, dry mop or vacuum cleaner. Wash with a sponge or cloth wrung out of warm soapy water. Rinse and wipe dry. For a very dirty floor use one ounce of sodium hydrosulphite (a colour remover, from household stores) dissolved in one gallon of warm water. Waxing is optional.

UNGLAZED: Dust with a brush or broom. Wash with warm water containing one ounce per gallon of washing powder that contains trisodium phosphate, or, equally effective, washing soda. Use a sponge or cloth; rinse thoroughly. If especially dirty you can use a stronger solution, but rinse the bricks thoroughly with clear water. Floors of unglazed brick are sometimes sealed. In this case, self-polishing waxes may be used to provide a gloss and make them easier to clean.

Brick fireplaces that have faded can be cleaned according to the directions given above. The colour can be restored by brushing them over with a cold water paint (consult your paint dealer). Sometimes it is still possible to get 'bath bricks', in various colours, for crushing and adding to water. A special red polish is also sold under the trade name of 'Cardinal'.

Bri-Nylon Trade name of an ICI product. Fluffy and soft to the touch. See *Nylon* and follow instructions on the label.

Brocade A rich fabric, usually of silk, satin or velvet. It is shot through with gold or silver threads and often ornamented with raised designs of leaves, flowers, etc.

Brocades should be dry-cleaned by an expert. To press: place the material right side down on the ironing board and cover it with a piece of thin white cloth or tissue paper. Do not dampen. Press with a warm, never hot, iron.

Bronze Our word 'bronze' comes from the Italian *bronzo*, meaning brass. Today's bronze is an alloy of copper and tin, sometimes containing a little zinc and lead. Formerly this alloy was included in the term 'brass'.

Solid bronze is often given a coating of clear lacquer at the factory to protect the finish. Lacquered bronze needs only dusting and occasional wiping with a damp cloth. Should the lacquer crack or peel, have it redone.

Unlacquered bronze can be washed if required with mild soap or detergent and water. Sometimes hot vinegar is used. Rinse and wipe dry with a clean soft cloth. To brighten bronze, rub it with a dry cloth dipped in whiting or rottenstone powder, or with a polish made for bronze.

Bronze-finished steel is often mistaken for solid bronze. When spots of corrosion appear and a little rubbing reveals a steel base,

then you need bronze lacquer or metal paint. Or the article could be electroplated with a dark copper.

Bronze, an alloy, cannot be applied by electrolysis. However, a new process has been developed recently by means of which molten metals, including alloys, can be sprayed on metal surfaces. Large objects can be touched up by this method or done over very satisfactorily. It is worth looking out for a firm that does this work if you have a nice lamp that needs to be refinished.

Broom A good modern broom is weighted to swing, has a handle that is easy to grip, and sometimes, a built-in device so you can hang it up. A broom should never stand on its bristles if you want it to give good service. If yours is not equipped with a ring for hanging, put a screw hook in the end, or bore a hole through the top of the handle and knot a piece of string through it. New bristle brooms will last longer if dipped in cold salted water before use. This does not apply to nylon and plastic.

Brushes If you are muddling along with an inadequate supply of brushes, the time has come to take an inventory of what you have and investigate the array of new and attractive models available.

There is a special brush for almost every job and the right one will cut down work time. A long-handled bristle brush is handy for porches and certain types of floors. When laundering, a small soft brush is indispensable for removing spots on materials which are damaged by rubbing. A nylon bristle by the sink enables you to use very hot water for washing up as you will not need to put your hands in it. Nylon is also good for bath and lavatory brushes. So keep a good supply and take care of them.

HAIRBRUSHES: Hairbrushes made of animal bristles should be cleaned regularly by washing in warm soapsuds, or suds to which one or two teaspoons of ammonia have been added. Rinse them thoroughly and dry them on a towel placed in the shade, with the bristles down. When they are nearly dry, turn them, bristles up, and place them in the sun if you can find any. A little alum (about half a teaspoonful) in the final rinsing water will stiffen sluggish hair bristles. Hairbrushes with nylon bristles are washed in lukewarm soapsuds and rinsed till the water is clear. Brushes with nylon backs and nylon bristles can be sterilized by boiling.

PAINTBRUSHES: Generally speaking, the material used as a thinner for the paint you are using will clean the brush after you have finished using it. Different types of commercial paintbrush cleaners are on the market. These will do a good job if you follow the directions on the containers carefully. Some have a starch base and contain soda compounds such as trisodium phosphate. Others contain mixtures of paint solvents to enable them to deal with a variety of paints.

Clean your paintbrush directly you have finished using it. Here are some notes for the different types. Brushes used with shellac should be cleaned with spirit then washed with soap and water. Brushes used for water-type paints are cleaned in water, or with water and a detergent. Rinse and hang to dry.

Paintbrushes used with lacquer are cleaned with lacquer thinner, or acetone. Wash with a detergent and hang up to dry.

Brushes used for oil paints, varnishes and enamel are cleaned with turpentine or turps substitute, then washed with water and a detergent. Hang them up to dry.

Brushes used for rubberized and synthetic resin paints, which are mixed with water instead of oil, can be cleaned with water containing a detergent.

Nylon brushes are cleaned in much the same way as other brushes, except that it is a good idea to work out as much of the paint as possible first. Pour a little paint thinner on to the brush and work out the paint on a newspaper or board. Then clean the brush in the thinner. If necessary leave it suspended in the thinner overnight, then work it out in the morning, rinse with clean thinner and wash with a detergent. Do not use spirit to clean nylon brushes, and do not use nylon brushes for shellac or the bristles will soften.

IMPORTANT NOTE: Paintbrushes should always be hung up to dry after being washed. They should never be allowed to soak in any solution containing water or the bristles will be loosened. If your paint project is to be continued within a few days suspend your brush in a jar containing linseed oil and turpentine (this is for oil paint). The mixture may be half and half, or less than half turpentine. The bristles will remain soft and pliable. When you want to use the brush again, wipe the bristles very carefully with a clean cloth, then rinse them with turpentine if required.

It is a good idea to wrap your clean dry brushes in paper or cellophane with the tips exposed, when storing them, as this keeps the bristles straight. Let them lie flat, if stored when dry. Or hang them, bristles down, in a rack.

Buckram A fabric stiffened by impregnating with starch etc. Dry clean only.

Bulbs See *Electric Bulbs*.

Butyrate See *Cellulosics*.

Calico A plain-woven cotton fabric, taking its name from the Indian town of origin. See *Cotton*.

Camel Hair A fabric made from camel and dromedary. Dry-clean only.

Candelabra See *Crystal* and *Lighting Fixtures*.

Candles Soiled or finger-marked candles can be cleaned with a soft cloth moistened with spirit.

Candlesticks Pour warm water into the candleholder to soften and remove old wax. To remove wax from outer surfaces of candlesticks cover your finger with a soft cloth and push the wax off gently with your finger-nail. Never use a knife.

Wash china candlesticks with warm soapy water, rinse and dry. Wash crystal candlesticks in water containing a synthetic detergent. Rinse and polish with a clean, lintless cloth.

Metal candlesticks are cleaned according to directions for the metals of which they are made. Candlesticks of weighted or hollow silver should not be immersed in hot water. Lacquered metal candlesticks need only be wiped with a damp cloth. Hot water and soap will damage the lacquer. See *China, Silver, Brass*, etc.

Candlewick See *Bedspreads*.

Cane Furniture See *Furniture*.

Carafe See *Glass*.

Carpets and Rugs For good appearance and better wear, carpets and rugs should be kept free of surface dust that dims their colours and of the sharp particles of grit which, unless regularly removed, become embedded and cut their fibres. Areas of heavy traffic and random spills can be cleaned up easily if you keep a small carpet sweeper handy. Once a week rugs should be vacuum-cleaned thoroughly. Go over each area at least seven times. Spilled food should be removed promptly and spots and stains should be attended to when they occur, to avoid setting.

At least once a year, carpets and rugs should be shampooed by a professional or at home with one of the appliances designed for the task. Long-handled applicators with roller-type brushes and built-in tanks to hold liquid shampoo are available. By finger-tip control they spread a foam of shampoo evenly over the rug. The foam is allowed to dry, for several hours or overnight. As it dries it draws the dirt to the surface. When the rug is completely dry vacuum the dirt away. Small rugs can be shampooed by hand with special shampoos, but hand-cleaning a large rug or carpet is a back-breaking business and the results are not always satisfactory.

Before attempting to shampoo a rug or carpet yourself, clean it with a vacuum cleaner – on both sides if possible. If you use a carpet shampoo, read and follow exactly the directions on the container. If using a soap lather, test first in an inconspicuous place to make sure the colours are fast, then, with a soft cloth or brush, using a circular motion, clean a small area at a time. Scrape the lather off with a spatula and wipe away the remaining suds with a clean dry cloth. When the entire area has been cleaned, sponge it several times with clean water, taking care not to get it too wet. Finally, wipe with a dry cloth in the direction of the nap.

Absorbent powder cleaners can also be used. Follow the directions on the container.

If the pile of a rug has been crushed by heavy furniture, place a damp cloth over it and apply a hot iron, using no pressure.

Brush the spot briskly. Repeat, if necessary. Use this same method on the front and back of corners and edges that curl.

Stain-causing materials, spilled on rugs or carpets, should be cleaned up promptly as some stains become permanent if allowed to remain even a few hours. Reweaving the area is then the only solution. When a stain is fresh it can often be removed by sprinkling the area with lukewarm water.

For spilled foods and stains of unknown origin, follow this procedure. With a blunt knife or spatula remove the solid part of the stain. Next blot up the liquid with a paper towel or slightly moistened sponge or cloth. Then

sponge the stain with a clean white unstarched cloth, dampened with lukewarm water, working always from the centre of the stain towards the edge. Do not scrub roughly; wipe and pat gently to avoid disturbing the pile. If a spot still shows when the area has

dried completely, sponge it again with a detergent solution (one teaspoon of liquid detergent and one teaspoon of white vinegar in two cups of water). Rinse by sponging with a cloth or sponge squeezed out of clear lukewarm water. Do not get the carpet too wet. Raise the damp part if you can so that the air can circulate, or dry it with an electric fan or the exhaust from your vacuum cleaner. For greasy stains use a cleaning fluid, sponging from the centre of the stain towards the edge.

If the stain requires the use of a special cleaning solution, apply it with a medicine dropper. For difficult or special stains see the section on textile stains. Follow the directions given, using the methods outlined here.

And now, before moving on to special types of carpeting, let's run through some do's and don'ts that apply to them all. *Don't* get rugs or carpets too wet during shampooing, and *don't* let furniture stand on a damp carpet if you can avoid it. If you can't avoid it, *do* slip folded waxed paper under table and chair legs to prevent stains from the casters. (The waxed paper containers in cereal packets will do very well.) *Don't* walk on a dampened carpet. If traffic cannot be prevented, make a path by spreading uncoloured wrapping paper. *Don't* attempt to pull off sprouting ends of yarn. Snip them off with sharp scissors. *Do* snip off fibre ends singed by dropped cigarettes – and sponge the place with detergent solution (and speak sternly to the offender). *Do* turn rugs around now and then so that the wear will be evenly distributed and *do* if possible, move stair carpet up or down a little every year if possible. *Don't* overlook the value of the rubber or plastic gadgets available for putting under casters to keep furniture stationary and to avoid crushing the pile. *Don't* take chances with moths and carpet beetles; protect wool and wool blends with suitable insecticides. (See *Moths – Clothes*.) Cotton rugs and carpeting made entirely of synthetic fibres are not attacked unless spotted with food. *Do* air manageable rugs in the sunshine occasionally, if you can. It freshens them and kills insect larvae.

COTTON RUGS, scatter size, can be washed in your washing machine or in a large bowl if the colours are fast. Use plenty of mild suds made with soap and a water softener, or detergent, and rinse with large amounts of water. Do not wring or twist them but hang them dripping, straight on the line in the shade. Shake chenille rugs out lightly now and then and, when dry, shake them vigorously to fluff them up. Oval and round rugs may be laid flat on the grass, or on paper, to dry without losing their shape. For cleaning large cotton rugs or carpets in place (fitted), consult your local carpet specialist.

FIBRE, GRASS AND SISAL RUGS are vacuum-cleaned or brushed on both sides with a stiff brush and wiped occasionally with a damp cloth. Roll them up frequently to clean the floor underneath, as dirt sifts through them. When very soiled, send them to a cleaner. Special rug paints can be used to freshen faded rugs of this type. If you undertake this job, be sure to put plenty of newspapers underneath. Use the paint thinly and work it into all crevices with a stiff brush.

FUR RUGS, when mounted on heavy flannel or wool, can be cleaned with a coarse absorbent. (See the list of materials useful in cleaning.) Spread the absorbent over the rug then brush it out. Repeat this process, using fresh absorbent each time, until the rug is clean.

Fur rugs otherwise mounted, or unmounted, are cleaned by wiping the fur surface with a cloth wrung out of mild, lukewarm suds made with a synthetic detergent. Be very careful not to get the pelt wet. Wipe with a cloth wrung out of clear lukewarm water and repeat till all traces of detergent have been removed from the fur. Blueing can be used in the last rinse if the fur is white. (See p. 172.) Dry flat on the floor. Moths love a fur rug so take precautions, especially if you are storing it. See *Furs*.

HOOKED RUGS are made by looping wool or cotton strips through a cloth base. They must not be beaten or shaken or these loops will be loosened and the backing broken. Sprouting ends can be clipped off safely if the rug is closely looped. These rugs, whether of wool or cotton, are best cleaned by a professional. The rotary scrubbing method is usually recommended.

Ordinary care of hooked rugs is the same as for other rugs.

NYLON RUGS: Nylon carpets and rugs do not require any special treatment. Remove spots and clean them according to the directions given for wool rugs. If spot cleaning disturbs the pile, this can usually be corrected by blotting the area in the direction of the pile lay. If you shampoo the rug, rinse it thoroughly. Vacuum the rug five or six times if you use an absorbent powder. Residues of either type of cleaner attract dirt to any carpeting. See also *Antistatic*.

MATTING may be swept with a soft brush or cleaned with a vacuum cleaner. Once a week, after it has been cleaned, it should be rolled up so that the floor underneath can be thoroughly cleaned. This is important because dirt sifts right through the matting. Occasionally wipe the matting with a damp cloth, wrung out of clear water, or water containing one or two teaspoons of ammonia. Don't soak the matting or you may get a nasty smell.

NUMDAH RUGS from India are made of matted goat's hair. They are not woven. Their routine care is the same as for other wool rugs. Don't ever shake them. Have them dry-cleaned; they cannot be washed.

RESIZING: If your rug has gone limp, it probably needs resizing. This should be done professionally. See also instructions for *Rug Anchor*.

Carpet Sweeper A carpet sweeper should be emptied and cleaned after each use. Snip tangled hair or string with scissors and you can remove it easily from the brush. If badly worn, get a new brush. Sweeper parts should be oiled about once a month for smooth service.

A carpet sweeper should be either hung up or rested on its side, when stored.

Cashmere Originally the word 'cashmere' applied to a rich shawl, made in Kashmir. Later the meaning was extended to the down-soft woollens fashioned from the fine hair which grows at the roots of the hair of Cashmere goats. In modern usage cashmere is applied to a variety of soft woollen materials. Your cashmere sweater probably comes to you through the co-operation of that

'hornless, long-necked, elastic-footed animal with the adipose hump' – the camel.

Fine woollens deserve the most scrupulous care. In washing cashmeres follow carefully the directions given for woollens, using the finest of detergents. See *Woollens, Sweaters*.

Cast Iron See *Pots and Pans*.

Cavalry Twill Heavy fabric with pronounced grooves. Used for cavalry breeches, slacks, raincoats etc. may be wool, cotton or man-made fibres. Dry-clean.

Ceiling See *Walls and Ceilings*.

Celanse Acetate fibre produced by Courtaulds. See *Acetate*.

Cellar See *Basement*.

Cellulose Sponge See *Sponge (Cellulose)*.

Cellulosics One of the ten main classes of plastics. Cellulosics are of four types: *acetate, butyrate, ethylcellulose*, and *nitrate*. Each type has characteristics that qualify it for specific jobs. All cellulosics are extremely durable even when the sections used are thin. They are light in weight and are available in a full range of bright and pastel colours – opaque, transparent and translucent.

Cellulosics will take hard use and knocks without breaking and are quite difficult to scratch, but only *butyrate*, which has high water resistance, is designed for outdoor use. The other three types will stand normal moisture. These plastics are not affected by freezing temperatures, but should be kept away from high heat, such as provided by ovens and direct flames. All are tasteless and non-toxic. *Butyrate* alone has a slight odour. *Nitrate* is highly flammable.

Cellulosic plastics are used for toys, partitions, lamp shades, shelf coverings, storage boxes, vacuum parts, ice crushers, frames for eye-glasses, pipe and tool handles. Wash them in warm water with mild soap. (They will not stand boiling water.) Do not use abrasives. Protect all types from nail polish, polish remover, and acetone. *Acetate* and *butyrate* are also damaged by spirits and alkalies. *Butyrate* and *ethylcellulose* are damaged by cleaning fluids. See also *Plastics*.

Celon A nylon fabric made by Court-aulds. The fibre is soft and the white stays white after repeated washing. It is flame resistant and is used for dress fabrics, knitwear, upholstery etc. Wash in hand-hot water, warm rinse, drip dry. If ironing is necessary use a warm iron.

Cement (Unpainted) Sweep with a soft broom or vacuum cleaner. Wash with a wet mop or scrub with a brush and rinse. For a thorough cleaning add from two to four tablespoons of washing soda, or trisodium phosphate, to a pail of water and wash with a mop or scrubbing brush. (A long-handled scrubbing brush makes the job easier.) Rinse with clear water and allow to dry.

Stubborn grease stains can be sprinkled with washing soda, or trisodium phosphate moistened with water, and allowed to stand for about an hour. Rinse, and the stain should be gone. If not, repeat the process.

Another method is to sprinkle the stain with an absorbent such as fuller's earth; let it stand for a while, then sweep it up.

Cement patios can be hosed down with water, scrubbed with a stiff broom dipped in thick detergent suds, then rinsed. If grease stains persist, wet the cement, sprinkle washing-up detergent on them. Let the detergent remain on them for a few minutes, then rinse with a kettle of boiling water. PAINTED : Sweep with a soft broom or vacuum cleaner. Wash with warm soapy water and rinse with a cloth wrung out of clear water. If badly marked, use a mild scouring powder. Rinse with a cloth wrung out of clear water. Dry.

Concrete flooring is being used today for home interiors, some-times with colour added to the cement mixture before it is laid, or the floor is painted with a good floor paint. Self-polishing wax is sometimes used on hard-finished cement and painted cement floors. TO WATERPROOF: A coating of sodium or potassium silicate (water glass) will give cement a hard waterproof surface and prevent dust being trodden into other parts of the house. New floors, however, should age three to six months before it is applied. Use one pint of water glass, available at house-hold stores, to four pints of water. Apply to clean dry cement with a brush or mop and let it dry for twenty-four hours. Rinse with clear water, allow to dry, and recoat. Three or four coatings are desirable for a good hard finish. Special sealers are also made for cement floors. Consult a local specialist or write to an appropriate firm.

Ceramics The art of making porcelain

and earthenware. The potter's art. See *Pottery, Porcelain, China, Earthenware* and *Tile*.

Cesspool See *Septic Tank*.

Chamois Chamois leather polishers should be washed after use in lukewarm suds made of mild pure flakes. Since this leather tears easily when wet, clean it by squeezing the suds through it repeatedly. Do not rub. Rinse in lukewarm water, squeeze out excess water. (Do not wring or twist.) Dry in the shade. Pull it gently this way and that several times while drying to keep the leather soft.

See also *Gloves*.

Chandeliers Dust them when you clean the room. Clean them according to the material of which they are made.

See *Brass, Iron, Crystal*, etc.

Checking See *Furniture*.

Chenille See *Bedspreads*.

Chiffon A soft light fabric made of silk or nylon, or rayon, and other man-made fibres. Silk chiffon should be dry-cleaned. For others, see *Nylon*, etc.

Chimney If a fireplace is used normally, the chimney should be cleaned once a year. If normal use involves burning resinous woods such as pine, more frequent cleaning may be necessary as more soot will be accumulated and the fire hazard will be greater.

A professional chimney cleaner is the best man for the job. He will probably use a specially designed vacuum cleaner and remove the soot with neatness and dispatch. However, if there is someone rugged about, the following home method can be used:

Fill a sack with straw and weight it with a stone or brick. Tie a long rope to it securely. Cover the fireplace opening with a wet cloth to safeguard furnishings. Lower the sack into the chimney and move it up and down the sides to scrape off the soot.

Fire prevention authorities view with doubt other soot-removing procedures such as adding salt to the fire.

As a further precaution, keep your chimney in good repair. Have it checked for loose bricks, cracks, etc. when it is cleaned.

China (Chinaware) Chinaware, as its name suggests, was made originally in the Land of the Lotus, whence it was first exported to Europe in the sixteenth century. It is usually a translucent earthenware and the Chinese made some of their finest from kaolin, a fine porcelain clay named from the hill that supplied it. Some English and French china is made of clay and calcined (powdered by heat) bones. This type is called 'bone china'. Porcelain is just another name for fine translucent chinaware. The term 'china' like the term 'porcelain', has been extended to include materials far from the realm of fine craftsmanship. Loosely, earthenware is called 'china'. A bath is sometimes identified as 'porcelain'.

The general rule for washing china calls for clean hot water, a mild synthetic detergent, rinsing and drying. Long soaking, hard rubbing and the use of cleaning powders or steel wool damage the glaze and the pattern. In fact with very lovely pieces not used for food or drink, some people content themselves with wiping them over with a damp cloth, then a dry one. Avoid pouring hot water on cold dishes or cold water on hot dishes, to avoid breakages.

China used for egg dishes should be rinsed promptly with cold water, then washed. Hot water will cook the egg to the plate and make it difficult to remove. Tea and coffee stains can be removed by rubbing them with a soft wet cloth that has been dipped into bicarbonate of soda. Commercial products such as 'Chemico' and Liquid Gumption may also be used. Also enzyme detergents. See p. 177. However, it is better to avoid the stains in the first place by not letting tea or coffee stand in cups and saucers.

Chinaware and earthenware vary in the treatment they will stand. Ceramic engineers today are producing dinnerware that is not harmed by boiling water or prolonged soaking; other china, especially very old china, is damaged by such treatment. The instructions which follow are general, safe for all types.

If you have fine china and value it accordingly, you will wash it by hand immediately after use, using a mild detergent if necessary. Salads, salted foods, gravies and similar foods that leave china wet or damp may have an injurious effect if allowed to stand long on china. Soaking china in water may soften ingredients used in its decoration and is especially damaging to gold trimming. Rinsing in water that is too hot, or pouring scalding water over china, sometimes meshes the glaze with fine cracks. This is called 'crazing'.

For hand-washing china, use a plastic bowl to avoid chipping, or put a vat in the sink. Aluminium pans mark china with fine pencil-like lines which are difficult to remove. Electric dishwashers, using harsh detergents, are for everyday china – not delicate, fragile old china and fine dinnerware.

China with raised ornaments may be cleaned with a soft brush.

Prized china should be stacked carefully, as the footing is often unglazed and can scratch the piece on which it is carelessly placed. For storage cover you stack plates with plastic covers or wrap them with a plastic film, such as saran, to protect them from dust. Hang your cups from properly spaced cup hooks. It's a good idea to protect delicate tea pot spouts with soft paper. See also *Electric Dishwasher.*

Chintz Chintz is a kind of cloth, usually cotton, printed in colourful designs of flowers, etc. Glazed chintz has a glossy finish, produced by first treating the material with a sizing, then rolling it between heated cylinders. Wash chintz according to directions given under *Curtains and Draperies.* When the glaze wears off, as it does after a number of launderings, it can be restored professionally. However, you can produce a fairly good glaze by dipping the chintz into a thin solution of clear starch to which a small amount of wax has been added. Use paraffin or candle wax and stir thoroughly into the starch solution while it is boiling hot. For a pair of curtains use a piece about the size of a walnut. Iron on the right side. It might be a good idea to test your starch first on a scrap of cloth to be sure that it gives the desired effect.

Chromium Chromium is a soft, silver-coloured, rustproof metal discovered in 1797. It is prepared from its oxide and never found in its metallic state. Chromium takes its name from the lovely colours which its compounds give to minerals into whose composition they enter. In its highest degree of oxidation it forms a chemical salt, ruby red in colour. Chromium salts are used in making dyes and paints.

As a metal, chromium is used as a plating on plumbing fixtures, for metal furniture, electric appliances, etc., and is easily recognized by its bluish sheen. It is also used in making stainless steel.

Household chromium usually needs only to be wiped with a soft, damp cloth and polished with a dry one. If very sticky it may be washed with a mild soap or detergent. A little paraffin on a damp cloth, or bicarbonate of soda on a dry one, is excellent for gummy kitchen lighting fixtures, etc.

Harsh metal polishes and cleaning powders should never be used on chromium. They are unnecessary and wear off the plating. Should sputtering grease burn on it, rub it off with a very little silver polish. Salt is injurious to chromium and should not be allowed to remain on it. Taps, water pipes, etc. that have become green with corrosion can only be replated or replaced.

Clock Clock wheels get tired and worn out pushing against congealed oil.

Have your clock cleaned and oiled, preferably once a year, unless the works are sealed, as in electric clocks.

Cloisonné In this type of enamelling each tiny part of the design is first outlined by wire bands. Enamel paste (powered glass and water) is then filled in and fused under high temperature. Sometimes the whole piece is coated with lacquer. You can wash cloisonné as you would a china dish, with a mild detergent and warm water. Rinse and wipe dry with a soft cloth. Use no abrasives or harsh cleaners.

Cloqué A compound or double-woven fabric, often in silk, Tricel or Courtelle. Wash in warm water with mild soap. Do not iron.

Clothes Your clothes will look better and last longer if you follow a few simple rules for their care. Hang them up properly. Keep them clean. Mend them promptly.

The time to put your dress or coat on a hanger is when you take it off, not after it has draped a chair for several hours. (However ironable clothes should be ironed after, rather than before, use.) When hanging clothes they should be buttoned or zipped up so that they won't sag out of shape. Brush woollens carefully after wearing them; it is easier to whisk the dust out then than after it has become embedded in the fabric.

Spots and stains are more easily removed when fresh. If you know what caused the stain and the proper agent for removing it, proceed quickly. If this is not possible because you are out visiting then send the garment to the cleaners as soon as possible.

In removing clothes, take care not to pull at them. Manoeuvre zippers gently; don't lose your head if you have apparently been locked in or out of your clothes. A little gentle coaxing will release you from your trap. If a piece of cotton is caught in the zip be careful not to try and force it open.

Sew on that button before you lose it.

Mend that burst seam before it becomes a tear. Your garment will then be ready for the next time, when you may be in a hurry.

Place hats, well brushed, on a hatstand or pack them carefully in a box, using tissue paper to keep them in shape. Mothproof woollens after cleaning if they are to be stored. Put shoe trees in your shoes or, if you don't like trees, pack tissue paper into the toes.

Good idea: to air garments out of doors before putting them away. This helps them to get back into shape and will reduce perspiration odour.

See also *Shoes, Moths* (page 163) and Section 2, *Stains*.

Clothes Cupboard A clothes cupboard should be completely emptied and tidied from time to time. This is a good opportunity for throwing away garments no longer worn (or sending them to a jumble sale). If possible, take coats and suits out of doors, brush them and leave them for a good airing. Dust all boxes, suitcases, hatstands, etc. Clean the walls of the cupboard, the lighting fixtures, and the hooks. Put fresh paper on the shelves and replace the things neatly, each in its allocated place. Resolve to keep it that way.

Clothes Dryer See *Automatic Dryer*.

Clothesline If your clothesline is soiled you may ruin the spotless wash you are about to fling to the breeze. Wipe it carefully with a damp cloth before using it. To make a new rope line pliable, boil it for several minutes and rinse it in hot water. Plastic rope and rustless wire are often used for clotheslines today.

Clothes Pegs Give wooden pegs a wash in hot soapsuds if they become grimy. Use mild soap and warm water if they are plastic. An easy way to wash clothes pegs is to put them in a nylon mesh bag and place them in your washing machine. But don't do this with plastic pegs!

Coffee Maker If you are fastidious about your coffee, you will have to be fastidious about your coffee maker. If it is not kept scrupulously clean, traces of oil that remain in it will grow rancid and give the coffee a bitter taste.

If yours is an electric percolator, wash the removable pieces with sudsy water, scald and dry. Wash the inside with warm soapy water after each use. Rinse with clear hot water and dry. Wipe the outside with a cloth wrung out of soapy water, being careful not to wet the heating element unless it is sealed. Wipe with a cloth wrung out of clear water and polish with a clean soft cloth.

ALUMINIUM COFFEE MAKER Dissolve two teaspoons of a cleaner such as 'Chemico' or 'Liquid Gumption' in one cup of hot water and put the solution in the bowl of your coffee maker. Fill the bowl to the top cup marking with boiling water. Let the solution stand for twenty minutes. Do *not* perk. With the solution still in the bowl, thoroughly scrub the stem of the pump and basket assembly with a small brush. (If this method has not been used before it may be necessary to repeat this entire cleaning operation.)

Next, fill the bowl with plain water and add ¼ cup of vinegar. Let it remain for thirty minutes

C

with the basket submerged. Wash and rinse. Always disconnect your electric percolator immediately after use. The spouts and tubes require special attention at least once a week. Using a small brush clean these parts carefully with soap and water. Rinse with hot water.

If your coffee has been off-taste due to oil deposits on the metal, apply the following treatment.

COFFEE MAKERS OTHER THAN ALUMINIUM: Dissolve two teaspoons of a washing-up detergent (the less it 'suds' the better) in one cup of hot water. Put the solution in the bowl of the coffee maker and add enough hot water to fill the bowl to top cup level (but don't quite fill it if the detergent makes rather a lot of suds). Let the coffee maker go through the complete brewing cycle. (It may be necessary to repeat this operation if the method has not been used before.)

Next, fill the bowl with water, mix in a tablespoon of bicarbonate of soda, and again let the coffee maker go through the complete brewing cycle. Wash and rinse. Prevent future accumulations of oil by washing your coffee maker thoroughly after each use, paying particular attention to the spout and tube. A soaped steel-wool pad can be used to brighten the exterior of aluminium coffee makers and the stem and basket assembly. Do not use it on the interior. A plastic basket can be sweetened by rubbing it with bicarbonate of soda.

Leave your coffee maker un-assembled after cleaning, to air.

NOTE: Contrary to popular belief, coffee grounds are not good for the kitchen drain. They will clog it up if they get mixed with grease.

Combs Clean combs made of hard rubber or bone or metal by letting them stand for ten minutes in a basin of warm water containing two tablespoons of household ammonia. Scrub with a small brush. Rinse and dry. Spirit and Lysol solutions are also good cleaners and disinfectants for hard rubber or bone combs. Pure nylon combs can be sterilized by boiling.

Wash other plastics in warm (never hot) water, using a mild soap. No ammonia or other chemical which might soften or discolour the plastic.

Cooker See *Electric Cooker, Gas Cooker*.

Concrete See *Cement*.

Copper Copper is a red metal, found in a pure state and in many ores. It gets its name from the island of Cyprus and was first called cyprium metal, or cyprium.

Copper cooking utensils must be kept scrupulously clean to avoid the formation of 'green rust', a copper carbonate compound produced by the action of vegetable juices on the metal. 'Green rust', like all copper compounds, is toxic. It is for this reason that most copper utensils today are lined with chromium or tin.

This lining must be replaced as soon as it becomes worn. The reason for going to all this trouble, and using copper for cooking, is that it is so excellent a conductor of heat.

Newly purchased copper vessels are likely to be covered with a protective film of lacquer. This must be removed before they are used. Cover the utensil with boiling water and let it stand till the water has cooled and the lacquer will peel off. Wash copper utensils and ornamental pieces (if not lacquered) with soap and water, rinse and dry. Spots caused by corrosion can be removed if rubbed with 1, hot vinegar and salt. 2, lemon juice and salt. 3, copper cleaner. 4, buttermilk. Rinse immediately and dry. Burned-in grease can be removed with mild scouring powder. For 'green rust' use a paste made by mixing a little oxalic acid solution. Sometimes soapsuds and ammonia will do the trick.

Polishes for copper are available commercially, but a good home-made polish can be prepared by mixing equal parts of salt, vinegar and flour. Rub the copper with this mixture until it is perfectly clean, then wash in hot suds, rinse and polish. Or you can use whiting and rottenstone mixed to a paste with olive oil. Always wash copper thoroughly with soapsuds after using acids or commercial polishes or it will retarnish rapidly.

Wash lacquered ornamental copper in warm, soapy water, if required. Rinse with warm water and wipe dry. Do not polish. Do not use hot water or allow it to soak, as this might crack the lacquer.

Coral Coral is the general term for the hard calcareous skeleton secreted by the marine polyps for their homes. See *Jewellery*.

Corduroy This word comes from the French phrase *corde du roi* (king's cord). Today's corduroy, tough and durable, is the mainstay of many children's wardrobes.

Most cotton corduroys are fast-dyed and completely washable. Clean bad spots with a soft brush before washing. Extract the suds, then rinse several times in luke-warm water. Tumble-dry garment or dry on hangers after a brief spin. Clothing to be air-dried should be wet when hung out. When completely dry, brush it in a one-way direction with a soft brush. Corduroy looks better if it is not ironed.

Corfam A material made by Du Pont from a urethane material reinforced with polyester. Used for handbags, sports equipment, shoe uppers, etc. It is flexible and water repellent. Resists scuffing. Clean with damp cloth. Polish occasionally with a wax polish.

Cork Cork stoppers can be sterilized by boiling. Cork used as, for instance, the handle on your glass coffee maker can be rubbed clean with emery paper or emery cloth. See also *Cork Tile*.

Cork Tile Cork tiles, pleasantly springy, are sealed at the factory by steel disc polishing or with special coatings. Naturally porous, they are protected by sealing from stains and abrasions. Quality tiles, correctly laid, are maintained by waxing them carefully and frequently. Any type of wax can be used, but polishing waxes are considered best. They give better results on the waxy glaze provided by modern sealers and eliminate the need to use water, sometimes damaging to cork floors.

Penetrating sealers that can be applied at home are sometimes used to improve the appearance of improperly sealed or badly worn cork floors. Select a reliable product, recommended for this specific job or for wood. If resealing seems impractical, try going over the tiles carefully with steel wool dipped in a liquid or paste polishing wax. Wipe away the soiled wax as you work and finish thoroughly by 'buffing' the floor (i.e. rubbing it over with a cloth with a pushing and sweeping movement).

Cotton (Untreated) Cotton has been used as a textile fibre for so long and in such widely separated parts of the world that no one can be sure where the plant originated or who used it first.

Beautiful cotton prints were produced in India long before Alexander's conquests, and in the Americas the weaving of cotton was an ancient art in Mexico and Peru before the white men came. Ready-made for spinning, cotton is produced today in every country where it will grow and is far and away the world's leading textile fibre. It lends itself to innumerable weaves, from sheer lawn and organdie to velvet, corduroy, and carpeting. It can be dyed and printed easily in endless variety. Cotton clothing is absorbent and therefore comfortable and cool to wear. It can be laundered in very hot water – even boiled. Cotton can be mercerized to make it lustrous, dirt repellent, and easier to iron. It can be woven in a special way to make it wind-and-water resistant. It can be finished with synthetic resins that convert it to wash and wear, and by silicone compounds that adapt it to rain-wear without sealing the open spaces that permit a fabric to 'breathe'. Grease-and-oil resistant cottons are available too. The treatments seem almost endless. Some of the finishes disappear with laundering; others are more or less permanent. Most of them do not require any special treatment.

White and coloured cottons should always be washed sep-arately. For run-of-the-mill cloth-ing and household 'linens', use hot water and a strong soap (with a softener if the water is hard) or a detergent. Hot water gets them cleaner and most dyes will stand it. However, if you have any doubt, squeeze a sample or inconspicuous corner of the material in a bowl of lukewarm water for a few minutes.

If the water colours the dye is not fast. Wash the article separately, by hand, using a mild soap or deter-gent and lukewarm-to-cool water. Rinse it in clear cool water im-mediately in a Turkish towel to remove as much water as possible. Unroll immediately and place it in the shade. Iron it while it is still damp, with a warm iron. (Some cotton dyes are meant to 'bleed'.)

Stains on cotton materials should be treated before they are washed because many are set by hot water and detergents. Sponge greasy stains with cleaning fluid and treat others according to directions given for them in the section on stains. Pretreat also especially soiled areas such as neckbands and cuffs by working into them with a soft brush or sponge thick suds of the detergent you plan to use in washing them. Oversoiled garments – work shirts, play clothes, loose covers, curtains – are more easily and completely cleaned if they are allowed to soak for ten or twenty minutes in water containing a detergent or a non-precipitating water softener. If the clothes are greasy, add half a cup of ammonia to the soak water. (The soak may be an agitated prewash in your machine, with lukewarm water and about half as much detergent as you would use in washing them.)

Untreated white cottons without resin finishes can be bleached if desired with either a chlorine or peroxy bleach. Follow the direc-tions on the container. (Blueing and optical whiteners are optional.) Starching gives cotton a neat appearance and helps retard soiling. Follow the directions given for the type you select.

For drip and dry cottons, see *Permanent Press*.

Courtelle An acrylic fibre produced by Courtaulds. It is moth-proof, resistant to mildew and quick drying. Will not stretch or shrink. Made up into a number of different fabrics including jersey, tweed, etc. Wash according to instructions on label which usually suggest warm water, cold rinse. Iron with cool iron.

Crêpe Name given to fabric with puckered, pebbled or crinkled surface. Wash in hand-hot water, rinse, remove excess moisture, iron on wrong side while still damp with warm iron.

Crêpe de Chine Hard wearing, lightweight fabric made of silk, terylene or rayon. See *Silk*, etc.

Creslan Acrylic fibre made in USA. Wash as for Acrilan, Orlon.

Cretonne A printed cotton fabric, heavier than chintz. The name is sometimes given to printed spun rayon fabrics. Wash in hand-hot suds. Iron with hot iron while still damp. Loose covers should be replaced partly ironed while still damp. For starching see *Chintz*.

Crimplene A polyester fabric by ICI. Fabrics of Crimplene drape well. Wash as Terylene, jersey or according to instructions on label.

Crochet Crocheted articles can be dry-cleaned or laundered like knitted clothing. See *Sweater, Bedspreads*.

Crystal This word comes from a Greek word meaning both 'ice' or 'clear ice', and 'rock crystal', since the ancients believed that rock crystal was a modified and permanent form of ice. Rock crystal, or, specifically, quartz, is used in jewellery today but the word 'crystal' is applied commonly to an especially fine type of clear, colourless glass.

Crystal glass contains a great deal of oxide of lead and thus is heavier than ordinary glass. It is used for fine tableware and for ornamental pieces, including cut glass. Crystal is cleaned like any fine glassware, but requires specially delicate handling.

When cleaning crystal candelabra and chandeliers, take them apart, being extremely careful not to bend or break the delicate hooks by which they are hung. Wash the crystals carefully in warm water, using a synthetic detergent. Rinse in clear water of the same temperature and dry with a soft, lintless cloth (i.e. not fluffy) or let them dry on a paper towel. Replace the prisms as before.

See *Glass, Jewellery, Quartz*.

Cuprammonium Rayon See *Rayon*.

Curtains and Draperies Sunlight and weather weaken delicate cotton curtains but synthetics (polyester, glass, nylon, etc.) are impervious to such hazards. Handle them gently to avoid snags and don't let them get really dirty.

Soak untreated white cotton curtains (organdie, dimity, net, etc.) for ten or fifteen minutes in cool or lukewarm water before washing to loosen accumulated dust. Lift them gently, drain off the dirty water, then wash them in thick, lukewarm suds. If the curtains are still dirty, make fresh suds and repeat. Handle the curtains gently at all times. Squeeze the suds through them. Do not rub, wring or twist the fabric if you are washing them by hand. Let the water drain off. Rinse at least three times in lukewarm water, adding blueing, if desired, to the last rinse. Starch cottons lightly (but not organdie). Many women prefer to hand-launder curtains. However, if you use a washing machine (not for glass fibres) run it from three to five minutes for the first wash and no more than two for the second and let the rinse water drain off or absorb it in a Turkish towel.

Coloured cotton curtains should be washed separately and should not be soaked unless colourfast. If not colourfast follow the instructions given under *Cotton*. Dry in the shade or indoors. Hang white cotton curtains lengthwise on a tight line, with the hems even to make ironing easier. When nearly dry iron with a warm iron on the reverse side, following the lengthwise threads.

Rayon requires special care because the fibres are sometimes weak when wet. Do not soak rayon curtains; wash them twice instead. Use lukewarm suds and squeeze the water through the material, keeping it under water at all times. Do not rub or twist. Repeat in second suds. Rinse several times in lukewarm water. Fold lengthwise then across, for the last rinse, dipping the curtain up and down in the water. Lay on a Turkish towel, then roll up lightly to absorb moisture. When of proper dampness, iron with a warm iron.

Rayons are tricky to iron and your guide is the manufacturer's label. Set the dial for rayon and press on the wrong side. Iron the hems first, then iron lengthwise, following the threads. Do not iron across the curtain. Silk curtains should not be too wet when ironed or they will be papery. Use a warm iron and work on the reverse side of the curtain, ironing the hems, then lengthwise.

Dacron, Orlon and nylon curtains should be washed by hand unless the directions say they are machine washable. Shake out the dust and pour a little detergent on badly soiled areas. Fold them in lukewarm suds made with a strong detergent. (Wash white curtains separately; any bleach can be used.) Rinse thoroughly but do not wring. Drip dry.

If the label says the curtains are machine washable, use the synthetic setting and remove them before the final spin-dry cycle for drip drying, or tumble-dry them on the wash-and-wear setting. For yellowed curtains see *Synthetic Textiles* and *Dacron*.

If the curtains have become limp and you want to stiffen them, use an instant laundry starch, following the directions on the packet. For best results iron with a steam iron at the rayon or synthetic setting, sponging lightly areas that have become dry, with a damp sponge.

Cotton and lace net curtains should be measured carefully before they are laundered. Since they are very delicate and the threads are easily broken or stretched, such curtains are often washed in a muslin bag. Otherwise follow the directions given for cotton curtains. Ecru and cream-coloured curtains can be retinted by adding a strong solution of tea or coffee (or both) slowly to hot water until the desired shade has been produced on a sample of muslin.

Lace curtains of natural fibres look best if they are stiffened with gelatine or gum arabic, and these finishes are preferred by some for sheer cottons, such as organdie and batiste. See *Starch and Special Finishes*.

Plastic curtains are washed with mild soap or detergent and warm water. Rinse in warm water. Do not iron.

See also *Glass Cloth* and *Shower Curtain*.

Cushion See *Furniture – Upholstered, Pillows, Floor Cushions*.

Cut Glass Crystal, or flint, glass that has been ornamented with designs that have been cut or ground into it with polishing wheels. See *Glass*.

Cutlery Whether made of carbon steel, stainless steel or chrome-plated, knives should not be allowed to soak in water because this damages and loosens the handles and blades. Always dry thoroughly.

If you have invested in fine, forged blades, have them sharpened occasionally by a professional grinder. You can keep them keen by whetting them on a carving steel or sharpening stone. Cheap cutlery needs frequent sharpening and will not keep an edge for long enough to make professional treatment worthwhile. In sharpening knives on a steel or stone, hold the blade at an angle of about 15° for best results. If using a rotary grinder (the kind that has little sharpening wheels), pull the blade through repeatedly. Do not push it back and forth.

Knives with serrated edges depend upon notches for their cutting ability. They are never sharpened.

Store your knives in a cutlery rack to safeguard their points and edges and as a safety precaution.

Do not use a good knife as a cooking fork or pancake turner because heat damages some blades. And don't let your fine knives be used to cut paper or string, or to sharpen pencils. Do not put knives with plastic or wooden handles in a washing up machine.

Dacron Dacron is the trade name for a polyester fibre by Du Pont, made for stiffness and resilience. It is spun from a condensation product of ethylene glycol and terephthalic acid.

Dacron fabrics and blends resist wrinkles, are comfortable to wear, dry quickly, and do not require ironing if laundered properly. They range from suitings and knitwear to a variety of dress materials, and sheer materials for blouses, lingerie and curtains.

Dacron is heat sensitive; hot cigarette ash will burn holes in it. It tends to accumulate static electricity. Blends with other fibres decrease its sensitivity to heat.

When dealing with clothing made of 100 per cent Dacron, high-percentage blends, and durable press Dacrons, follow any special directions given by the manufacturer. Dacron can be dry-cleaned by standard processes or washed according to the directions given under *Drip Dry*. If touching up with an iron is needed, use a low temperature setting (rayon). Here are some tips from Du Pont on special problems.

The occasional use of bleach will help keep Dacron white. Any kind can be used unless the label warns against chlorine bleach.

Durable press materials and those containing spandex tend to become yellow when chlorine bleach is used; use a peroxy bleach instead.

Greying or yellowing of white Dacron can be caused by: an insufficient amount of soap or detergent during laundering, the use of soap and hard water without a water softener, washing coloured articles with white articles, overloading the washing machine, inadequate rinsing, or the use of chlorine bleach on a chlorine-sensitive finish. Before attempting to correct the condition, try to identify the cause.

To restore whiteness, try first an especially vigorous wash. Treat one item at a time, or a load of not more than four lbs. The cloths should be covered by at least two inches of water to permit them to move freely during the washing cycle. If the agitator is adjustable, set it for maximum agitation. Use hot water (145°F to 160°F). Fill the machine and add one cup of strong detergent and one cup of non-precipitating water softener (e.g. Calgon). Add the garments, set the timer for a 15-minute wash, and start the machine. Add one cup of water softener to a hot deep rinse. Complete the cycle. Repeat the treatment if necessary. (The article will probably require ironing after this treatment.) If the results are still not satisfactory, try the alkali soak described under *Drip Dry*.

If the discolouration is due to insufficient rinsing or the use of soap in hard water, try this reconditioning method:–Fill the machine with hot water (140°F) and add one to two cups of a non-precipitating water softener. (Do *not* add soap, detergent,

bleach, or any other washing aid.) Add the clothes and run them through the complete wash and rinse cycles. Suds which may occur on the surface of the water are evidence that soap film is being removed from the fibres. It may be necessary to repeat this procedure several times before suds cease to form, indicating that the soap or detergent film has been removed completely.

For white fabrics that have yellowed because chlorine bleach has been used on a resin finish, or because they have picked up dyes from coloured clothing, try this: To one gallon of hot water in a glass or enamelled container add one tablespoon of a packet of colour remover. Soak the garment in this solution for five to ten minutes, rinse thoroughly and wash. (Do not use colour remover in your washing machine. Follow instructions on the packet.)

See also *Drip Dry*, *Pillow*, *Quilts*.

Damask A figured fabric originally made in Damascus. It is now of cotton, linen and man-made fibres. Wash according to fibre.

Decanter See *Glass*.

Deep Freeze See *Electric Freezer*.

Delft See *Pottery*.

Denim A heavy or medium weight fabric of cotton or cotton and rayon mixture. For washing see *Cotton*, *Rayon*. Iron while still damp.

Diamond The diamond, hardest of known substances, 'consists of pure carbon, crystallized in regular octahedrons and allied forms, either pure white or variously tinted'. It is brother to graphite (in a 'lead' pencil) and to charcoal. Sheer geological chance produced it and endowed it with lasting beauty. An artful craftsman cuts and polishes it to flash fire.

But, if your diamond is to flash fire, it must be kept scrupulously clean so that light, striking at every facet, breaks down into rainbow colours. If your diamond is dirty and gummed up with soap, you might as well be wearing glass. A diamond that is worn every day needs a special cleaning at least once a month.

Slip your ring onto a hairpin or grip and dip it into a solution of hot water and synthetic detergent. Then use an eyebrow brush to loosen the dirt at the back of the setting. Soap and water, plus a little ammonia, will also clean a diamond nicely. Use your little brush, rinse thoroughly and dry with soft tissue.

For a professional cleaning, as given by a jeweller, boil your diamond in soapsuds. Use mild white flakes (not too many) and a few drops of ammonia. When the solution has come to the boil, place your diamond in a wire tea strainer and dip it into the suds for a moment or two. Let it cool, then rinse it carefully. Next dip it into a small bowl of white spirit, to cut any remaining foam, and lay it in jeweller's sawdust or on tissue paper, to dry. The spirit evaporates in an instant, leaving your diamond sparkling.

Do not boil diamond jewellery if it contains any other precious or semi-precious stone.

Dishcloth or mop Rinse and hang to dry. Sponge cloths are damaged by household bleach.

Dishes If you wash your dishes by hand a little preparation is advisable. The first step is to scrape food off, using a paper towel or rubber scraper, and rinse. Cold water for milk, egg, flour, oatmeal and other starches; warm for other foods.

Now make hot suds with a synthetic detergent or mild soap and get to work with mop, brush, cloth or cellulose sponge. If you use soap a little ammonia will help with the greasy things, but avoid it if you are using your best china, especially if it is ornamented with gold or silver. (Ammonia will perhaps soften these.) In any case most people these days use washing up liquid detergents which take care of grease.

The rule is: glassware first (to be dried with non-fluffy cloth), silver second, china third, pots and pans last. Rinse in hot water and wipe or allow them to dry in a rack. However, though detergent advertisements never admit it, many of them do leave streaks, and some women prefer to dry their dishes with a cloth after they have drained in the rack for a short time. Be specially careful to dry glassware and silver carefully for a good shine.

See also, *China, Glass, Electric Dishwasher*, etc.

Dishwasher See *Electric Dishwasher*.

Disposable Clothing This is made of specially prepared paper and when it is soiled you throw it away. Babies' nappies and women's briefs are well known, but more and more items of disposable clothing are constantly coming on to the market.

Drains Flush drains after use with plenty of hot water. This helps keep them free from grease and leaves the famous 'S' bend filled with clean, fresh water. Drains in hand basins and baths should be kept free of hair and fluff. If yours have those pipe-like stoppers that will lift out, clean them thoroughly at least once a week. On other types hair, etc., can often be removed by means of a wire bent into a hook. A little washing soda down the kitchen drain once a month helps prevent it from becoming sluggish, as it cuts out grease.

Sometimes very hot water will suffice to open a sluggish drain. Pour it down then run in plenty of hot water. If this doesn't work, a thorough treatment with washing soda may do the trick. Dissolve one pound of soda in three gallons of boiling water and pour it down the drain. This treatment is usually sufficient for a bathroom drain. If, however, the drain is clogged with a solid object you will have to unscrew the 'gooseneck', the curved section of pipe under the sink, which serves as a trap. Turn off the water, cover your wrench with a cloth to prevent it from scratching the finish and unscrew the cap at the base of the U-shaped section of pipe, allowing the water to drain into a bowl placed underneath. If the object does not come through with the water apply the bent wire treatment. Commercial products that will clean drains include enzyme 'soaking' powders.

Lye is a last resort for a grease-clogged kitchen drain. It is poisonous and corrosive and must be used with the utmost caution. Lye must not touch porcelain enamel, which it damages instantly upon contact, and it must not touch your skin, as it can cause severe burns. Commercial drain cleaners (e.g. Brillo, Clearway) may contain lye in a specially prepared form.

Mechanical aids to open drains include the rubber-cupped gadget on a stick, a suction implement, and the flexible steel, clean out auger, which plumbers sometimes call a 'snake'. If you reach the stage where you need a 'snake' you had better call for help.

Draperies Dust heavy drapes when you clean the room, using a hand vacuum or the upholstery attachment of your vacuum cleaner. Failing these, use a brush of medium stiffness. Work always from the top down. Regular dusting will stretch the time between cleaning and keep your house from smelling dusty.

Lined draperies, even when made of sheer material, are difficult to wash at home. However, if you know they are washable and want to do them yourself, snip the lining loose on all but one side to avoid uneven shrinking. Heavy draperies and those of doubtful washing potential should be sent to a dry cleaner.

Cretonnes and coloured cottons and linens, if colour fast, can be washed at home with care. If you are uncertain about the dyes, test them first by squeezing out a sample, or inconspicuous corner, in a basin of lukewarm water. The water will become discoloured if the dyes are not completely fast. This does not mean that the material will not wash; it does mean, though, that care must be taken. Wash each piece separately in lukewarm suds, and, after rinsing, spread it flat on a large Turkish towel and roll it up to extract as much moisture as possible. Unroll immediately and hang it to dry, making sure that the surfaces do not touch, in a place where it will dry as quickly as possible ... but not in the sun.

Fabrics known to be colourfast can be washed with assurance in good stiff suds made with lukewarm water. Rinse well and hang straight on the line, or indoors, avoiding direct sunlight. Draperies should be ironed lengthwise of the material, on the wrong side, except glazed chintz, which looks best if ironed on the right side. See also *Cotton, Rayon, Chintz, Cretonne*, etc. for special instructions.

Drill A twill fabric. Treat as *Denim*.

Drip Dry Sometimes known as 'Wash and Wear', the term is applied to garments made of synthetic textiles with a 'memory' which enables them to return to their original creaseless state when properly washed and drip dried. Such textiles include nylon, polyesters, acrylics and their blends.

When instructions have been provided by the manufacturer, follow them. Otherwise, use these directions, based mainly on material provided by the Du Pont Company for Orlon, nylon and high percentage blends of these fibres.

Before washing, to ensure best results, pretreat badly soiled areas by rubbing in strong liquid detergent or a paste made with a detergent powder. Cleaning fluids can be used on oily stains. Remove any trimming such as ribbon bows, which may not be washable.

Hand wash articles of delicate construction. Always wash white and coloured clothing separately. If a little touching-up ironing is needed, use either a steam iron, or dry iron at a rayon or synthetic setting.

Dry Cleaning Dry cleaning at home is not recommended because of the hazards involved. Inflammable or explosive cleaning fluids are dangerous when used in large amounts. Improper use of nonflammable fluids containing carbon tetrachloride may result in severe poisoning. A report in an American magazine said: 'A single teaspoon of any of the tetrachloride preparations, taken internally, or

the fumes from one cup may cause death.

'Repeated contact of the skin with the liquid may also produce a toxic reaction'. Newer and less toxic is chlorothene which is also nonflammable, see Section 4.

Duragold A tarnish-proof alloy that resembles gold. Rub with chamois or soft cloth.

Duralumin An alloy of aluminium containing 3 to 4 per cent of copper and fractional percentages of manganese and magnesium. Duralumin has a satiny finish, does not tarnish or stain and can be washed with soap and water. Rinse and polish with a soft cloth. Duralumin is equal to soft steel in strength and hardness. It is used for bowls, trays, candlesticks, etc.

Dustbins It is possible to buy pleasant-looking plastic dustbins which are easily cleaned and whose lids are soundless. They should be lined with paper or with the dustbin liners now on the market. Or each contribution can be securely wrapped in newspapers to avoid smells and make life sweeter for the dustmen. Wash the bin frequently with hot suds, using a little disinfectant if desired. Dry and air well. All these apply equally to the pedal bins used in kitchens.

Duster A soiled, gritty duster does more harm than good, it engraves fine scratches on polished surfaces. Make a habit of whisking it through hot suds occasionally. Rinse it thoroughly and hang it to dry out-of-doors if possible.

If you like an oiled duster put a few drops of lemon oil on it. For a 'dustless' duster add a little paraffin.

Do not use an oiled duster on a waxed surface. For safety, store it in a tin with a lid.

Dusting Brush Soft dusting brushes

should be washed occasionally in mild, lukewarm suds, then rinsed and hung in the fresh air to dry. Always hang up when storing to protect the bristles.

Dusting Mop See *Mop* (*Dry*).

Dustpan Give it a bath now and then with soap and warm water. Hang it with the edge towards the wall to discourage denting. If the edge does get bent, take time to straighten it out, or you will find yourself chasing dirt halfway across the room every time you use it.

It is possible to get long-handled dustpans (as well as brushes) for those who are disabled, stout, or merely lazy. Unnecessary to stoop.

Dynel Dynel, a Union Carbide (United States) textile fibre, is spun from the chemical compounds acrylonitrile and vinyl chloride, and is classified as a modacrylic. It is used for blankets, draperies, pile fabrics, men's socks, infants' wear, blends for suits, shoe fabrics, rainwear, ski suits, shirtings and carpets. Dynel are wool-like, warm to the touch, and capable of providing a wide variety of textures, ranging from cashmere-soft fabrics to harsh 'wools' and 'mohair'. This versatility is accomplished by varying the size of the filament. Dynel is quick-drying, resilient, warm, fire-resistant, practically shrinkproof, and

insects would rather die than eat the stuff. Mildew and fungus leave it unharmed.

Dynel can be washed by hand or in the washing machine. If desired, it can be dry-cleaned by standard methods. Follow instructions on the tag. There are no limitations on soaps or detergents that can be used, but washing with a mild soap is suggested – as for other fabrics. Keep the water temperature below 170°F. This is quite hot, hotter than the hand can stand. Bleaches do not harm it, but do not use acetone as a spot remover.

The only limitation in finishing 100 per cent Dynel articles is that drying, pressing or ironing temperatures should not exceed 170°F. Generally, if articles of 100 per cent Dynel are hung out while damp, creases will fall out and no ironing or pressing will be necessary. If you *do* want to press it, use a dry cover cloth over the fabric and set the temperature control low.

When Dynel is blended with 50 per cent or more of another fibre, such as rayon, cotton or wool, in apparel, it is generally recommended that a cool iron should be used and that pressing should be on the reverse side.

If Dynel garments are sent to the laundry or dry cleaner, tell them they are Dynel and require their special instructions. See *Blanket* (*Synthetic*) and *Synthetic Textiles*.

Earthenware The term earthenware is applied to non-vitrified, opaque dinnerware and cooking ware, more appropriately called pottery.

Modern earthenware table services are not translucent like china but are often a high class product, beautifully designed and decorated, and finely glazed. Some of it is oven-proof. Treat it as you would good china.

Partially glazed earthenware intended for cooking requires careful handling because it chips easily and breaks if exposed to sudden temperature changes. Do not place it in cool water when it is hot or in hot water when it is cold. Do not let it soak very long.

Good cooking-ware of this type can be used on surface burners as well as in the oven provided the heat is turned low at the start and increased gradually. It should never be placed on the fire empty. When the vessel and its contents have been warmed thoroughly, full heat may be used. If used for frying, put the fat in the pan while it is cold and heat it slowly to the right temperature. See *China* and *Dishes*.

Electric Appliances These are general instructions for electric equipment, as each item is treated separately on the pages that follow. If you are buying new equipment look for the 'Kite' mark, which signifies the approval of the British Electrical Approvals Board.

The two most common causes of trouble with electric equipment are faulty plugs and worn flexes or cords. Tighten loose prongs in plugs by turning the little screws that hold the wires. If a prong is broken, discard the plug and get a new one. Replace cords as soon as they begin to fray.

Always disconnect electric appliances before attempting to clean them and never immerse them in water unless your instructions say it is safe. Disconnect toasters, heaters and other equipment when they are not in use.

Use your equipment on the voltage indicated and use the cord that belongs to that particular appliance. Cords are not all the same, even if the plug fits. Do not overload a circuit or you will get a blown fuse.

'And', says my favourite electrician, 'please say to oil 'em'. Sealed motors do not require oiling, but failure to oil the kind that do require it sends more electrical equipment back to the factory than any other cause. Always use the amount and kind of oil specified by the manufacturer. Too much oil is as bad as too little. If you are in doubt about when, where and how to oil, ask your dealer's advice.

Electric Bulbs Dust your electric bulbs as regularly as you dust your room. Wash them about once a month if you want to get full watt value. To do this, disconnect the lamp, then wipe the bulbs carefully with a cloth wrung out of warm suds, taking care not to get the metal part wet. Or use an aerosol window cleaner. Wipe dry. Wash reflecting bowls as well.

Blackened electric bulbs burn 20 per cent less efficiently than new ones. Better replace. Dusty shades, reflectors and glass fixtures can absorb as much as one fourth of a bulb's light.

Electric Cooker Clean the outside enamelled surfaces, after the range has cooled, with a cloth wrung out of warm water and soap or detergent. Rinse with a cloth wrung out of warm water. Wipe dry. If food has stuck to the surface, use a soapy plastic sponge or nylon mesh pad. If spilled foods are wiped up promptly, you won't often have the problem of burned-on food. Use a dry cloth if the surface is hot. To forestall a variety of problems try to avoid overheating, splutters and spills, sudden sharp blows, acids and alkalies.

Be sure the switch is off before attempting to clean the heating units. After each meal, when the stove has cooled, wipe the rims of the units with a damp cloth, being careful not to pull or twist the wires. Spilled foods should be burned off open units. Place a pan of water on the burner, turn the switch to high, and heat until the food remnants have been completely charred. When the unit has cooled, lift it out with a palette knife and brush off the charred bits. Clean the rim on which the unit rests, using a mild cleanser or fine steel wool. Wipe with a cloth wrung out of detergent suds, rinse and dry. Wash the surfaces of enclosed units in the same way.

Reflector pans under the units are usually removable and can be washed with other utensils. It is important that they should be kept shining because they help the heat output of the units. Wash them frequently. Spills, boil-overs, and grease splutters should be removed as soon as the burner has cooled. Soaking the pans for a few minutes in hot detergent suds will remove most of the deposits. Rub stubborn spots with a plastic sponge or nylon mesh pad, or use steel wool lightly. If food has burned on, use one of the strong aerosol cleaners suggested for ovens. Some manufacturers suggest using a silicone spray on these pans to make cleaning easier. However such a coating is removed when the pans are washed. Well cookers and pressure cookers should be washed after each use. Do not leave food in them.

The grill and the grill rack should be removed and cleaned carefully after use and grease splutters should be wiped off to prevent burning them onto the enamel the next time the grill is used.

The newest electric ovens are self cleaning; the door locks, and deposits are burned off at high heat. Other ovens are easier to clean if spills and splutters are cleaned up promptly. If deposits are allowed to accumulate and are burned on, cleaning the oven becomes a major task.

For a lightly soiled oven, use hot detergent suds, or hot water containing ammonia or washing soda. A half cup of ammonia, left overnight in a closed oven, helps loosen grease and burned-on food so that its surfaces are easy to clean.

For a neglected oven use a strong aerosol oven cleaner such as Shift, following exactly the directions given on the container. There is also a useful little gadget, Mansion Oven Pad, which contains enough cleanser to clean an oven thoroughly and is shaped to fit into every corner. There is no need to heat the oven before using this pad. A silicone spray applied to the clean oven will make it easier to clean next time. Cover the floor around the stove with newspapers before you apply the spray because if any falls on the floor it will make it dangerously slippery. (Recoat the oven with silicone spray after cleaning it with a detergent.)

If the oven door has a glass window, clean that by rubbing it with a damp cloth dipped in bicarbonate of soda.

If your electric stove has a removable oven vent, remove it and wash it with the other things. Otherwise wipe it with a cloth wrung out of suds, rinse and dry.

Have your electric stove checked

periodically by the serviceman for your locality. This will ensure maximum efficiency and forestall some troubles.

Electric Cords and Flexes Electric cords and flexes should be replaced promptly if they are damaged. This insures against short circuits and electric shock. Inspect your cords regularly for wear and tear.

Before connecting, or disconnecting, a cord from an outlet controlled by a switch, turn it off. This prevents sparking and eventual wearing away of the contacts.

In disconnecting a cord from a wall socket, pull on the plug, not the cord. Jerking plugs out by the cord strains and loosens the copper wires inside and is likely to break or bend the prongs of the plug. Always be sure your hands are dry when you are handling 'live' cords.

Do not switch the cords indiscriminately from one appliance to another, but use the one that belongs to it. Keep cords clean by wiping them with a clean dry cloth. If a cord becomes greasy, disconnect it and wash it with soap and water. Be sure a washed cord is thoroughly dry before you use it again.

Heat also can injure both cord and insulation. Never wrap the cord around an electric iron or a heater while the appliance is still warm. Store your electric cords loosely coiled in a box or drawer or hang them, coiled, over a peg.

Electric Dishwasher An electric dishwasher does not require a great deal of attention for, after washing and rinsing the dishes, it thoroughly rinses itself. The instructions which follow may have to be varied for your particular model.

Electric dishwashers use strongly alkaline detergents, and soap powders should never be substituted for them. Use the amount stipulated on the box or in your instruction leaflet. Too much detergent blankets the water with suds so that the dishes are not effectively cleaned, and sometimes builds up on dinnerware an unsightly chalky deposit that masks the decoration and is difficult to remove. Strangely enough, this film often appears in soft-water areas where the amount of detergent needed is less than stipulated. For effective drying the temperature of the water should be between 140°F and 160°F (60°C and 70°C).

Dishes and pans should be free of all insoluble matter before being placed in the trays. If they are not, food bits may lodge in the drain and flood the dishwasher. Arrange plates, glassware, silver and pans according to your model. Heat-sensitive plastics and woodenware, including kitchenware with wooden handles, highgloss aluminium ware, coloured aluminium, and lacquered metals, insulated cups and glasses, expensive glassware, and ironware should not be put in a dishwasher. Think twice before you use it for very fine or delicate china. A manufacturer of high-quality china warns that detergents for dishwashers vary in harshness and that some of them remove platinum and gilt decorations. Those with metal baskets unprotected with plastic coatings remove gold and platinum bands by abrasion. Ask your dealer if he can replace the baskets.

To remove chalky deposits left on dinnerware and glasses, place the affected pieces in the dishwasher (but *not* silver and pans). Place a cup filled with chlorine bleach (e.g. Parazone) on the bottom rack. Operate the machine for five minutes. Stop the machine and empty the cup which is now filled with water. Fill the cup with vinegar, replace it in the dishwasher, and finish the cycle. Repeat the vinegar cycle. Finish with a complete cycle, using plain hot water. The deposit is loosened by the bleach and removed by the vinegar. Some manufacturers recommend using two cups filled with vinegar for this operation (without the bleach), followed by a complete cycle with dishwasher detergent.

If your dishwasher needs a special cleaning, after a period of use, take out the trays and other removable parts, and wipe the interior with a damp cloth. A mild cleansing powder can be used if necessary.

Wipe the exterior of your dishwasher occasionally with a sponge or cloth squeezed out of suds. The finish will become less soiled if a special appliance wax is used, but do not apply it to plastic buttons or metal trimming. Do not use household cleaners or cleaning fluids. Wipe off spills promptly with a soapy sponge.

Electric Fan Most new electric fans are lubricated at the factory. Ask about this when you are buying one. Afterwards, plan to oil your fan about once a year. A few drops are all you need.

To clean an electric fan, first disconnect it. Then wipe the blades and motor casing with a damp cloth. If the casing is very dirty, use a cloth wrung out of soapsuds, taking great care not to let any moisture get inside the casing. Rinse and dry.

When storing your electric fan, cover it completely with paper or cloth (an old pillowcase is fine) to prevent dust from settling on the motor casing and blades.

Electric Flex See *Electric Cords*.

Electric Freezer or Deep Freeze
The routine care of a home freezer is slight. For the outside of enamelled cabinets manufacturers sometimes recommend an emulsified cleaning wax. Or you can use mild soap or a detergent and warm water. Do not use abrasives.

Defrosting is called for when the accumulation in the cabinet becomes thick enough to interfere with the closing of the lid. Too much frost slows down the freezing operation and the general efficiency of the unit. The electric current need not be switched off for routine defrosting. If desirable, remove the food packages to your refrigerator, or place them, thickly wrapped in newspaper, on a nearby table. (If it is necessary to remove the food, turn the control to the coldest position twelve hours in advance so that the packages will be less likely to thaw.) Scrape down the frost with a wooden paddle or plastic scraper and scoop it out with a piece of cardboard. Do not use any sharp instrument which might damage the cabinet.

The finned condenser of the freezer, behind the louvered panel at the base of the freezer in the front, should be cleaned once a year to maintain highest efficiency. Remove the panel and clean the fins with a stiff brush or vacuum cleaner attachment. It is as well to start this operation in the early summer before the hot weather begins.

If the frost has turned to ice, or if food odour has developed, a thorough cleaning is needed. First remove all food packages to a large box, thickly insulated with newspapers, and cover the box with a thick blanket. If the weather is hot, add dry ice, (frozen carbon dioxide) usually available from a shop where frozen food or ice cream is sold.

After all the food has been removed, turn the current off and leave the door partially open to facilitate thawing. If necessary, run cold water over refrigerated surfaces to hasten melting. Finish with your scraper. Wash the inside carefully with lukewarm water, containing about a tablespoon of bicarbonate of soda per quart. Rinse with clear, lukewarm water and wipe dry with soft cloths. Turn the current on, let the freezer run for about half an hour, then replace the food.

If you are going away for a long time and wish the freezer to remain off, clean the unit thoroughly, as described, and *leave the door open* or you'll find a splendid crop of fungus in it on your return.

Should the electric current be interrupted, keep the lid closed as much as possible to conserve refrigeration. It takes forty-four hours for food in a fully loaded freezer to *begin* to thaw. In partially loaded freezers, the food thaws a little faster.

Experts consider it safe to refreeze foods if the temperature rises to no higher than 40°F (5°C). In an emergency try to get about twenty-five pounds of dry ice from a nearby frozen-food or ice-cream store and sprinkle it over the frozen-food packages. If you cannot get dry ice, try to find a shopkeeper who will store the food for you temporarily.

Electric Fruit Extractor Disconnect after using. Wipe the housing of the motor with a cloth wrung out of soapsuds and rinse with a cloth wrung out of clear water. Wipe dry. Wash the removable parts, dry and replace. Apply oil according to the manufacturer's instructions. Do *not* immerse your extractor in water.

Electric Frying Pan Disconnect the flex from the outlet, then from the pan. Let it cool. Do not immerse the heating element unless it is water-sealed. Wash in hot sudsy water, rinse in clean, hot water, and dry thoroughly. Pans made of cast aluminium may be darkened by strongly alkaline detergents or very hot water. Acid foods tend to cause pitting of aluminium surfaces. Never let them stand in your frying pan.

and rinse out any residue promptly. Avoid the use of steel wool, metal scrapers, abrasives on silicone-treated and 'Teflon' coated surfaces. See *Silicones*, page 183.

Electric Garbage Grinder An electric garbage grinder does away with a good deal of mess and fuss in the kitchen by shredding waste foods into fine particles and washing them down the drain. In operating a grinder, you should follow the directions for your model.

A garbage grinder will dispose of vegetable refuse, fruit pips and rinds, egg shells, lobster, crab and shrimp shells, and soft foods. It can even gnaw bones to bits but *not* metal, including tin foil, glass, cloth, string, rubber, china or cartilage.

The opening, or top, of the garbage grinder replaces the usual sink drain and the rest of the compact unit is under the sink. The top of the grinder, turned to various positions indicated on the dial, acts as a sink stopper or as a strainer, without causing the machine to go into action. When turned to the operating position, the top is locked in place and the motor is ready to be started simply by turning on the cold water.

An electric garbage grinder requires little care. No oiling is necessary because the motor is permanently lubricated. The interior never has to be cleaned because the unit scours itself each time it is used. About once a week, however, it should be flushed out. To do this, close the opening, run two or three inches of cold water into the sink, and (with the cold water still running) turn the top to the 'on' position. Let the unit operate until the sink has been emptied. Do *not* use any drain-cleaning chemicals. They are not needed and their action is harmful.

If a forbidden item, such as bottle cap or piece of broken china, accidentally gets into your garbage grinder, the motor will protest by becoming unusually noisy. When this happens, turn the motor off, remove the top, and take out the foreign material. The grinder *will* not and *cannot* bite you, because the motor cannot run while the top is off. And you can't get your fingers inside without removing it.

An electric garbage grinder can be installed in practically any sink with a three-and-a-half to four-inch drain opening that connects with a municipal sewage system or septic tank of the proper capacity. It cannot be used in connection with a cesspool system. If you are thinking of installing one, check the building laws in your area first because the sewer systems of some cities are not adequate and garbage grinders are therefore not allowed.

Electric Heater Dust and dirt cut down the efficiency of electric room heaters just as dirty bulbs and reflectors cut down light. Always disconnect the flex when dusting, cleaning or polishing. If your heater has a fan, oil it at least once a year. The reflectors of sun bowl lamps should be kept brightly polished for maximum efficiency. Slip off the guard and polish it with a suitable fine polish. Sometimes, when this type of heater fails to function, the heating element is loose. Before running to an electrician, be sure the whole thing is disconnected and try to tighten the element. It may twist into a socket just like a light bulb.

Keep your electric heater away from swinging draperies, papers, clothing and small children. Never let it get wet and never touch it when your hands are damp. There have been tragedies resulting from people handling electric equipment when in the bath. Always disconnect a heater when not in use. Even if it has a switch.

When storing, cover with cloth or paper to keep out the dust, and choose a cool, dry place.

Electric Heating Pad Here are the general rules for their care:

Inside the pad is a network of fine wires, and if one of these is broken the whole thing will go out of gear. To avoid breaking these wires do not crush or fold the pad and do not carry it by the flex. Grasp it by the pad instead. Let the pad cool before you put it away. Then coil the cord loosely and store it in a cool, dark, dry place.

Never fasten the pad with pins or metal clips. If you are going to put it next to the body, put it into a little cover. This will also have the advantage of keeping it clean. Unless your model is moistureproof do not use it over a wet dressing or if you are sweating profusely – unless it is inserted in a moistureproof casing. The casing should be examined constantly to make sure it has no holes or cracks or blisters. If the casing has deteriorated it should be replaced.

Electric Iron Most electric irons are chromium plated and therefore rust and tarnish proof. Always disconnect the iron as soon as you have finished your work and allow it to cool before putting away. If the base has become stained with starch, wipe it with a cloth wrung out of hot suds. To remove melted nylon, heat the iron till the nylon is soft, then scrape it off with a wooden spatula. If necessary a mild abrasive, such as whiting or silver polish, may be used to clean the base, but be careful as the chromium plating is easily damaged. Rinse afterwards with a cloth wrung out of clear water. On irons with aluminium bases (known as sole plates) fine steel wool can be used to remove stains. Stroke lightly, lengthwise of the iron. Use a soapy sponge or nylon mesh pad on 'Teflon' coated sole plates.

Never scrape an iron with a knife to remove starch or anything else, and avoid ironing over zip fasteners, hooks or buttons which might scratch the plating. From time to time rub the sole plate with beeswax, being careful to wipe off the surplus on a piece of old cloth or paper. This will keep the iron smooth.

If the plating on the sole plate of your iron has been damaged, you can have it replated (or replaced) at the factory.

PRECAUTIONS: Do not store your iron, or wrap the cord round it while it is still warm. Try not to drop it. Dropping causes more casualties to electric irons than anything else. Replace worn cords promptly. In ironing, don't press too hard. It's the contact of heat with the damp cloth that removes creases, so why wear yourself out? See also *Steam Iron*.

Electric Ironer See *Rotary Ironer*.

Electric Kettle To prevent furring special shells are sold to put inside the kettle. A marble will also do the trick. These must, of course, be discarded when furred. Descaling fluids for removing fur are also sold. Or, fill the kettle with cold water, add one level dessertspoon of borax and bring to the boil. Pour the water away, rub softened deposit with a scourer and rinse. A gentler method is to add a few tablespoons of water softener (Calgon) to the filled kettle and bring it to the boil. Leave till cold, then rinse out. Repeat if necessary.

Electric Lamps See *Lamp-Electric* and *Sun Lamp*.

Electric Mixer After using your mixer, detach the beaters, or other attachments, wash and dry them. Wash the bowls according to the material of which they are made. Do not knock the beaters against the mixing bowls, as this bends the beaters and chips the bowls. Use a spatula or, better still, a rubber mixer, to scrape out the remaining food.

Wipe the motor casing with a damp cloth. Do not immerse it in water or rinse it under the tap. If water gets inside the motor may be damaged. Oiling the motor is not required in most models since the motor is usually sealed. Do not overwork the motor by forcing it to mix more than its stated capacity. Keep the mixer covered when not in use to keep it quite clean.

Electric Percolator See *Coffee Maker*.

Electric Plugs If the prongs holding the wires are loose, tighten the two little screws that hold them in place. If the prongs are broken or bent, get a new plug. Remove plugs from their outlets after switching off the controls (if any) and grasp the plug not the flex. Yanking out the flex is likely to break the little copper wires inside the casing or to pull the wires away from the screws which fasten them to the plug.

Electric Polisher When operating an electric floor polisher you are not supposed to bear down on the handle, but you *are* supposed to remember to oil it, according to the manufacturer's instructions, probably about once a month. Use only on the voltage indicated.

For best results let the polish dry for at least thirty minutes before you start work.

Electric Refrigerator See *Refrigerator*.

Emerald The emerald, a variety of the mineral beryl, is a deep, clear green in colour and, if of gem quality, transparent. It is believed that the peculiar shade of green which characterizes the emerald is due to the presence of small amounts of chromium. The finest emeralds come from the region of Muzo, in Colombia, South America. Large crystals, which are less valuable, are found in North Carolina and in Siberia. See *Jewellery*.

Enamelware Enamelware is made by fusing a special kind of glass on a steel base. It must be handled carefully to avoid chipping and cracking. Sudden changes of temperature will also cause enamel to crack so don't pour boiling water into a cold pan or cold liquid into a hot pan. When using enamelware pots and pans heat them slowly. Enamelware absorbs heat quickly but spreads it unevenly. If the heat is too great, foods will scorch and heat stains will appear at the bottom of the vessel.

Ordinary cleaning calls for soap and warm water, rinsing and drying. Do not use metal scrapers or sponges, scouring powders or steel wool. To remove stuck food, put cold water in the pan and let it remain until the food is soft enough to wash off. If food has burned, let the pan cool, then run water into it. Add baking soda (about two teaspoons per quart), and boil. This will loosen the burned food so that it can be removed easily with a rubber scraper or plastic sponge.

Light stains can often be removed from enamelware by rubbing them with a damp cloth dipped in baking soda (bicarbonate of soda). For stubborn stains use chlorine bleach. If the stain is in the bottom of the pan, let the bleach stand in the pan till the stain vanishes. If elsewhere, cover the stain with a cloth saturated with the bleach. Be careful to wash very thoroughly after using bleach.

Acids should not be allowed to stand on enamel surfaces because they damage the finish, leaving a rough spot. Acid foods, such as tomatoes, rhubarb and citrus fruits, should never be stored in an enamelled vessel. Antimony, a toxic metal, is sometimes used in its manufacture and the acids *could* break it down to form poisonous compounds. There is no record of food poisoning traceable to food cooked in enamelware vessels, but cases have been traced to acid foods prepared and allowed to *stand* in them over an extended period.

Enamelware is varied to meet specific requirements: ordinary ware, stain-resistant, acidproof, etc. Kitchen enamelware should not form part of the equipment of home photographers.

Faience See *Pottery.*

Faille A ribbed fabric in silk or acetate rayon and other man-made fabrics. See material concerned.

Fan See *Electric Fan.*

Feathers See *Pillows.*

Felts A fabric made of wool, fur or other materials, matted, not woven. Felt hats can be brushed and the surface dirt removed with a clean rubber sponge. For a

special beauty treatment steam the hat gently, using the spout of a kettle. Steam the crown first, turning the hat slowly until the surface has been covered, then brush it lightly in the direction of the nap. Steam the brim and brush it. Do not get the hat too wet or it will shrink.

Felt Base Floor Covering A floor covering made of paper felt and asphalt, coated with oil paint. It is cared for like linoleum.

Felt Flooring Heavy quality felt which will not stand up to rough handling. Brush with stiff brush or use a vacuum cleaner with slow strokes. Spots and stains may respond to a cloth wrung out of mild synthetic detergent suds. Greasy marks should be treated with carbon tetrachloride.

Fibreglass Trade-mark for a variety of products made from glass fibres. See *Glass Fibres, Glass Cloth.*

Fire Tools See *Andirons.*

Fireplace Ever since the days of the cave man, an open fire has been a comfort and pleasure to the human race. The fireplace in your room is the focus of attention and deserves special care so that it may be attractive in appearance. While it is an almost irresistible impulse to toss scraps of paper and other waste objects into it, try to resist the urge. Otherwise your fireplace will be as charming as a dustbin.

The ashes from last night's fire *should* be removed in the morning and a new fire laid. The hearth should be carefully brushed and the damper closed to prevent dust from blowing about the room. Most of us, in fact, do no such thing. The next day's fire is much easier to light and burns better if the warm ashes stay there. Let the flames die down before you retire and cover the embers with ashes as a fire precaution. Put a fire guard in front.

Occasionally the hearth requires special cleaning and the method will be determined by the material of which it is made. Soot stains can be removed from stone fireplaces by the following method:

Make a soft soap by adding about a quart of hot water to four ounces of yellow laundry soap and heating till the soap has completely dissolved. When the mixture has cooled add half a pound of powdered pumice and half a cup of household ammonia. Mix well. After brushing off as much of the soot as possible, apply a coating of your mixture to the stone with a clean brush. Let it remain for about half an hour, then scrub it off with a stiff brush and warm water. Rinse thoroughly with warm water.

For the cleaning of other types of facings, see *Brick Floors*, *Glazed*, *Slate* and *Marble*. See also *Andirons*.
NOTE: Remember that your lovely open fire is illegal if you live in a smokeless zone unless you use a smokeless fuel.

Fireproof Finish A label which states that a material is 'fireproof' gives the manufacturer's assurance that it has total resistance to destruction by fire. 'Flameproof' means that it may change its physical form but will not support combustion. 'Flame-resistant' and 'fire-retardant' mean that the material will not burn readily.

A fire-retardant solution for home use can be made by dissolving seven ounces of boracic acid in two quarts of hot water. Make a paste by mixing the boracic acid with a little water and add it and the borax to the water. Rinse articles in the solution and let them dry. If not washed or exposed to weather, the treated cloth will be flame resistant for about a year. This solution should not be used on rayons or resin-treated cottons.

For rayons and resin-treated cottons (creaseproof, drip dry, etc.) use a mixture made by adding twelve ounces of diammonium phosphate (chemist) to two quarts of water.

For Christmas trees, a solution of sodium metasilicate may be sprayed on.

Flannel A plain or twill woven fabric made wholly or partly from wool. Heavy flannels (trousers, etc.) should be dry-cleaned, but lighter garments may be washed at home. See *Woollens*.

Flannelette A soft lightweight fabric with a slightly raised face in cotton. It is made in various blends including rayon. Wash as 'wool' or 'rayon' or according to manufacturer's instructions.

Flatplate Ironer Follow the manufacturer's instructions in using your flatplate ironer. The care and cleaning of it is comparatively simple, but make it routine for best results.

A moisture cup, located under the lapboard, catches moisture as it is pressed out of clothes on this type of electric ironer; empty it after each ironing, oftener if necessary.

Wax the aluminium shoe occasionally to keep it slick. When necessary, clean it with a cloth wrung out of warm suds. After drying rewax the shoe, using paraffin or beeswax.

Every now and then shake out and fluff up the padding. This freshens it and makes it last longer. To ensure even wear, reverse the position of the padding after fluffing it.

Keep the muslin cover clean by laundering it frequently. Liquid wax, applied occasionally to the exterior of the ironer, will keep the finish clean and provide it with a protective coating. Use a kind recommended for such equipment by your dealer.

Protect your ironer from dust by keeping it covered when not in use.

Flex See *Electric Cords.*

Floors If you are planning to do a thorough job on a floor, move the furniture out, clean the rugs on both sides and roll them up, then go to work according to the type of floor with which you are dealing. The appearance of the floor affects the appearance of the entire room, and it is not too difficult to keep a floor nice if you follow the correct cleaning procedure.

WORD OF WARNING: If you are washing a floor, plan your exit before you start so you won't be stranded in a corner. Otherwise you will either have to shout for newspapers or walk right across the area of your strenuous endeavour. This advice is even more important if you are doing a paint or varnish job.

For cleaning procedure look up the floor according to the finish: *Woodwork, Linoleum,* etc.

Floor Cushions See *Rug Anchor.*

Foam Rubber Foam rubber is produced from latex, the liquid exudation of rubber trees. The liquid latex is beaten into a froth, by means of machines that resemble giant egg beaters. It is then poured into moulds and heat-treated to set its shape. The result is a very fine-textured material that is moist to the touch, mildew-proof, non-allergic, light, soft and porous. It is used for pillows, mattresses, cush-

ioning for chairs, as a non-slip backing for rugs, etc. Usually it is in a continuous piece. Shredded foam rubber is made from scraps, sometimes mixed with adhesives and pressed; it is less satisfactory.

Being porous, foam rubber permits free circulation of air through it, a sort of breathing action, which keeps it clean and dustfree, cool and comfortable. Foam rubber pillows do not lump or mat and foam rubber mattresses do not have to be turned. They can be cleaned with the dusting attachment of the vacuum cleaner, either in or out of their covers. They should never need washing.

However, if a foam rubber pillow has to be washed, preferably hand wash it in its cover. Use cool or lukewarm water and a mild detergent and handle the pillow carefully because it is weak when wet. If you use a machine set it for the lowest possible agitator speed and wash no longer than 10 minutes. Rinse at the same slow speed. Put it in a pillow case and hang it to dry, away from sunlight or direct heat. If you use a tumble dryer, first squeeze out excess water, and, *using no heat*, let it tumble in the air cycle.

Rugs backed with foam should be shampooed. Hang them pile-side down to dry, out of the sun and away from direct heat. Follow directions given for pillows.

Foam rubber is slow drying. Use an electric fan to hasten the process, if possible.

To clean upholstery covering over foam rubber cushioning, use a dry-foam cleaner and try not to get the cushioning wet. Zippered seat covers can be removed for cleaning. Never use mineral spirit solvents (benzine, etc.), carbon tetrachloride, or strong chlorine solutions on fabrics encasing foam rubber.

Foliage See *Stains: Grass, Flowers*, page 142–3.

Folk Weave Loosely woven material made from coarse yarn. Test for colour fastness and wash in warm suds. Iron with medium hot iron while still damp, stretch gently where necessary.

Formica A trade-mark for laminated plastics, made of synthetic resins and cloth or paper. Clean with soap or cleanser, but *not* steel wool. Porcelain cleansers may be used for stubborn stains.

Fortisan Fortisan is the trade name of a Celanese rayon, very fine yet exceedingly strong. Although this fibre is produced from pure cellulose like other rayons it is entirely different from them. The difference is due to an exclusive process by which the molecules forming a strand of Fortisan are aligned to run parallel to the direction of the strand. This structure gives Fortisan extraordinary resistance to shrinking and stretching and accounts for its tremendous strength. Its manufacturers say that it is about twice as strong as the rayon cords used to strengthen automobile tyres, yet can be spun into filaments finer than those of any other fibre natural or man-made.

This gossamer quality of Fortisan filaments makes possible a wide range of gauzes, sheer curtain materials, and lightweight casement draperies. All-Fortisan textiles have dimensional stability and excellent resistance to the effects of sunlight.

Fortisan is absorbent and is often blended with low-moisture yarns such as acetate, Arnel, nylon, or Dacron. Follow instructions on the label for laundering or dry cleaning.

Foulard See *Surah*.

Foundation Garment See *Girdles*.

Fountain Pen Every time a fountain pen is filled it should be flushed out several times with ink to clear it of dried or clotted particles of ink.

To fill a pen properly dip the point into clean ink deep enough to cover the crevice above the point. It is through this crevice, not the point, that the ink enters. Let the pen stay in the ink for about 10 seconds to give the ink sack time to fill. Shake the pen hard as you remove it from the bottle to rid it of surplus ink. Wipe the outside carefully with a clean cloth or paper handkerchief, paying particular attention to the crevice and point. Do not use a blotter around the point as particles from it may clog the pen.

If a pen has been badly neglected, or has not been used for some time, flush it repeatedly with warm water to remove dried or clotted ink. If water is not effective, flush the pen with ammonia, then flush it thoroughly with warm water. Shake the water out carefully. Fill the pen as directed above.

Freezer See *Electric Freezer*.

Fringe On washable materials, such as bedspreads, comb out fringe while it is still wet and it will be comparatively easy. Straighten rug fringes by flipping them out with your hand, then manipulating your vacuum cleaner carefully.

Frying Pan Clean it according to the material of which it is made. See *Glass, Copper, Electric Frying Pan, Pots and Pans*.

Fur Fabrics – or 'Fun' Furs Made of various natural and man-made fibres. Cotton and rayon fur fabrics are best dry-cleaned; nylon, acrylic, etc. according to manufacturer's instructions, or see *Nylon Fur*.

Furniture No matter what the material, furniture eventually reaches a point where it needs more than dusting and polishing to make it look clean and gleaming. Different materials call for different cleaning methods. Let's begin with furniture of finished wood, then tackle the others alphabetically.

WOODEN FURNITURE is usually finished with varnish or lacquer, sometimes with shellac, and rubbed to a high polish. To dust use a clean, dry, hemmed duster and give each piece a little extra rub to keep it lustrous. Dirty cloths damage the finish. Unhemmed ones leave more fluff. Oiled and treated dusters should be used only on furniture polished with an oil polish. Do not use them on waxed surfaces if you want to re-wax them. Oil will gum up the finish.

Even the finest furniture, which receives regular care, accumulates a scum of dirt after a while and needs to be cleaned. De luxe lacquered pieces call for special treatment. (See *Piano*.) For the usual finishes use an emulsified oil cleaner-polish, soap and water, or furniture wash. To clean finished furniture with soap, make rich suds, using pure, white soap or soap flakes and warm water. Dip a soft cloth into the suds, squeeze it as dry as you can and wash a small area. Rinse promptly with a second cloth, wrung out of clear, warm water. Wipe dry. Move to an adjoining area and repeat this routine until the entire piece has been thoroughly cleaned. Use a soft brush on carved pieces. If your suds go flat, mix a fresh, clean batch. When dry, polish.

CAUTION: Never let water stand on the surface. Work carefully, but quickly. Polish.

If the furniture has been finished with a cheap grade of shellac or varnish, it may look whitish after the washing process. If the finish is varnish, go over it with a soft cloth dampened with pure, raw linseed oil. If shellacked, use a cloth very slightly dampened with spirit and apply it lightly. Too much spirit will damage the shellac.

To prepare a soapless furniture wash add three tablespoons of raw, or boiled, linseed oil and two tablespoons of gum turpentine to one quart of hot water. Mix it and allow it to cool. Apply the wash with a soft cloth, well wrung out, covering a small area at a time. Wipe each part dry as you proceed. Polish afterwards.

If the piece of furniture under special care has been badly neglected and looks as if refinishing may be the only solution, try this procedure first.

Dust the piece and then wash it as described above. If using the wash, add a little more turpentine, but test to be sure the finish will stand it. Next dip a cloth in linseed oil (either boiled or raw), then in powdered rottenstone or fine pumice, and rub it over a small area in the direction of the grain. Wipe with a cloth moistened with plain linseed oil. Proceed in this manner until the entire surface has been cleaned, then polish with a flannel cloth. Make minor repairs, then give the whole thing a final polishing. Either oil or wax polishes may be used over the linseed.

POLISHING furniture is not a task to be undertaken lightly, if you want to do a good job and not have to repeat it for at least a season. After cleaning the furniture as described, apply the polish of your choice sparingly (too much polish, whether oil or wax, makes the whole job harder), following *exactly* the manufacturer's directions for polishing. Rub with the grain, using a soft cloth, until a clean finger will leave no mark on the finish. Rub finally with a soft cotton flannel polisher. There is no substitute for hard, thorough rubbing.

For a really good job on chests and desks with drawers, unscrew and remove the handles before cleaning and polishing. On carved legs, etc., apply the polish with a brush wrapped inside the cloth and give it a rub the same way before wielding your final polisher.

There are many shades of opinion on the merits of different furniture polishes and you will have to make your own choice. If using a commercial stand-by, follow the directions on the container. Lemon oil, liquid and paste waxes, all are good if used properly. Use a light-coloured wax on yellow furniture, dark on mahogany. Yellow furniture darkens with time, even if light wax is used, and there apparently is no solution to the problem.

Some women prefer to mix their own polish. Raw linseed oil and turpentine in equal parts is an old recipe. Another mixture consists of equal parts of boiled linseed oil (see page 180), turpentine and vinegar. The chief thing to remember in using any polish is to apply a very thin coating and a lot of elbow grease. Otherwise you will get a gummy, dust-catching surface.

For specific stains see Section 2.

BAMBOO, cane, reed, wicker and rattan furniture should be dusted with an untreated cloth or with a cloth dampened with water. Or you can use the dusting attachment of your vacuum cleaner, which is ideal for crevices. To prevent drying out and splitting this type of furniture should be wet thoroughly about once a year. Put it outside and treat it to a fine spray from the garden hose or place it under the bathroom shower. If such furniture needs washing use mild pure suds containing a little ammonia. Rinse with clear water. Dry thoroughly. Once a year treat it to a coat of shellac. If painted, follow the directions for painted furniture. (Do not use water if the finish on the furniture is damaged by it.)

LEATHER-upholstered furniture should be dry-dusted with an untreated cloth and cleaned, as required, with saddle soap or with a thick suds made of mild, pure soap. Use as little water as possible. If using saddle soap, obtained at a hardware store or shoe shop, follow the directions on the container. Wipe off soap traces with a damp cloth and, when thoroughly dry, polish briskly with a soft, dry cloth.

To prevent leather from drying out and cracking, rub it once or twice a year with castor oil, neat's-foot oil or a good commercial leather conditioner. On light-coloured leathers use a white conditioner or white Vaseline, since most oils tend to darken leather.

After rubbing the oil in thoroughly with your finger tips or with a clean, soft cloth, wipe off every trace with another cloth. If oil remains on the leather, clothing will be soiled.

If using neat's-foot oil, remember that, while it is an excellent leather conditioner and is readily absorbed, it leaves a dull, rather than a glossy, finish. Do *not* use mineral (paraffin) oil. It is not good for leather. Do *not* wax leather furniture.

See also *Leather Goods*.

MARBLE FURNITURE: See *Marble*.

METAL furniture should be dusted regularly and cleaned according to the particular metal of which it is made. It seldom requires more than dusting. See *Aluminium, Chromium, Magnesium, Iron*, etc.

PAINTED furniture is more easily cleaned if it is kept waxed. For cleaning instructions see *Walls and Ceilings* and *Paint Cleaners*.

PLASTIC furniture should be dusted regularly. A damp cloth is usually all that is needed to remove spilled foods. It can be washed with lukewarm water and a mild soap or detergent. Rinse with a cloth wrung out of clear warm water and wipe dry. Do not use chemical cleaners or chemical aids, such as ammonia, on plastic furniture or table tops with plastic finishes. See *Plastics, Acrylic Plastics*, etc.

REED FURNITURE: See *Bamboo* above.

RUSTIC furniture should be given an annual coating of varnish to safeguard it against damage from weather and insects.

UPHOLSTERED furniture attracts as much dust as a mahogany table top. Don't neglect it just because the dust is less visible. On cleaning days remove the cushions and clean all surfaces with the up-holstery attachment of your vacuum cleaner, or with a good stiff brush. Pay special attention to seams and tufts. After dusting, fluff up the cushions and replace them. An occasional airing out-of-doors gives feather cushions a new lease of life and benefits all types.

CAUTION: If your cushions are stuffed with down, don't use your vacuum cleaner on them. It will pull the feathers through and you will spend the afternoon plucking them.

Spots should be removed from upholstery as soon as possible after being made. Follow the directions given for the particular stain in Section 2 of this book. Always test an inconspicuous portion, or sample, first for colour-fastness if using water and for any possible reaction to the chemicals called for.

There are reliable professional cleaning services that will do an all-over cleaning of upholstered furniture. Some will do it in the home. However, you can do a pretty good job yourself on most materials, except pile fabrics like velvet and plush. Use a good upholstery shampoo or soap lather, which you can make yourself. A dry-cleaning fluid can be used on materials that won't stand water.

Should you choose upholstery shampoo, get the kind that makes a thick soapless lather. To make your own, dissolve about six tablespoons of pure, white soap flakes in a pint of boiling water, adding two teaspoons of ammonia *or* two tablespoons of borax as a softener, if desired. Let the mixture stand until it jells, then whip it like mad with an egg beater. Whether you are using a chemical shampoo or soap, remember that it is the lather you want for this job. The fabric must absorb as little moisture as possible.

Using a small, soft brush, clean an area about eight inches square, applying the lather until that portion is clean. Now wipe it with a clean cloth or sponge, squeezed out of clear warm water. Proceed to an adjoining area and work in this manner until the entire surface has been cleaned. Do not use the cleaned furniture until it is absolutely dry. Do not dry it in the sun as colours may be damaged. An electric fan will speed drying.

For vinyl upholstery see *Vinyl*.

See *Foam Rubber* for special instructions.

WICKER furniture. See *Bamboo*, above.

Furs Furs represent a considerable investment and are best stored and cleaned by a professional who operates under a guarantee. If they must be stored at home during the summer months, place them in a container with paradichlorobenzene (para) crystals, or naphthalene flakes or balls, and seal all openings. Sprays recommended for mothproofing woollens should *not* be used on furs.

Gabardine A smooth twill fabric made from cotton, wool and blends of cotton and wool, and also blends with man-made fibres such as nylon. Being closely woven with the twill running at a steep angle it is almost showerproof. Proofing finishes are also sometimes applied to increase resistance to rain. Gabardine is often used for wax-proofed rainwear. To maintain the spread of wax-proofing, warm the gabardine by the fire occasionally. Gabardine rainwear and coats should be professionally dry-cleaned. Lighter garments may be washed in hand-hot suds, and ironed when slightly damp with a medium hot iron.

Georgette A fine sheer fabric which may be made of pure wool, cotton, silk or many man-made fibres. Fabric of pure silk or wool is delicate and should be sent to a dry cleaner unless the manufacturer's instructions state otherwise. The man-made fibres should be washed according to instructions on the label. If no label then proceed as follows:

Wash gently in warm soapflakes or mild detergent, having measured garment to avoid shrinkage and tested it for colour fastness, squeeze garment in the suds, rinse thoroughly. Lay garment on Turkish towel, ease back to shape and original measurements, roll it in the towel, squeeze gently. Shake it, hang away from heat. When almost dry iron on wrong side with as hot an iron as the fabric will take. Iron till completely dry – measure constantly to retain original size.

Galoshes See *Rubber*.

Garbage Grinder See *Electric Garbage Grinder*.

Garden Tools Clean your garden equipment in the autumn and put it away carefully if you want to find it in good condition in the spring. Rust and corrosion take a heavy toll of tools that are stored improperly.

Scrape the mud from hand tools, remove rusty spots with steel wool, and coat the metal with lubricating oil. Wash off all traces of fertilizer from spreaders and, when they have dried, rub the metal with oil. (Fertilizers attract moisture and invite rust.) Insecticides left in a sprayer can ruin it in a single season by corroding the metal. Store your sprayer empty, clean, and dry. A neglected hose, containing water, can freeze and spring a leak. Store it on a reel or coiled on a dry flat surface. (Worn sections of a hose can be joined with new couplings.)

Drain leftover fuel from the gas tanks and carburettors of the garden tractor and power mower to prevent gum deposit. With the engine warm, drain off the oil, then refill the crank-case with fresh oil. Remove the sparking plug, squirt a teaspoonful of oil into the firing chamber, give the flywheel a few turns to spread the oil, and replace the sparking plug. Cover the exhaust pipe to protect it from moisture.

Garnet A mineral species including many varieties. While garnets conform to the same general formula, they differ widely in composition and colour. Most garnets are red, but some are white, brown, yellow, green and black.

The precious garnet, valued as a gem, is a deep, transparent red. A brilliant, bright green garnet, of gem quality, is found in Siberia.

See *Jewellery*.

Gas Cooker If you are careful to wipe up spilled foods immediately, you will be able to keep your gas cooker shining and won't have to give it a thorough scrubbing often. Grease and food that are allowed to burn on resent being removed.

Always let your cooker cool off before attempting a beauty treatment. Clean the enamelled parts with a cloth wrung out of hot suds, made with soap or a detergent. Rinse with clear, hot water and wipe dry. If food has burned on, use a plastic sponge, or nylon mesh pad.

For a thorough cleaning remove the pans beneath the burners and grates and wash them in hot detergent suds. Rinse with clear water and dry. Now for the burners. Use soap, a heavy-duty detergent, or washing soda, and a stiff brush. A good soak in a very hot solution of any of these cleaners loosens grease and makes its removal easier, or put them in a pan (not aluminium) with water and soda and boil them. Use two tablespoons of soda to a gallon of water.

Whatever method you choose, pay particular attention to the gas orifices in the end of the gas cock, through which gas flows to the burners. Clean out the ports (little holes) in the burners with a wire or hairpin if they fail to light. Rinse thoroughly and dry, open side down, in the oven or in the open air.

Return the drip tray, burners and grates to position and light each burner to be sure it is operating correctly. If you have a model without a drip tray, try lining the surface with aluminium foil.

Follow the directions given under *Electric Cooker* in dealing with the oven.

A blue, even flame is maintained when gas and air reach the burner in the correct mixture. Too little air will make the flame burn yellow. Such a flame is inefficient and blackens the bottoms of pots and pans. Clean the ports in the burner (little holes) and make sure the air shutter (located at the turn-on end of the burner's arm) is opened slightly to admit air.

If the pilot light on your range goes out lift off the top and clean the pilot with a fine wire, as dust or soot probably has clogged it. Relight. To increase the flame, turn the little screw to the left. To decrease, turn it to the right.

The flue outlet of your cooker should be kept open at all times. If it is clogged it will not only cause your oven burners to operate inefficiently but will be dangerous.

It is a good idea to have your cooker inspected periodically by a reliable service mechanic. He can check whether it is sitting level, whether the oven control is operating accurately and whether the burners and pilot light are adjusted for maximum efficiency. Ask your dealer or fuel company about this service.

Gas Refrigerator See *Refrigerator*.

Gas Water Heater See *Water Heater*.

Gems See *Diamond, Pearl, Quartz*, etc., and *Jewellery*.

Gilding This term describes the golden surface created by covering a substance with a thin layer of gold leaf, or with a thin coating of gold in powder or liquid form. The cleaning method depends upon the kind of gilding and, since it is impossible for anyone but a professional to determine the type, it is best not to experiment.

Regular dusting is the best way to keep gilded objects clean. If more than dusting is needed, a dry-cleaning fluid is safer than one containing water, I have been advised by a museum expert.

If the gilding still looks impossible after cleaning fluid has been used, have it redone by an expert or, if it isn't worth that, get some gilding and do it yourself.

Gingham A striped or checked fabric,

sometimes woven of cotton or spun rayon, sometimes in Terylene/cotton, or in a wool blend. Wash in hand-hot suds. (Warm if colourfastness is in doubt.) Iron while still slightly damp with medium hot iron.

Girdles Before washing a girdle, close the zipper and be sure the clasps are open. Pretreat spots, then wash by hand or machine with a mild soap or detergent in cool to lukewarm water. If a bleach is needed, use a peroxy type. Chlorine bleach yellows spandex. After rinsing, roll the garment in a towel to extract water and hang it to dry in an airy place. Do not place it near a source of heat or in the sun. Use of a dryer is not recommended, but if pressed for time tumble dry it at a moderate temperature, usually indicated by a medium or wash-and-wear setting.

Wash latex rubber girdles by hand. Pat them dry with a towel and dust them generously with talcum powder.

For personal daintiness and to ensure satisfactory wear, wash girdles frequently. Oily soil and perspiration reduce their elasticity.

Glass Glass is made by fusing silica with alkalies, metal oxides and salts. Clean it according to the article into which it is made.

TABLE GLASS: The rule in washing dishes is glassware first, silver second, dishes third and pans last. This gives you clean hot suds for your table glass. Use a synthetic detergent. Rinse in clear hot water and let it drain dry. Or, if you wish, polish glass with a non-fluffy cloth. If a detergent is used, drying is not necessary. (Drain your choice glassware on a soft cloth to avoid chipping.)

STEMWARE: Always lift it by the stem, rather than the cup; it is less likely to be broken. Do not jumble it in the washing up bowl but dip each piece carefully to avoid broken stems and chipped edges. GILT AND SILVER ORNAMENTATION: Will soak off if the water is too hot or if the glassware remains too long in warm suds. Use a synthetic detergent. Do *not* use ammonia, washing soda or harsh soaps. Do not wash glassware with metallic trim in an automatic dishwasher. CUT GLASS is flint, or crystal, glass that has been ornamented with designs cut or ground into it with polishing wheels. It is cleaned like other glassware, but a soft brush helps greatly. Rinse carefully. Expensive crystal goblets that have been chipped at the edges can receive first aid from a good glazier. Ask your nearest store where this can be done. COOKING UTENSILS made of glass can be cleaned with any cleanser desired and chemicals in food will not affect them. Steel wool (or a metal sponge) is helpful when food has burned or stuck on. Avoid sudden changes in temperature as for all glassware. STAINS OR CLOUDINESS: In glass vases, carafes, cruets, etc., these yield to ammonia. Fill them with water containing a teaspoon or two of ammonia and let them stand for several hours, or overnight. Wash and rinse. This method works almost as well for mineral deposit. Or you can try shaking tea leaves, plus vinegar, around in the vessel. See also *Windows, Mirrors, Crystal, Glass Cloth* and *Glass Fibres*.

Glass Cloth The silky superstrong fibres which compose glass cloth are obtained mainly by melting glass marbles of special composition in an electric furnace and letting the melted glass flow through numerous tiny holes in the bottom. The filament is stretched to the desired fineness as it is reeled. One marble three-quarters of an inch in diameter spins about 95 miles of filament.

Glass cloth has many industrial uses, being fireproof and practically unaffected by chemicals. It will stand high heat, does not transmit electricity, and is not attacked by mildew, rot, or insects and it does not age. All of these qualities recommend it also for its main home use – curtains and draperies. Curtains made of glass do not shrink, stretch, sag, or wrinkle. They absorb little water and can be washed and rehung in a matter of minutes.

For curtains it appears in a range of colours as dainty marquisettes and casement cloth, and for draperies there is a variety of weights and weaves, piece-dyed or printed in attractive patterns.

Hand-washing is recommended for glass curtains and they are very easy to do since the fibre cannot absorb soil. Use hot suds made with any mild soap or detergent. Squeeze the cloth through the suds and through two rinses. (Never machine-wash, rub, twist, or mangle glass materials.) Roll the curtains gently in a Turkish towel to remove excess water, then rehang them while they are still damp. Smooth the hems with your fingers. Instructions for washing glass draperies are practically the same, but be sure to remove first any hooks or fastenings that might snag the material. Since glass draperies do not absorb water, they are very light to handle. After washing in hot suds and thorough rinsing, the draperies can be rolled in a towel or hung over a shower curtain rod to remove excess water. Hang them while they are damp.

Straighten the hems. They will dry crease free. Sometimes wiping with a damp cloth is all that is needed to remove soil from glass draperies. CAUTION: Although glass cloth has high tensile strength, it will not stand excessive rubbing or abrasion. Never wring or twist curtains or draperies during washing. Do not hang them on a line with clothes pegs. Do not let them flap against window sills, floors, or chairs. Hang them just short of the floor or windowsill and slightly away from protruding window ledges. Cover the tip of the curtain rod with cloth before slipping the curtain onto it. *Never iron glass cloth. Never send it to a dry cleaner.* See also *Glass Fibres*.

Glasses See *Glass* and *Spectacles*.

Glass Fibres Glass fibres, of which glass cloth is woven, are used also for stuffing pillows and cot eiderdowns. Such articles are light in weight, will not wad up and will not burn. They are non-allergenic and warm. Provided the covering used on the pillows or eiderdowns is not harmed by water, they are hand washable in lukewarm to cool water. Squeeze the suds through the material repeatedly and rinse. Do not rub or twist.

Fibreglass lamp shades diffuse light in a close approximation of sunlight. To make them, soft, glittering fibre glass mat is compressed into a fire-resistant sheet with millions of tiny facets to reflect and diffuse light. They are made in different sizes and colours, with a variety of trim, and can be cleaned by wiping with a damp cloth.

See also *Glass Cloth*.

Glazed Finish A finish which gives a shiny appearance to cotton, rayon, acetate, and nylon. Some of these finishes are lost in the first washing.

Others last for some time. Look for the label 'permanent'. Follow any laundering instructions given.

Gloves, Fabric Gloves are washed OFF the hands in mild, warm soapsuds. Squeeze the suds through the fabric repeatedly. Do not rub, wring or twist. Use a little brush on bad spots. Rinse thoroughly, ease into shape and dry either flat on a towel or over a rod.

LEATHER: Gloves not stamped washable should be dry-cleaned. Washable gloves should be handled according to the manufacturer's instructions. Generally speaking, they are best washed in mild, warm soapsuds while they are on the hands, except for chamois and doeskin, which tear easily when wet. Avoid rubbing. Instead squeeze and press the suds through the leather, using a soft brush on spots. When clean, let a little water run inside the gloves and slip them off the hands. Rinse several times in lukewarm water.

Place the gloves in the fold of a Turkish towel and pat them gently to remove excess water. Puff them out by blowing into them, stretch them gently lengthwise and allow them to dry flat on a towel, away from sunlight and artificial heat. When they are nearly dry, stretch them gently this way and that in order to soften the leather, or put them on your hands and rub them carefully. Should your leather gloves dry stiff, fold them in a damp towel and gently fingerpress them until they are soft.

Gold Gold is one of the earth's most precious metals. It cannot be injured by exposure to the air and is the most ductile and malleable of all metals. Gold can be beaten so thin that one gram will cover 53 square inches. In jewellery parlance, pure gold is termed 24-

carat. The term 'carat' is used in all countries and the common qualities are 10-carat, 14-carat and 18-carat. Twelve-carat means that the article is half pure gold, the rest consisting of baser metals such as nickel, copper or silver. Commercial jewellery is not made of pure gold as it is considered too soft to be practical.

'Gold-filled' or 'rolled gold plate' means that gold has been affixed by soldering or welding, etc., to a surface of base metal. 'Goldplated' articles contain the least amount of gold, the article being merely dipped into a solution containing gold and lightly coated by an electro process.

Since gold does not tarnish, it requires little care other than washing and drying as for other jewellery. Go easy on gold plate or it will soon lose its coating. Gold-plated jewellery that is worn regularly needs replating about once a year. See also *Jewellery*.

Handkerchief Paper handkerchiefs are sanitary only when disposed of in a sanitary fashion. Pin a paper bag to the side of the bed, or secure it to the bed table with cellulose tape, when a child has a cold, and ask him to drop used hankies into it. If possible, burn bag and all.

Hats See *Straw Hats*, *Felt*, *Velvet*.

Hearth See *Fireplace*.

Heater See *Electric Heater* and *Water Heater*.

Heating System Whether your heating system uses coal, oil or gas, it is a good idea to have it checked and the furnace cleaned once a year. The end of the heating season is a good time to have this done. Your fuel company probably can handle the job or recommend an expert. Have your hot-water unit checked at the same time.

Home Freezer See *Electric Freezer*.

Hopsack A loosely woven fabric of plain weave in which the yarns are used in pairs instead of singly. Can be of various materials. Dryclean.

Horn Horn is often used as handles for carving sets, etc. Such sets should go in and out of the dish suds quickly, be rinsed promptly and dried. Never let them soak in water as this tends to loosen the cement used to hold the handles. Do not place cutlery with horn handles in an automatic dishwasher.

Hot-Water Heater See *Water Heater*.

Iron See *Electric Iron* and *Steam Iron*.

Ironer See *Rotary Ironer* and *Flatplate Ironer*.

Iron Furniture Iron furniture for outdoor use must be kept well painted to prevent rust. If you are beginning from scratch, coat it first with red lead or aluminium paint, after removing every trace of rust with a wire brush, steel wool or emery cloth. If rust remains under the paint it will go on spreading. Apply two or more coats of ornamental paint.

Ironing Drip-dry clothing, synthetic permanent-press curtains, and bed linens, paper napkins and kitchen towels, and place mats that can be wiped clean with a damp cloth have lessened the ironing load. You can reduce it further by being fussy about the way you hang up the wash. (If you don't have a dryer, that is.)

Many articles need not be ironed if they are hung straight or put on hangers and stretchers. These include cotton knitwear, Turkish towels, dungarees and sheets.

Fold the hems of sheets together, right side out, and pin them by the hems straight on the line: straighten the selvages. Put terry cloth robes, seersucker dresses, and corduroy shirts on rustproof coat hangers.

Untreated cotton curtains can be folded lengthwise and ironed double. Other articles that can be ironed folded include everyday napkins and tablecloths, linen and cotton huckaback towels, sheets and pillowcases. Fold sheets meticulously as you take them from the line, smooth them with your hands and place them on the shelf. The same goes for tea towels.

GENERAL RULES: Now that we have disposed of most of the ironing in our own way, it may be well to look into some general rules for the successful ironing of the things we are particular about.

Rule One: Have the clothes dampened uniformly and of proper dampness for the particular material. If you can snatch them from the line or dryer when just right to iron, you will find that they iron better and you will be spared the operation of sprinkling.

Rule Two: Iron first those articles which require the least heat ... in this order: nylons and other synthetics, acetate, rayon, silk, wool, cotton and linen. If you plan it that way you won't have to wait for the iron to cool, or risk scorch-ing something nice because you thought the thing had cooled enough.

Other Rules, mainly applicable to linens and cottons. Other materials require special directions, so look up the ones about which you are doubtful. Each is listed separately as *Woollens*, *Rayon*, *Nylon*, etc.

Iron clothes in straight strokes WITH the thread of the material until they are dry.

Iron clothes on the right side except when it is desired to bring out the pattern of the fabric.

Iron embroidery and cotton lace on the wrong side, on a thick soft pad, to bring out the pattern.

Iron crêpe weaves, such as seersuckers, when dry.

Iron first those parts of the garment which, while the rest of the garment is being ironed, hang off the board. Place paper under the board to prevent long pieces from picking up dust.

Fold flat pieces to a size convenient for storing. Fold sheets, tablecloths and other large pieces lengthwise first, then crosswise, until the desired size is reached. Fold towels and pillowcases lengthwise in thirds, then crosswise. (If you want to fold them crosswise first, go ahead and do it.) Napkins and handkerchiefs may be folded in squares.

Allow all pieces to dry thoroughly before putting them away. If possible, hang them on a rack to dry out after ironing. See also *Electric Iron* and *Steam Iron*.

Ironing Accessories A well-planned laundry and proper equipment make ironing a great deal easier. Adjustable ironing boards that enable the worker to stand or sit, plastic sprinkling bottles that can be squeezed to produce a fine, even spray, and flex holders are some of the gadgets now available to you if you look in the right stores.

Ironing Board An ironing board should be mounted firmly and should be correct in height for *you*. It should be padded neatly and the cover kept clean by frequent laundering.

The height of your ironing board is correct when, if you rest the palms of your hands on the working surface, your arms are bent slightly at the elbows. Many ironing boards are adjustable, allowing the ironer to stand or sit.

Wash and bleach your ironing board cover like any other white cotton material. Asbestos covers can be washed on the board with a soft brush or cloth and soap and water. A little household bleach can be added to help remove scorch stains. Rinse with clear water. If the cover is removed for washing, replace it on the board while it is wet and allow it to dry in place. The tendency of asbestos covers to lint disappears with use.

When ironing, don't clutter your board with things already ironed or ready to be ironed. If you cramp your working space you are more likely to burn yourself or knock over your iron.

Ivory Ivory objects of natural finish (not tinted, gilded or otherwise decorated) can be washed in mild soapsuds. Rinse carefully and wipe dry. Ivory yellows naturally with age and more rapidly if kept in a place where light does not reach it. Very yellowed ivory handles, etc., can be restored to their original white finish by scraping, but your jeweller should be the one to do it. Knives, etc., with ivory handles should not be allowed to soak in water because

the cement holding them to the blades may be loosened by such treatment.

See *Piano* for a discussion of the keyboard.

Jade Chemically, jade is a silicate of calcium or magnesium. It is tough and compact and has an oily, or resinous, appearance when polished. Although it is best known in shades of green, jade is found also in delicate pink and pure white.

Jade ornaments usually need only to be dusted. However, they may be washed in mild, warm soapsuds. Rinse carefully and wipe dry.

See also *Jewellery*.

Jet Jet is sometimes called black amber. It is a hard, compact form of lignite (brown coal), capable of taking a high polish, and once in vogue for buttons, pins and other jewellery. If not decorated with materials damaged by water, it can be washed.

See following entry, *Jewellery*.

Jewellery To look its best jewellery should be kept clean. It should also be stored properly. Jumbling it together in a box or jewellery case invites damage. A diamond will easily nick and scratch other gems as well as metal settings. If you haven't a proper box, wrap each piece in tissue paper.

Care should be taken also when you are wearing jewellery. Leave your good rings and your watch at home when you play tennis or golf. Screw earrings on tightly to avoid dropping them. Have the settings of valuable stones and the strings of good necklaces checked periodically by your jeweller as a precaution against loss.

The cleaning of jewellery depends upon the materials of which it is made. Valuable jewellery, of precious metals and stones, loses its sparkle if it is not kept clean. Soap and dirt collect quickly on the backs of all stones and around mountings, dimming their brilliance. For cleaning, jewellers recommend hot sudsy water and a little brush. A little ammonia helps loosen dirt, but should be omitted for pearls. Scrub and pat each piece with the brush so that the bristles get into every part of the setting. Rinse in clear hot water and dry with a soft bit of cloth or tissue paper.

Gold jewellery can be rubbed up gently with a soft piece of chamois, but go softly on gold-plated articles or the metal will be worn off. Such pieces can be replated at a moderate price when they begin to look shabby. Wash silver jewellery with soap or detergent and hot water, polish it with a good brand of silver polish, wash it again and rinse well or the tarnish will reappear quickly. Polish dry.

Stone bead necklaces (of topaz, amethyst, crystal, etc.) should be restrung frequently, especially if the beads are heavy or have sharp edges. Some experts advise having this done once a year. Investigate having them strung on fine chain.

Costume jewellery is cleaned with soap or detergent and water also, but use lukewarm water instead of hot to avoid cracking rhinestones, tinted glass, etc. Rinse in water of the same temperature. If desired, settings can be given special attention by tipping a toothpick with cotton, moistening this with alcohol and going over the stones. Work quickly. Water that is too hot or too long a soaking may loosen cement. Sponge plastics with mild lukewarm suds, rinse with a cloth dampened with clear lukewarm water and wipe

dry. (No soaking, no hot water, no alcohol or ammonia.)

Wooden jewellery may be wiped with a soft cloth, wrung out of cool water. Polish by rubbing it gently with the palm of your hand.

A tip is to clean stone beads and lightly tarnished metals with dry baking soda on a brush.

Diamonds and pearls, among the jewels, require special attention and are treated in their own right. See *Diamond, Pearl, Watch, Silver, Gold, Platinum*, etc., for additional information.

Kapok Mattresses and pillows stuffed with kapok need frequent airing and sunning to keep them fluffy and prolong their service. Turn the mattress often. Kapok pillows cannot be washed.

Kettle Electric kettles should always be switched off when being refilled, or emptied.

To prevent scaling put a marble inside, or one of the special shells sold for the purpose. Fluids are sold for removing scale and fur. Otherwise, fill the kettle with cold water, add one level dessertspoon of borax, bring to boil. Pour away water and if you can get to the inside, rub off the softened deposit and rinse. Repeat if necessary. A gentler method suggested for electric kettles is to add a few tablespoonfuls of Calgon water softener to the filled kettle and bring to boil. Leave till cold then rinse. Repeat if necessary.

To keep a picnic kettle from rusting, dry thoroughly and store with two lumps of sugar inside.

Knife See *Cutlery*.

Knitted Woollens See *Sweater* and *Woollens*.

Kodel Trade name for a polyester fibre notable for its heat resistance. It can be ironed satisfactorily at a very low temperature and also at a temperature as high as 425°F, the setting for light cottons and rayon. This makes possible blends with cotton and linen, which must be pressed with a fairly hot iron to look their best, and blends with wool and man-made fibres which require a lower setting. Kodel is undamaged by alkalies, acids, solvents, and dry-cleaning agents normally encountered by fabrics. It can be dyed readily in a wide range of fast colours.

Kodel fabrics may be automatic wash and wear, wash and wear, easy care, or dry cleanable, so you will have to consult the label. Most of them are drip dry, however. For these follow the directions given under *Drip Dry*.

Lace Baste flat cotton and linen laces to a piece of muslin and wash in mild lukewarm suds. They will not need to be ironed. Small lace articles can be washed by shaking them up in a fruit jar, partly filled with warm soapy water. Rinse them in the same way and dry them flat on a Turkish towel. If necessary, use rustproof pins to hold them in shape.

To restore body to laces that have lost their finish dip them in a gum arabic solution. (See *Starch and Special Finishes*.) Stretch over a flat surface to dry. They will not require ironing.

If lace *is* to be ironed put it upside down on the board and press the wrong side. Straight lace edgings are ironed from the centre outward. Iron lace ruffles from the outer edge inward.

Lace tablecloths can be drycleaned or washed. Stretch them into shape while they are drying.

Lacquer (Oriental) Lacquered trays, boxes, etc., can be cleaned with liquid wax, applied with a clean soft cloth. Polish gently with a second cloth.

Lacquered Furniture See *Piano* and *Furniture*.

Lacquered Metals Lacquered metals need only to be dusted. They may be washed, however, with warm water and a mild soap or detergent. If desired, give them a protective coating of wax.

Lambs' Wool See *Woollens*.

Laminated Fabrics See *Bonded Fabrics*.

Lamp – Electric Disconnect the lamp and remove, for cleaning, bulbs, reflector and shade. Dust with the soft brush of your vacuum cleaner or with a cloth. Glass and plastic globes and reflectors may be washed in warm suds. Rinse and dry carefully. Wipe the bulbs with a damp cloth, taking care not to wet the metal base, and replace them.

Metal lamp bases, if not lacquered, may be polished. (See *Brass, Silver, Bronze*, etc.) Lacquered metals should be dusted and occasionally waxed. Lacquered surfaces that have been damaged by harsh cleaning methods and show cracks or spots of corrosion should be redone.

Sometimes the factory where they were made will service them. Clean tole (painted metal) with a soft cloth, either dry or damp.

Crystal bases are best cleaned with a cloth wrung out of clear water or water containing a synthetic detergent. Rinse with a cloth wrung out of clear water and polish softly with a lintless cloth.

Bases of porcelain, glazed pottery and china can be cleaned with a cloth wrung out of warm mild suds. Use a soft little brush to get at nooks and crannies. Rinse with a cloth wrung out of clear water and wipe dry.

Clean marble and alabaster

lamp bases according to the directions given under *Marble*.

Lampshades Dust them regularly as you would other furniture, using the little round brush of your vacuum cleaner or a soft cloth. Dry-clean all hand-painted silk, linen and chintz shades. Water will damage a painted pattern on silk and shrink linen and cotton.

Silk, rayon and nylon shades can be washed, provided the shade is sewed, *not glued*, to the frames and the trimmings are colourfast. Dip the shade in and out of a tub of tepid suds, made with mild, pure soap, or synthetic detergent. Rinse twice in clear, tepid water. Let it drip for a few moments, then let it dry in front of an electric fan, if possible, turning the shade frequently around and over. Quick drying is important because the water may rust the metal frame and stain the fabric. Do not dry silk shades in the sun.

Silk and rayon shades that are glued to the frames (sewed shades too, if desired) can be dry-cleaned.

Real parchment shades should be dusted regularly with an untreated duster and conditioned periodically with neat's-foot oil or castor oil to prevent the leather from drying out. Clean imitation parchment occasionally with liquid wax. Shades of metallic paper seldom need more than dusting. Paraffin (mineral) oil mixed with a little turpentine (one tablespoon of turpentine to one-half cup of paraffin oil) is recommended for an occasional beauty treatment. Wipe away any surplus carefully. Plastic shades can be wiped with a cloth moistened with cool, soapy water. Rinse with a cloth wrung from clear water and dry. Shades made of fibreglass need only to be wiped with a damp cloth.

Lawn A fine material made from cotton or 100 per cent polyester or a blend of cotton and polyester or from Vincel cotton blends. Wash by hand or very briefly in machine. Hand hot water and rich lather. Rinse thoroughly and wring or spin-dry. Iron while slightly damp. Hot iron for cotton, coolish iron for Terylene or Terylene blends.

Leather Clothing Leather clothing goes to the dry cleaner unless labelled washable. Follow directions on the label.

Leatherette A type of artificial leather.

Leather Goods Leather luggage, handbags, briefcases, etc., will retain a smart appearance and wear indefinitely if they are given the proper care. The reason leather cracks, peels and powders is that it dries out. Neat's-foot oil, lanolin and castor oil are all good leather conditioners. Mineral oil (paraffin oil) and linseed oil should *not* be used.

Before oil is applied the leather should be cleaned by careful dusting, or by washing with a cloth wrung out of pure soapsuds, or with saddle soap, according to directions given on the container. Oily spots may be removed with a dry-cleaning fluid.

Neat's-foot oil should be applied while the leather is slightly damp and should be rubbed in with the fingers or a pad of soft cloth. Let it stand on the leather. It will soon soak in, leaving it soft and dry. If the leather is extremely dry repeat the oiling the following day. The only drawback to neat's-foot oil is that the leather is difficult to polish afterwards, so use lanolin, castor oil, or a fifty-fifty combination of the two on glossy or polished leathers. Or you can use half lanolin and half neat's-foot oil. Use white Vaseline on white and light-coloured leather.

CAUTION: These directions do not apply to suede or patent leather. See *Shoes* and *Suede*. See also *Books, Furniture, Mildew, Gloves, Chamois*.
ARTIFICIAL: Artificial leather is made by coating textiles with pyroxylin, rubber, plastics, etc., grained to look like leather. Wipe with a damp sponge or with a sponge wrung out of mild suds. Rinse with a sponge wrung out of clear water. Wipe dry.

Leather Tile Leather tiles, used for floors and walls, are factory-finished with a special lacquer that makes them resistant to stains, scratches and abrasion. They are maintained with polishing waxes, either liquid or paste, which clean as they are applied.

Lighting Fixtures Candelabra often present a problem because it is difficult to know what metal they are made of and whether the metal has been lacquered, plated or gilded. But don't toss out a chandelier because it looks shabby until you have consulted a reliable dealer in electric equipment or a hardware man. If hard pressed, you can gild or silver it yourself. And it may need only a new coat of lacquer.

Linen Fibres of the flax plant were woven into fine cloth in Egypt in 4800 BC and are still highly prized today. Linen, while extremely durable, lends itself to exquisitely fine weaves and is appropriately cherished by women who take pride in the appearance of their dinner tables. As a general term, 'linen' has been extended to include all bed coverings, table coverings and towels.

In laundering untreated linens, follow the directions given for cotton materials. Do not use chlorine bleaches on crease-resistant linen clothing. They are likely to produce a stain and weaken the fibres. Unless more than the usual stiffening is desired, they do not need to be starched. Iron linens when very thoroughly dampened, on the wrong side. Use a reasonably hot iron.

Linens that are to be stored should be washed in soft, or softened, water. Use softened water for rinsing too. (Iron in hard water is left in residue in linens. Over a long period of time it rusts, leaving little brown dots.) See also *Permanent Press*.

Linen Cupboard Keep the door shut when you are cleaning nearby but try to air your linen cupboard daily. Linens should be sorted and kept in neat piles, the guest towels and other special linen carefully hidden in a corner where the family won't grab them. Put linen just back from the laundry on the bottom of each pile so that articles will rotate in use and wear uniformly.

During special cleaning, remove all linen to a safe place and clean the walls, shelves, floor and lighting fixtures thoroughly, according to the material. Air the closet for several hours, then re-line the shelves with fresh paper and replace your linen. This is a good time to check on possible needs.

Linoleum Linoleum is made by applying to a canvas base a coating of hot, oxidized linseed oil, rosin, powdered cork and pigments. Sweep it or dust it with an *unoiled* mop. Wash with a cloth or mop wrung out of hot water containing an unbuilt synthetic detergent, mild soap, or washing soda. Rinse with a cloth or mop wrung out of clear hot water. Wipe dry. Clean a small area at a time until the floor has been finished. It is important that the cloths used be well wrung out as water rots linoleum. So does oil. Never let either stand on it. Harsh soaps contain alkalies that also are damaging. Scouring powders cut into the sealed surface.

Waxing helps preserve linoleum, enhances its appearance and makes it easier to clean. It is especially important for printed linoleum because the design is on the surface and tends to wear away. To remove old wax, wash the floor with a strong solution of your favourite floor cleaner. On linoleum you have your choice of self-polishing, liquid or paste wax. If you use liquid or paste wax apply it very sparingly over a small area at a time and rub it in thoroughly. Then polish with a weighted buffer or an electric waxer. Wax looks best when applied in a miserly fashion; it takes a better polish and is less likely to be slippery. A waxed floor often needs only to be damp-mopped. Self-polishing waxes are generally preferred for kitchen linoleum.

Be wary of special finishes for linoleum. Varnish, shellac and lacquer are not recommended as a finish. They cause cracks, ridges and discolouration. Worn or dis-coloured linoleum can be painted with floor or deck paint.

IMITATION: Wash with a cloth or mop wrung out of warm, rather than hot, soapy water. Rinse with a cloth wrung out of clear warm water. Wipe dry. Imitation linoleum can be varnished, if desired, to preserve the pattern.

Loose Covers Have your loose covers dry-cleaned if you are not sure that they are washable. If both fabric and bindings are colourfast and shrinkproof, or allowance has been made for shrinkage, they can be safely washed.

It is not difficult to wash slip covers by machine. The first step is to vacuum them or brush them thoroughly, paying particular attention to seams and bindings. Step two is to remove conspicuous spots and stains by wetting them and brushing them with soap or detergent. Ripped seams should be mended, zippers or other fasteners closed.

For washing, use soap or a synthetic detergent, and warm water if the colour is delicate. Wash the covers and rinse them twice. If very soiled, you may want to give them a second brief washing, followed by rinses. Do not spin them too long to avoid setting wrinkles.

Loose covers dried on a line should be turned inside out and placed in the shade. Pin the front of a chair seat straight to one line and the top of the back to a parallel line. This encourages quick drying and an even distribution of moisture.

Chintz and linen fabrics may require all-over ironing. Iron glazed chintz on the right side to bring up the sheen. If it does not have a permanent finish use a light starch containing wax. (See

Chintz.) For loose covers of other materials that do not need all-over ironing, iron the ruffles or pleats while the material is still damp, then place the loose covers on the chairs to finish drying. This saves work, and the loose covers fit better.

Lucite Trade name for an acrylic plastic. See *Acrylic Plastics* and *Plastics.*

Lurex Trade name for metallic and plastic thread made by giving aluminium foil a coating which withstands washing and dry-cleaning. The thread, which comes in several colours, does not tarnish. Wash according to main fibre – e.g. cotton, silk, nylon. For unwashable materials sponge to remove spots. Warm iron, NEVER hot.

Magnesite A flooring made by mixing assorted stones in a substance similar to concrete, cutting it down and polishing it. See *Stone Floors.*

Magnesium Magnesium is a bluish white metal, one-third lighter than aluminium. It is obtained by intricate processes from sea water and a bath full of ocean will yield about one pound. In thin ribbon strips and in powder form magnesium is highly flammable, emitting a brilliant white light. In this form it is used for flares at airfields, etc. But don't let this worry you if you have a new magnesium pancake griddle. The metal is incombustible *except* when powdered or cut in the thinnest of strips.

Magnesium is used for all sorts of cooking utensils, for piano frames, garden furniture, ladders and other objects. It is valuable because of its light weight and because it does not rust, tarnish, or corrode.

Magnesium furniture requires no particular care, just dusting and ordinary washing. But watch your magnesium ladder and garden furniture when the wind begins to blow.

Magnesium griddles are often given a protective coating of wax at the factory. This should be removed with a cleaning powder and medium hot water before the utensil is used. Dry and coat the entire cooking area with vegetable shortening or cooking oil before placing it over the heat.

With use, a magnesium griddle loses its bright silver colour and takes on a deep, rich, gunmetal lustre. It is then giving its best cooking service so do not try to remove it. Just clean your griddle with a light application of cleanser or steel wool.

Mahogany See *Furniture (Wooden).*

Majolica A type of glazed pottery made in Italy, etc. See *Pottery.*

Mantel Be fussy about your mantel because a fireplace is always the focal point of a room. Clean it according to the material of which it is made and do not allow it to become cluttered. See *Marble, Walls and Ceilings (Painted),* etc.

Manufacturer Manufacturers of reliable household equipment are anxious that you should get satisfaction and pleasure from them. When repairs are needed, or parts are lost, a courteous note addressed even to a giant corporation will often bring surprising results.

The name and address of the company is usually stamped somewhere on the equipment, along with a number indicating the model. Or you can find the address in your booklet of instructions if you saved it. The care and maintenance departments of the different companies will often repair your electric iron, mend your doll, send you a new handle for your tea kettle and replace small parts of other equipment. They will take up as their own the problem of finding a suitable repairman for your refrigerator, sometimes going to a great deal of trouble and expense to please you. And, believe it or not, there will be times when you won't even be charged.

This is called 'public relations', which sounds a little formidable. Public relations, however, means the importance of pleasing you, the consumer, and that is very good business. So, before you throw away the electric iron or fire extinguisher that the local man says isn't worth fixing, send it to the factory and find out. Pack it securely and fasten your stamped letter of explanations to the box with cellulose tape. That makes things easier at the other end. It may take a little time but, when you get your equipment back, the chances are it will work like new.

Marble Marble is a form of limestone, more or less crystalline, or granular in structure. It is found in many colours and combinations of colours, also in pure white and black and patterned in strange designs. While subdued colours predominate brilliant reds, yellows, blues and greens also are seen, blended in fantastic patterns.

Polished marble in good condition needs only to be dusted or wiped with a soft damp cloth. If it has been soiled through neglect or improper maintenance, the situation can usually be corrected by applying suitable cleaners or stain removers. On polished marble, if a damp cloth will not suffice, use a cloth wrung out of suds made with Ivory or Lux soap flakes. Rinse thoroughly and wipe dry with chamois to prevent streaking. A mild detergent solution can be used as a one-time cleaner on very soiled marble. (Do *not* use strong detergents.) Even a mild detergent should not be used repeatedly because yellowing or other surface change may result on some types of marble. After cleaning, apply a sealer.

Marble furniture is cleaned by the method described for polished marble. Spilled foods, cosmetics, and drinks should be wiped up promptly, a rule which applies to all fine furniture. Fruit juices, carbonated drinks, and foods containing acids produce dull areas that look like stains but are actually etchings, revealing the colour of the unpolished marble which is always lighter. Minor etchings and scratches can usually be removed by patient rubbing with powdered tin oxide (putty powder). Sprinkle the powder on the surface and rub vigorously with a moistened felt pad or chamois. When the shine has been restored, rinse the surface with clean water and dry it thoroughly with a soft cloth. Preferably, apply a sealer to the clean marble after the proper interval.

Marble floors are cleaned with detergent. Wet the floor with clean water, sprinkle it with detergent, then mop or scrub the floor. Clean a small area at a time and remove the soiled water promptly. Rinse with a clean mop. If some areas are badly soiled, give them this special treatment: Mix the detergent with water to the consistency of thick cream and apply it to the soiled marble. Let it dry, then rinse it off thoroughly with clean water. If the floor looks dusty or white when it is dry, too much detergent has been used or the floor has been incompletely rinsed. Rinse it again. Sealed marble floors can be damp-mopped.

Stains on marble, as on other materials, are easier to remove if they are treated promptly. Remove the material that has caused the stain, then apply the proper stain remover. Solvents recommended are alcohol, acetone, lighter fluid, and inflammable cleaning fluids. The best bleach is hydrogen peroxide (35 per cent). Deep stains may require patient poulticing. A poultice is made by mixing a stain remover with detergent or whiting.

Oil and grease stains are usually dark in the centre shading to light. For these, use one of the solvents listed, applied in a poultice or on a white blotter covered with glass or plastic film to hold in the moisture. Repeat as often as necessary. Rinse.

For rust stains, use a poultice made with a commercial rust remover. Rinse thoroughly.

Organic stains (yellow to rose) from coloured paper, foliage, tobacco, tea, coffee, and cosmetics are removed with hydrogen peroxide. Apply it directly to a flat surface, as a poultice to a vertical surface. Add a few drops of ammonia and let it remain until the bubbling stops. Rinse with water.

For ink stains (except those caused by metallic inks) use hydrogen peroxide. Apply it directly to the stain and rinse after a few minutes.

If the marble is etched slightly by a stain remover, polish it with putty powder, as previously described.

If your marble needs refinishing, consult your local dealer. It is not easy to do it yourself.

Marocain A medium weight crêpe fabric, now usually made in acetate. Wash in warm suds, rinse at once. When almost dry stretch under warm iron to original shape.

Matting See *Carpets and Rugs.*

Mattress Mattresses accumulate dust and should be cleaned periodically with the upholstery attachment of your vacuum cleaner or a good stiff broom. An occasional sun and air bath will help keep them fresh and clean. If badly soiled, clean them with soap foam or upholstery shampoo, following the directions given for *Furniture – Upholstered.*

To ensure long wear and comfortable service, a hair mattress should be turned frequently from side to side and from end to end. Makers of fine mattresses recommend turning them daily; you, however, probably care more for yourself than for the mattress to undertake it. Turn it, though, at least once a week. (Foam-rubber mattresses do not need to be turned).

If you have a good mattress that has become lumpy or has lost its bounce, think about having it remade. There are firms that specialize in this sort of thing. For a fraction of the cost of a new one, your mattress can be cleaned, sterilized and completely remade. Mattresses and inner springs also can be cut down in size and otherwise remodelled.

See also *Kapok* and *Foam Rubber*.

Melamine and Urea Melamine plastic is used for dinnerware, table and counter tops, cutlery handles, buttons, housings for electric shavers, and other appliances. Urea is used for buttons, bottle tops, electric plugs, and wall plates. Both plastics are hard to break but should be protected against sharp or severe blows.

Melamine and urea are odourless, nontoxic, and tasteless. They can be washed with soap or detergent in very hot water, but should not be subjected to oven heat or a direct flame. Freezing does not affect them. Alcohol, cleaning fluids, mild acids, and alkalies do not damage them; but keep abrasives away.

Dinnerware of melamine is in the high-quality bracket, but it can go into the dishwasher and emerge undamaged. Even boiling water will not soften it. Special washing compounds are available to remove stains. Baking soda will often remove light stains. Sodium perborate is usually effective for heavy stains. Heavy abrasives, including steel wool pads, should not be used. A mild detergent is suggested for automatic dishwashers. See also *Plastics*.

Metals The various metals used about the house are treated individually in this book, so look up *Gold, Silver, Monel, Aluminium*, etc., and also *Jewellery*. The surface of a metal must be scratched lightly with an appropriate abrasive if it is to shine. If the abrasive selected is too harsh, the scratches will show. If it is too soft, it will not polish the surface. Therefore the same polish cannot be used on all metals, since some are much softer than others.

Micarta A trade name for a laminated phenolic resin. See *Phenolic* and *Plastics*.

Mirrors Mirrors can be cleaned with a soft damp cloth wrung out of plain warm water, or water to which a little vinegar or ammonia has been added. Spray-on window cleaners can also be used. Polish with a lintless cloth or chamois leather. Moistened face or toilet tissue can be used for a quick cleanup of the bathroom mirror. Polish with dry tissue. In washing mirrors great care must be taken not to wet the backing. Don't let water seep in around the edges, or between the glass and the frame, or the mirror will be damaged.

Good mirrors that have become useless and unsightly through damaged backing can be resilvered. Consult your hardware dealer or furniture repairman about this. You may want to undertake it yourself, but it isn't easy. Clean mirror frames according to directions given under *Picture*.

Mixer See *Electric Mixer*.

Modacrylic As the name suggests, modacrylic textile fibres are modified acrylics. They contain less than 85 per cent (but must contain at least 35 per cent) of the chemical substance acrylonitrile. Modacrylics are sold under the trade names Dynel and Verel. Since the two fibres differ, each is listed. See *Dynel* and *Verel*.

Model Aircraft Cement See *Stains*, page 138.

Mohair A textile made of wool from the Angora goat. See *Woollens*.

Moiré A rippled fabric, ribbed or corded; after weaving it is subjected to heat and heavy pressure from rollers. Because of the ribbing, some parts are not flattened and the two surfaces show different reflections which give a watered effect. Dry-clean.

Monel Metal Monel metal is an alloy of nickel and copper, named for the French scientist who perfected it. Wipe Monel metal with a cloth wrung out of hot soapy water, or water with a detergent, rinse and rub dry. If desired, scour it with a fine cleaning powder.

Mop (Dry) Give it a good shake out-of-doors if you live in the country, to get rid of the dust. If you live in the city, shake it into a big paper bag or clean it with your vacuum cleaner. When dust clings tenaciously to the strings, the mop needs a bath. A mop made of cotton yarn should be soaked overnight in water containing soap or detergent. Wash it by plunging it up and down in the water. Remove hairs and lint. Rinse thoroughly, squeeze out excess water, and untangle the strings by 'combing' them with a pencil. Shake the mop to fluff the yarn and hang it to dry in an airy place, preferably outdoors. Some cotton mops, made to fit over metal frames, can be slipped off and washed by machine. Enclose them in a nylon mesh (or muslin) bag, to avoid unravelling the yarn.

Wool mops do not need to be washed often because dust is more easily shaken out of the yarn. Wash your wool mop, without previous

soaking, in lukewarm suds made with a mild synthetic detergent. Rinse in lukewarm water, squeeze out excess, shake to fluff, and dry in any airy place away from direct sun or any source of heat.

Mop (Oiled) Wash mops used for oiled floors like other dry mops, but make the suds stronger. When dry, add a few drops of oil polish to the strings and store the mop head in a closed metal can. Oiled mops and dusters sometimes ignite spontaneously and cause fires.

Mop (Wet) Mops used with cleaning compounds, soaps, and detergents usually need only to be rinsed thoroughly after use. Squeeze the water out of string mops and gently separate the strands. Press sponge mops as dry as possible and hang them in the shade. Cotton yarn mops can dry in the sun. They benefit by a trim now and then. Using sturdy scissors, snip off frayed ends. Mops should never be stored wet in a pail or on the floor. Hang them up to dry and when you store them. If put away damp, they are likely to mildew and develop an unpleasant odour. See *Sponge (Cellulose)*.

Moquette An upholstery fabric with heavy pile made from wool, cotton, Evlan and acrylics such as Courtelle and Acrilan. Most moquette must be dry-cleaned, but detachable acrylic covers may be washable. See manufacturer's instructions.

Mother-of-Pearl The rainbow substance which lines sea shells: nacre. See *Pearl Handles*.

Muslin A fine cotton fabric originating in the East. Wash in warm water, rinse thoroughly, iron with warm iron while still damp.

Nappies Nappy washing services, approved by physicians generally, are a boon to mothers, especially during the first few months. They provide the nappies as well as a container and laundry service.

If nappies are to be washed at home you will need a large, plastic or enamelware pail as a container for used nappies. Fill it with cold water and add a little detergent, if desired. Place the nappies in the pail to soak. If the nappy is soiled, shake or scrape off as much as you can and rub a little soap or detergent into the stained part before putting it to soak. (Paper nappy linings, strong and fleecy soft, or cleansing tissues, obviate this trouble).

Wash nappies with the baby's other clothes in plenty of hot water with any mild soap or detergent and rinse them thoroughly. Rinsing is as important as washing because, unless all traces of soap are removed, a baby's tender skin is likely to be irritated. If the water in your area is soft, two or three rinsings may be enough. If the water is hard, three or four rinsings may be required to remove all the soap. A little bleach can be used in the wash water if you rinse the nappies several times.

Boiling, ironing, or the use of a special rinse, may be necessary for an infant susceptible to nappy rash. Ask your doctor about this. Disposable paper nappies are

hygienic and convenient, but expensive. Use them if you are travelling with your baby. The newest in washable nappies fasten with press-together nylon tape. See '*Velcro.*'

Net See *Cotton*.

Nickel Nickel is a hard, silver-white, lustrous metal, usually used around the home as a plating over steel or copper. It also is used in the alloy, Monel metal. 'Nickel' is an abbreviation of the German *Kupfernickel* (copper mimic). It was first obtained from the copper-coloured ore, niccolite, in 1751. The designation implies some annoyance on the part of an early prospector. who thought he had found copper, The value of copper at that time was well known, while that of the new metal was a question mark.

Clean nickel with soap and water, rinse, then polish with a soft cloth. If this treatment is not sufficient, use whiting, or a fine cleaning powder, moistened with alcohol. Rinse and polish. Nickel darkens if it is not cleaned frequently.

Ninon A sheer fabric made from fine, twisted yarns. Originally silk, ninon is now usually acetate, nylon or polyester fibres. e.g. 'Terylene', 'Dacron'. See appropriate fabric.

Nitrate A plastic. See *Cellulosics*.

Nomex Nomex is the trade name for a new du Pont nylon that is unusually tough, resistant to high heat, and virtually unaffected by chemicals. Its main uses are industrial but ironing-board covers are being made of it and protective clothing for firemen, spacemen, truck drivers, auto racers, and workers in many industrial fields. Du Pont claims that a 'Nomex' ironing-board cover will not char, burn, ignite or melt if the hottest iron (500°F) is left face down on it for several months. 'Nomex' can be machine washed by standard methods, but do not use a chlorine bleach. It yellows white 'Nomex' and continued use degrades the fibre. Peroxy bleaches are safe.

Nylon Nylon, spun in a test tube from chemicals found in coal, air and water, was the first no-iron synthetic to achieve commercial success. It was first produced in 1928 by chemists engaged in basic research for the du Pont Company. Years of experimentation and testing followed. It made its bow to the public in 1940 in the guise of sheer, quick-drying hosiery and was acclaimed with cheers. Eighteen months later the stockings were unobtainable. Nylon had gone to war. It was making tough ropes for mountain troops, cord for bomber tyres, parachutes, military clothing, life rafts.

In 1945, nylon returned to the domestic field and the first drip dry clothing began to appear. The strong silky fibres were woven into gossamer hosiery; dainty lingerie with pleated net, lace and embroideries that never needed ironing; dresses, blouses and tough lightweight outdoor gear that could take real punishment. Nylon resists moths, mildew, ageing, and most chemicals. When properly heat-set, nylon materials will not stretch, but if stretch is wanted it can be achieved. Nylon textured under heat to resemble minute accordion pleats, coiled springs, loops and curls, not only retains its new form but springs back to it if pulled straight. This makes possible stretch clothing.

Nylon is easy to care for. Many spots can be sponged off with plain warm water if treated when fresh, and standard cleaning fluids can be used for greasy stains. Provided the dyes are fast, it can be machine laundered with heavy-duty detergents. It is heat-sensitive. White textiles should always be laundered separately because they tend to pick up tints from coloured clothing.

For laundering instructions see *Drip Dry*. See also *Antistatic, Sweaters, Synthetic, Curtains, Pile Coats*.

Nylon Fur Launder small items in hand hot water and soap-flakes or mild synthetic detergent. Squeeze fur in suds for several minutes, rinse in warm water, squeeze out moisture, dry out-of-doors if possible, away from direct heat.

For large garments with linings it is safer to use a dry shampoo according to instructions on the container.

Nylon Net, Flare Free Treated to make party garments safe. Wash as for nylon. Drip dry.

Nylon Plastic Nylon plastic is translucent or opaque, milky white when uncoloured and softly pastel when tinted, with a texture similar to horn. It is light in weight, rigid, yet slightly resilient. Although nylon will stand rough treatment and is not affected by freezing temperatures, it is not intended for continuous outdoor use.

Nylon plastic is used for tumblers that will bounce but not break, for brushes and bristles, combs, funnels and salad sets. Slide fasteners made of nylon can be ironed with a warm (never hot) iron. Dry-cleaning fluids will not damage them. Brushes with nylon bristles *and* nylon backs can be sterilized by boiling. (If the handles are transparent they are probably acrylic and cannot be boiled.)

Utensils made of nylon can go

into the automatic dishwasher and emerge unscathed. If dishes are piled on top of them they may lose their shape, but prompt rewashing will restore it. Nylon utensils used with coffee, mustard, beets and other coloured foods should be washed quickly to avoid stains.

Nylon plastic is not affected by chemicals. It cannot go into an oven or over a flame. Use no abrasives. See also *Plastics*.

Oilcloth Oilcloth is made by coating a textile with a mixture of linseed oil, whiting and pigment. It should not be folded when wet because of its tendency to crack along the folds and at the corners. Sunlight and strong heat also damage it. Remove food stains quickly, before they become set. Clean oilcloth by wiping it with a damp cloth or a cloth dampened in warm suds, made with a mild soap or detergent. Do not use harsh cleaning powders and do not set hot dishes on it. Alcohol, acetone and amyl acetate are especially damaging to the finish.

Oiled Floors See *Woodwork*.

Oil Heaters Oil heaters are perfectly safe when manufacturers' instructions are followed. Never move or refill an oil stove when it is alight. Trim wicks often. Use the paraffin recommended by the manufacturer. Buy a good make.

Oil Paintings If your oil painting is at all valuable, leave it strictly alone, except for dusting. Paintings seldom need first-aid treatment in the home. If any doubt exists about the condition of the painting, don't touch it until it can be examined by a professional restorer. The associate curator of a famous art museum reluctantly offers the following advice regarding the care of oil paintings:

'Superficial dust and dirt can be removed from an oil painting in sound condition by a light brushing with absorbent cotton or a soft brush. Either of these can be used dry or moistened with a petrol-type dry-cleaning fluid (inflammable; proper precautions must be taken). The canvas must be firmly and uniformly supported from the reverse while any pressure is being put upon the face of the painting.

'Paintings should not be treated, on front or back, with soap, water, breadcrumbs, erasers, raw potato, sliced onion or oil of any kind. Some of these may improve the appearance of a painting temporarily, but all can be harmful in inexperienced hands.

'A painting whose surface has become dull can frequently be brightened by the use of a good quality prepared wax emulsion cream furniture polish. If the manufacturer's directions for use on fine furniture are carefully followed, no harm should result and the thin film of wax left on the surface is a safe and moderately durable protection.

'*No other treatment* should be followed by inexperienced persons.'

Olefin Olefins are high-strength synthetic textile fibres based on polyethylene and polypropylene. They are resistant to stains, sunlight, ageing, acids, and alkalies. Mildew does not attack them. An outstanding quality is that they absorb moisture and thus have a low static level.

These fibres appear in blends with wool, acrylics, cotton and rayon for clothing. Alone, they are used for knitwear such as socks, sweaters and sports shirts and for bathing suits, lingerie, nappies and babies' pants, neckties and 'Ban-Lon' outer sportswear.

Olefin fibres are extremely light and therefore provide superior bulk and cover. Manufacturers say olefin textiles 'breathe' and thus do not become clammy and sticky. Household furnishings (upholstery, rugs) resist stains and spills, which are easily wiped up. Olefin clothing is machine washable in warm water and can be machine dried at a low temperature setting (140°F to 160°F). It requires little or no ironing. For touch-up, use a low setting. See also *Synthetic Textiles*.

Onyx Marble Onyx marble, sometimes called Oriental alabaster, is a translucent and particularly iridescent variety of carbonate of lime, bearing some resemblance to the stone, onyx. Hence its name. It is a material of great beauty and is used to make cases for clocks, vases, lamps and tabletops.

Ancient quarries in Egypt were rediscovered about 1850 and these furnish a highly prized quality of stone. However, the chief supply comes from Algeria, where a fine quality is obtained abundantly. More recently, a similar stone has been found in Mexico. This is called Mexican onyx or tecali marble.

Organdie Cotton organdie should be laundered in warm suds made with a mild, pure soap and handled gently so as not to distort the threads. Rinse carefully. If the organdie has a permanent finish, it will not require starch. After many washings, however, it probably will benefit from a light starch. Limp organdies require regular starching – one part basic mixture and one part water. Gelatine, gum arabic and gum tragacanth are preferred as a stiffening by some women. Organdies may be rolled while wet in a Turkish towel to absorb moisture. In this case they can be ironed almost immediately. If embroidered, iron on the reverse side.

Organza Organza, a sheer dress material similar to organdie but with more body and stiffness, is made of various fibres – silk, rayon, nylon. Follow the instructions on the hang tag for washing or dry cleaning.

Orlon 'Orlon' is the trade name for du Pont's acrylic fibre. It has many of the desirable characteristics of nylon. It is important where strength and low stretch are required. It washes easily, dries quickly, has good heat and moisture resistance, is not attacked by moths or mildew and can be set by heat so that it resumes its original shape and dimensions after washing.

'Orlon' is amost equal to nylon in tensile strength, withstands heat better, is more absorbent and has better covering, or bulking, ability. 'Orlon' is not affected by the acidic fumes that damage nylon. Most ordinary chemicals and solvents will not harm it. It is practically impervious to moths and other insects, moulds and bacteria.

'Orlon' continuous filament yarn is silklike, warm, dry and luxurious to the touch. 'Orlon' staple on the other hand, is like wool, warm and soft. While light in weight, 'Orlon' has the strength and feel of heavier materials and good recovery from wrinkles.

'Orlon' is used alone and in blends for sports shirts, blouses, sweaters, skirts, blankets, socks, work clothing, service uniforms, pleated materials, and pile coatings. Spots can be sponged off with water or cleaning fluids. It can be washed or dry cleaned according to the label. See *Acrylic Textiles, Sweaters, Blanket*. See also *Pile Coats*.

Paint Your procedure in cleaning a painted surface and your selection of a cleaner for the job probably will be influenced by several factors. If the surface is chipped, scuffed and needs redoing anyhow, you will no doubt proceed with scouring powders and strong cleaners and a what-the-heck attitude. If you rent your apartment or house, you probably won't be as particular as if you owned the place. If you own the place, you will be more careful, but, if you did that paint job yourself, you will give the surface tender, loving care.

Some paints are not washable. These include the water washes, such as calcimine and whitewash. Oil paints thinned with water ('Kemtone', etc.) are difficult to clean. Good oil paints, thinned with turpentine, and rubberized and synthetic resin paints can be cleaned satisfactorily if a proper method is selected.

For procedure see *Walls and Ceilings* and *Furniture*. For a discussion of various cleaners see *Paint Cleaners*. For Paint stains on textiles, see *Stains*, page 151–2.

Paintbrushes See *Brushes – Paint*.

Paintings See *Oil Paintings* and *Water Colour Paintings*.

Palladium Palladium is a silver-white metal, malleable and ductile, often used instead of platinum and sometimes called platinum. However, it is a much less expensive metal. Clean it like platinum See *Jewellery, Platinum*.

Parchment Parchment is made from skins of goats and sheep, especially dressed so that it may be written on. The skin is scraped with sharp instruments and rubbed with pum-ice until the desired thickness is obtained. See *Lampshades*.

Patent Leather Leather dressed so as to have a high gloss. See *Shoes*.

Pearl The pearl has been called the purest of gems because it requires neither cutting nor polishing. Pearls have been known and prized since ancient times and are found wherever mussels and oysters flourish. Chemically, pearls consist of layers of calcium carbonate and animal tissue, called nacre, which lines the shells. They are formed when an irritating particle, such as a grain of sand, invades the shell. Pearls are usually silvery white, or bluish white, but some are pink, yellow, copper-coloured, smoky brown, grey and black. Light-blue, purple and black pearls are found in the common clam. The finest grey and black pearls come from the Gulf of California. Pink pearls are of two varieties, those from the common conch shells of West Indian seas and those from fresh mussels, found in France, Scotland, Germany, and the United States. Ceylon, the Persian Gulf, Thursday Island and the west coast of Australia produce the most beautiful white pearls. Cultured pearls are made by injecting a small bead or similar object into a pearl oyster shell. Imitation pearls are usually made of glass coated with an essence of fish scales.

Pearls in rings and pins can be washed with mild soap or a synthetic detergent and water. Do not use ammonia. Pearl necklaces should be restrung at least once a year, or whenever they are loose on the string. To keep them clean, rub them gently and frequently with a piece of clean, soft chamois leather, taking care to rub between the beads. This will remove the film of dirt that collects on the pearls when they are worn. Do not use soap and water to clean a pearl necklace. Water will soon rot the thread.

Artificial pearls are cleaned in the same way as genuine pearls.
CAUTION: Acids dissolve pearls; high heat destroys them.

Pearl Handles Pearl handles are made of mother-of-pearl, the nacre that lines sea shells. They need only soap and water. No ammonia. Do not let pearl handles soak in water as this treatment may loosen the cement that holds them in place. Do not put them in your dishwasher.

Peau D'ange or 'Angel Skin', A dress fabric with a satin weave. Dry-clean.

Percolator See *Coffee Maker.*

Permanent Press i.e. Permanent Pleating. Permanent press clothing goes a step beyond drip dry in which the textile (synthetic and blends) is said to have a 'built-in' memory that enables it to return to its original, crease-free state when properly washed and drip dried. In permanent press, the garment also 'remembers' the shape that was 'locked in' when it was sewn and pressed. This is accomplished by treating fabrics (of synthetic and natural fibres and blends) with finishing agents which are 'cured' or 'set' by heat after the garment has been made.

Permanent-press techniques are constantly being improved and the result is an ever-increasing range of garments and household accessories which do not require ironing. Proper laundering will enable you to get the best possible results. If full instructions have not been provided by the manufacturer, follow these directions.

Launder permanent-press items promptly when they are slightly soiled. Some synthetic fibres included in them tend to absorb and hold oily soil.

Pretreat spots on moderately soiled clothing by rubbing them with liquid detergent or a paste made of powdered detergent and water. If doubtful of colour fastness, first test an inconspicuous area. Should fading result, remove oily stains with cleaning fluid and launder by hand with a mild detergent or soap. Rinse, roll loosely in a towel to remove excess water, then hang to dry. If the clothing is heavily soiled, measure out the amount of detergent for an entire load and apply it full strength to the most soiled area. Add hot water and let the clothes soak until the water is cool.

Wash in small loads, preferably with cool water. Use the wash-and-wear or durable-press (permanent) cycle if it is provided on your machine. Otherwise adjust the controls by hand to short wash, rinse, and spin cycles. If warm or hot water is needed to remove the dirt, rinse in cool water.

Also dry in small loads, about half of the dryer's capacity. This minimizes creasing. Again use the drip-dry or durable press cycle if available, or set the dryer for low or medium heat. At the end of the drying cycle, turn off the heat and let the clothes continue to tumble for a 10-minute cool-down period. Remove them as soon as the dryer stops, and hang or fold them.

The heat and tumbling action of an automatic dryer relaxes fibres and removes creases that appear during washing and wearing. If an automatic dryer is not available, shorten the final rinse spin in the washer by advancing the dial, or remove the garments while dripping wet and put them on rust-proof hangers to dry.

Water and fabric softeners can be used as desired. If a bleach is needed, a sodium perborate type is suggested because chlorine bleaches yellow some durable-press cottons. Stain removal is the same as for other fabrics but quick action is desirable because grease and other stains are harder to remove from some treated cottons. For touching up with an iron use the low setting.

If you wash by hand, drip dry. Permanent-press clothing can also be dry-cleaned. See also *Pleats*.

Pewter Pewter is a grey alloy of several metals, usually tin with lead, or tin with copper. It has been made in China for over 3,000 years. Since pewter is a soft metal, it should not be subjected to harsh polishes. For a dull finish rub it with rottenstone and olive oil, mixed to a paste. Use a soft cloth. Wash, rinse and wipe dry. For a bright finish use a paste made by mixing whiting and denatured alcohol. Let the paste dry on the pewter, then polish. Wash, rinse and dry. Special polishes are available for pewter.

Bad spots can be removed from pewter by rubbing them with grade 00 steel wool, dipped in olive oil, to prevent scratching.

Very old pewter sometimes acquires a brownish scale (museum scale) caused by climatic action on the tin in the alloy. This can be removed by soaking the pieces in a strong solution of lye. (See *Lye* for precautions.) Japanned pieces and those with wooden knobs and handles should not receive this treatment. Be sure the articles are covered completely. After allowing them to soak for about 15 minutes, remove them with tongs, rinse them carefully and scrub them with a stiff brush. It may be necessary to repeat this treatment a number of times to remove the scale completely. After it has been removed, the pewter may be polished in the usual way.

Phenolic There are two types of phenolic plastic, moulded and cast. Moulded phenolics are light in weight and very durable. They are hard to break or scratch. Limited in colour to blacks and browns, they are found in the home as TV and radio cabinets, pot and iron handles, wall panelling and other utilitarian furnishings.

Cast phenolic is decorative. It is produced in a full range of translucent, transparent, and opaque colours as well as in marbled effects. Pen desk sets, chessmen, clock cases, jewellery, teething rings, and cutlery handles are made of phenolic.

These plastics are unharmed by chemicals and by heat up to 300°F. They are not damaged by freezing temperatures. Do not subject them to high heat or place them near an open flame. They can be hand washed with very hot water containing soap or detergent, but cannot stand boiling water. Cleaning fluids do not affect them, but do not use abrasives. See also *Plastics*.

Piano 'A fine piano is a work of art. Therefore, to treat it roughly, carelessly or negligently is to commit a crime against a beautiful piece of expensive craftmanship. To pay a lot of money for a fine piano and then allow it to go to ruin for lack of expert care is not merely aesthetically wrong – it is bad business'.

This is the opinion of an expert on the subject of piano care, a director of acoustic research. Of what does piano care consist? The summary which follows has been compiled from information given by Steinway and Sons, makers of fine pianos for nearly a century.

TUNING: Proper care of a piano demands at least three, and preferably four, tunings a year, during spring, summer, autumn and winter. Pianos get out of tune, whether used or not, as the result of contraction and expansion due to atmospheric changes. Tuning does not affect the tone of a piano. It simply puts the strings in unison and at the proper pitch.

REGULATING: In addition to tuning, a piano requires tone and action regulating, and other servicing from time to time. All pianos tend to become more brilliant with use, owing to the constant pounding of the hammer felts against the steel strings. As the felt becomes hard through this pounding, the tone becomes more brilliant. If your piano should become too brilliant, regulating will restore the desired degree of mellowness, provided there is sufficient hammer felt left. Occasional action regulating is also desirable so that the mechanism may be smooth and responsive to the touch of the player. This is particularly desirable in damp climates, since the felt bushings in the action parts absorb moisture and swell, causing the action to become sluggish.

LOCATION: Your piano should be kept in a normal temperature and free from dampness. Dampness will cause rust on the metal parts and swelling of the action. It will also injure the finish of the case, and may raise the softer fibres of the sound-board.

Do not place your piano near hot water pipes, or stoves, or where one end may be hot and the other cold. Do not open opposite windows of a warm room, permitting cold draughts to blow on the piano. However well the finish may have endured weather testing, it may be seriously affected by rapid changes of temperature.

INTERIOR: Have the interior of your piano cleaned from time to time. This helps to prevent damage to the fine wool felts, which are liable to attack from moths. It also prevents corrosion of the strings and pins. Ask your tuner about moth-proofing the felts and hammers.

EXTERIOR AND KEYS: Do not use furniture polish or other preparations for polishing purposes, or any coarse fabrics on the case of a new piano. If dull, wipe it with a soft, damp (not wet) chamois or a soft, dampened cheesecloth. Then remove the moisture with a dry, soft cloth or chamois. (If the chamois is brand-new, soak it in water for 24 hours before using it.) If your piano is old, with a waxed or varnished case, clean it according to directions given under *Furniture*.

Do not place vases or other objects on your piano. They may leave pressure marks. Close the top when the piano is not in use, but expose the keyboard to light.

Ivory turns yellow if continuously kept from the light. If the keys become dusty or dirty, wipe them lengthwise with a soft, slightly dampened cloth and then follow with a soft, dry cloth.

PRECAUTION: If your piano is to be left in an unoccupied house for some time, place camphor where it will not affect the finish of any metal or wooden parts; place quantities of newspapers in the interior to absorb moisture and cover the top with a heavy flannel cover or blankets.

Steinway experts say that when the finish of a piano becomes scarred, checked, etc., it should be sent to the factory. There the finish will be removed down to the raw wood and the case completely refinished. Keys that have become very yellow can be removed and sent to the factory for scraping and repolishing by an ivory expert. However, their true colour is not white. The ivory is specially treated and bleached. It will not remain white indefinitely.

Picture Use an aerosol spray or any of the cleaning mixtures recommended for windows. Be careful not to let your cleaner seep between the frame and the glass and stain the picture or mat. Polish with paper towels or tissues.

Clean wooden frames by wiping them with a soft cloth wrung out of warm soapy water. Dry. Apply wax or oil polish, if desired.

Soiled gilt frames may be cleaned, if necessary, with a cloth moistened with a little dry-cleaning fluid. See also *Gilding*, *Oil Paintings* and *Water Colour Paintings*.

Pile Coats Coats and robes of 100 per cent nylon or 'Orlon' pile are washed according to the following directions, provided by du Pont, manufacturer of these fibres.

Before washing, pretreat stains with liquid detergent or a paste made with detergent and water. Remove grease spots with a dry-cleaning fluid. For washing use lukewarm water (100°F) and a heavy-duty detergent. Avoid twisting and other rough handling if you wash by hand. Rinse thoroughly in clear water. Do not wring.

If you use an automatic washer, set the machine for the highest water level possible. Let the coat go through the complete washing cycle if you intend to machine dry it. Otherwise, remove it dripping wet from the final rinse, place it on a strong rustproof hanger and let it drip dry. Straighten the seams and shape the collar and cuffs while the coat is wet.

If you use a dryer, set it for the lowest possible temperature and tumble dry the coat until it is damp dry. Remove it immediately from the dryer, place it on a hanger, and adjust as described.

Pilling Fibre ends of some fabrics tend to roll into little balls, or pills, which cling tightly to the surface. They are especially noticeable on sweaters. Washing and wearing increase the pilling. To minimize pilling, turn the garment inside out before washing. Some advise washing it in a mesh bag.

To remove pills, stretch the fabric snugly over a curved surface so that the pills stand up, and snip them off with scissors. Or shave them off carefully with a safety razor.

Pillows (Down and Feathers) Fluff them daily and air them at least once a month outdoors or on a chair by an open window. Fresh air puffs them up and gives them a new lease on life.

Pillows, often very neglected,

are entitled to a bath now and then and this service can be performed by any first-class laundry. Laundry washing service differs from a renovating job. In renovating a pillow the feathers are removed from the ticking and washed separately. New feathers and down are then added if needed. Worn ticking will be replaced. Ask your laundryman about this service.

If you are washing your own pillows, first make sure that there are no ripped seams and that the ticking is in good condition. Loose feathers can cause trouble in a washer or dryer. If the ticking is weak, plan to replace it and wash the feathers separately in a muslin bag. Also wash separately the feathers of heavily stuffed pillows.

To transfer the feathers, rip out the stitching at one end of the pillow, baste the bag securely around the opening, and shake the feathers into the bag. Tightly baste the opening of the filled bag.

If the ticking is sound, rip the stitching in opposite corners for an inch or so, then pin up the openings with a heavy safety pin. These slits provide outlets for air. (Pillows with eyelet ventilators do not require this.)

Fill the washer with warm water, add detergent for a normal load, and agitate to dissolve it. Wash two pillows together, or one at a time with enough bath towels to balance the load. Immerse the pillows in the suds until they are thoroughly wet, then agitate the washer for 10 minutes. Repeat the wash if the pillows are very soiled, using slightly less detergent. Complete the rinsing cycles, then give the pillows an extra rinse.

Before putting the pillows in the dryer, check the corners to make sure the safety pins are secure. Tumble for about an hour at the warmest setting, then reduce the heat and tumble them until they are dry. If you are not using a dryer, hang the pillows outdoors in the shade, using three or more clothes pegs. Fluff them every half hour or so and turn them so that they will dry uniformly. If they are not dry by night, bring them inside. Rehang them outdoors in the morning.

Pillows (Other Than Feather)

Washing is not recommended for foam-rubber pillows, but see *Foam Rubber* for emergency action. Kapok pillows are not washable. Polyester pillows can be hand washed if necessary, but do not machine wash them unless the manufacturer advises it. Tests by du Pont show that the batt structure tends to break down and become lumpy after four or five machine washings.

To hand wash a pillow stuffed with polyester batting, immerse it in lukewarm suds made preferably with a nonsudsing synthetic detergent for easy rinsing. Compress it repeatedly to create a flow of washing water through the pillow. Rinse thoroughly in lukewarm water. Compress gently to remove excess water. Air dry overnight, or spin in an automatic washer to remove excess water and dry in a tumbler-type dryer if available. Otherwise, hang it to dry.

The newest in 'Dacron' pillows has a nylon-zippered 'Dacron' and cotton, durable-press ticking over its nylon marquisette ticking. It is the ticking that becomes soiled, not the batting. You machine wash the outer casing.

The du Pont company recommends refreshing and refluffing 'Dacron' pillows several times a year by placing them (minus the outer casing, if there is one) in a dryer for about 20 minutes at high heat.

Piqué A fabric with rounded cords running from side to side. Wash according to material i.e. cotton, rayon, etc., or according to tag.

Plastic Coat Hangers Textile chemists recommend a thorough airing of clothes cleaned in coin-operated dry-cleaning establishments. The airing can be done outdoors or in a well-ventilated room. But do not use plastic hangers for this purpose. Enough solvent may be retained in shoulder pads or thick fabrics to soften the plastic. When this happens the garment sticks to the hanger and is difficult to remove without damage. The same warning applies to clothes that are exposed to the fumes of moth preventatives.

Plastic Dishes See *Melamine and Urea.*

Plastic Floor Coverings See *Vinyl Plastic Floors.*

Plastics 'Plastics' is a family name like 'cloth' or 'metal'. Just as there are many kinds of cloth and metal, there are many kinds of plastic, each with its individual characteristics and qualifications for certain jobs.

Plastics are synthetic, or man-made, materials which have been developed by chemists in search of durable and attractive substances to take the place of the more expensive natural materials such as wood and metal. All are made from combinations of carbon with oxygen, hydrogen, nitrogen, chlorine and sulphur. By varying the combination of these ingredients, the chemist can create a plastic to suit almost any need.

Plastics represent a wealthy industry which is still growing. In addition to serving as substitutes for natural products such as wood and metal in a variety of household articles, plastics are spun into textiles and used to form dirt, stain- and crease-resisting finishes. They are used in making wet-strength paper for grocery sacks, hand towels, money, tea bags, and transparent film for protecting foods, dishes, linens, clothing and silver. Sometimes they are an ingredient of paints and varnishes.

Plastics are divided into two main groups. Thermoplastic plastics soften when exposed to sufficient heat and harden when cooled. These include the *acrylics, cellulosics, nylon, polyethylene, polystyrene* and *vinyls.* Thermosetting plastics are plastics that are set permanently by heat into various shapes during forming. Heat applied later will not soften them. The thermosetting plastics include *phenolics, amino plastics* (melamine and urea), *cold-moulded polyesters, silicones,* and *casein.*

Plastics are easy to care for. All can be cleaned safely with warm water and soap and a very soft cloth. This is preferred to wiping them with a dry, or even a damp, cloth as there is a tendency for dust particles to scratch the surface of fine plastics unless they are lubricated. Soap and water provide that lubrication.

To provide more detailed information about plastics, what they will and will not do and the special care they require, plastics in household use are listed in this book alphabetically and a reference to their family branch is given. Thus, you might look up *Lucite* and find that it is an acrylic plastic. You would then look up *Acrylic Plastics* to learn more about it.

Plastic Sheeting Articles made of washable plastic sheeting (shower curtains, storage bags, covers for furniture and equipment) benefit by a brief machine washing now and then. Warm water helps keep the plastic soft and pliable. If the sheeting has a printed pattern, test it first for colour fastness. To do this, wipe a small inconspicuous area with full-strength liquid detergent on a cloth wrung out of hot water. If colour comes off, do not put the article in the washer. Just sponge it with lukewarm suds.

For machine-washing colourfast washable sheeting, use warm water and a small amount of detergent. Make the washing cycle short. If the water is hard, a suitable softener ('Calgon', 'Oakite') in the rinse water will prevent water spots. Place small articles in a mesh bag to keep them from being sucked into the pump or drain. Use slow agitation and spin speed if these controls are available. Agitate for two or three minutes, then spin off water. Do not put plastic articles through the wringer; such treatment can cause permanent creases. Just shake the water out, refill the tub with warm water, and rinse them briefly. Wipe dry with a clean towel, or hang to dry – away from sunlight and any source of heat.

SPECIAL NOTE: If a shower curtain is mildewed, brush off as much as possible, then wipe it with a chlorine bleach solution before placing it in the washer. For a soap-filled shower curtain, use only water softener in the washing water and agitate for five minutes. The soap film will provide sufficient detergent. Use the softener in the rinse water too. Rehang to dry.

Plastic Tile See *Polystyrene* and *Vinyl*.

Platinum Platinum ranks above gold among the precious metals. It is non-tarnishing and dull silver in colour. Platinum is very heavy, easily worked and is unaffected by all simple acids. It melts only at a very high temperature. These qualities make it extremely useful in chemical and other scientific processes. It also is used for jewellery.

Platinum was first discovered in South America and takes its name from the Spanish word, *plata* (silver), because of its resemblance to that metal. There is nothing tricky about cleaning platinum. If dirty from grease, etc., simply wash it with a detergent or soap and water, rinse and dry with tissues.

See also *Jewellery*.

Playing Cards Wipe plastic cards with a damp cloth. To clean paper cards wipe them carefully with a bit of cotton wool moistened with spirits of camphor. Dry with clean cotton wool.

Pleats First iron the hem, then iron the pleats from the bottom up. For a fussy job, pin each pleat to the ironing pad, taking care to place the pins so that the marks won't show. On wool use a press cloth and a warm iron and set it down gently on the cloth instead of using a gliding motion. Always leave wool slightly damp for best results in pressing.

Unless directions advise a different course, hand wash dresses and skirts with permanent pleats in cool or lukewarm water. Do not scrub or twist them. Remove them sopping wet from the final rinse and place on hangers to drip dry, with zippers or other fasteners closed. Adjust pleats with your fingers.

Separate skirts should be supported in at least three places to keep the bands straight. If quick drying is desired, roll into tubular form with the pleats parallel and beginning at the waistband, gently squeeze out excess water before hanging to dry.

While hand washing gives the best result, some pleated garments are machine washable. If the hang tag says the garment can be washed by machine, omit the water extraction cycle because it is likely to cause hard-to-remove wrinkles. Use lukewarm water (100°F) and detergent or soap with a water softener. Rinse thoroughly. Remove the garment dripping wet before the final spin-dry cycle and drip dry as described for hand washing.

If pressing is desirable, use a steam or dry iron on the synthetic setting. Press on the reverse side, after aligning the pleats, using a dampened press cloth. Let each pressed area cool before you lift or move the garment. Dacron polyester and Orlon acrylics can be cleaned and repleated by your dry cleaner.

'Plexiglas' Trade name for an acrylic plastic that made its début in World War II as the blister (nose, that is) on bombers. See *Acrylic Plastics*.

'Plexon' Plexon is a trade name for fabrics made of cotton, linen, synthetic and other yarns that have been treated with a fine plastic coating to give them extreme durability and make them immune to moisture, fading, stains and chemicals. Plexon can be made resistant to almost any chemical, as specified. Similarly the thickness of the coating can be varied, as desired.

Plexon fabrics are non-inflammable to self-extinguishing. They are damaged little by age or sunlight and are impervious to mildew and moths. Weak alkalies and acids affect them only slightly. Strong acids and alkalies vary from 'no effect' to 'decomposition', depending on the coating. Acetone, ethyl acetate and other lacquer solvents should be avoided.

Plexon is used for draperies, upholstery, handbags, shoes, lampshades and fashion accessories. Clean it by wiping it with a damp cloth or with a cloth wrung out of warm suds, made with soap or a detergent.

Plissé See *Seersucker*.

Plumbing See *Sink* and *Drains*.

Plush See *Upholstery*.

Polyester Polyester is a term used in classifying synthetic textile fibres according to their composition. In this group the fibre-forming substance is obtained mainly from dihydric alcohol and terephthalic acid.

Polyester textiles and their blends are notable because, correctly laundered, they do not require ironing. Their popularity for suits and dresses is still soaring. Polyester curtains are outstanding for their daintiness and ease of care. Sales of no-iron cotton-polyester sheets and pillow cases are zooming.

Polyester fibres are crisp to the touch, resilient, resistant to moisture and thus to stretching or sagging in damp weather. The first polyester fibre ('Terylene') was developed in England. Polyester textiles are sold under various other trade names such as 'Kodel' and 'Crimplene'. For laundering instructions see *Dacron*.

Polyethylene Versatile polyethylene may be rigid, semi-rigid, a film, or a coating. Semi-rigid polyethylene remains flexible even under refrigeration. It is so light in weight that it will float on water. Polyethylene is unbreakable even when dropped or crushed. In texture it is waxy, except as film, when it has a satiny transparent finish. Colours range the spectrum scale and may be translucent or opaque.

Polyethylene is used to make icecube trays that can be twisted to eject the ice, refrigerator food containers and mixing bowls that can be pinched to form pouring spouts, and bottles that can be squeezed. It is also used to make frozen food wraps that can be sealed without heat, refrigerator food bags, storage boxes, flashlights, pipe, and kitchenware.

Qualities which recommend polyethylene for the uses listed are that it resists heat and freezing, that it is impenetrable to water though it allows oxygen to pass through, and that it is not damaged by food acids and common chemicals. It is odourless, tasteless and nontoxic.

Articles made of polyethylene can be hand-washed with very hot water and soap or detergent. Brief contacts with boiling water during use will not harm such articles, but they should not be subjected to high heat or direct flames. Do not let cleaning fluids contact polyethylene; some cause damage. Do not use abrasives. Can go into the dishwasher. See also *Plastics*.

Polystyrene Polystyrene is a rigid plastic, seen in clear, colourless, transparent form and in a full range of transparent, opaque and translucent colours. An odd characteristic is that it produces a metallic sound when tapped with a spoon. Like the acrylics, polystyrene is able to pick up light and transmit it unseen, even around curves, to an opposite edge or groove.

Polystyrene is light in weight and unaffected by freezing temperatures, but not designed for outdoor use. It does not absorb moisture and is odourless, tasteless and nontoxic. The usual run of household acids, oils and alcohol do not harm it, but keep cleaning fluids, gasoline, nail polish and polisher, turpentine, acetone, and citrus rinds away. (Only the rinds are injurious; the juices cause no harm.)

Like all thermoplastics, polystyrene should not be subjected to high heat. It should never go into an oven or over a flame. Handle it with normal precautions, avoiding sharp knocks and twisting.

Polystyrene is used for rigid refrigerator boxes, canisters, storage boxes, picnicware, toys, refrigerator door liners and bins, lighting fixtures, costume jewellery, and housing for radios.

Hand-wash polystyrene with warm water and mild soap. Do not use abrasives. See also *Plastics*.

Polyvinyls are fire-resistant – some types stop burning as soon as the flame is removed, while others actually snuff out fire. Vinyls are light in weight and their colours will withstand long exposure to the sun without fading. All of these qualities recommend them for upholstery. Vinyl film can be stamped in dainty patterns, and the material can be hemmed, tucked, pleated and seamed by heat. When closely boxed, vinyls may develop a slight (not unpleasant) odour but this disappears with airing.

Hand-wash vinyl plastics with warm water and soap or synthetic detergent. Keep hot dishes and burning cigarettes away and, in cleaning, do not use carbon tetrachloride, ammonia, nail polish remover, acetone, or abrasives. Some vinyl products have a tendency to stick to, mar, or discolour lacquered surfaces when in close contact under certain conditions. If you are using moth or insect sprays, be careful not to spatter vinyl surfaces.

Pongee In Chinese, pongee is called 'punki' (own loom). It is a soft washable silk woven from filaments prepared from wild silkworms. The care of pongee is described under *Silk*.

Poplin A woven material with a rib effect caused by the warp being heavier than the weft. Poplin is usually cotton but may also be silk, wool and rayon. Wash according to fabric. Rayon and silk poplin should not be sprinkled if too dry for ironing. Instead it should be wrapped in a damp towel for about half an hour.

Porcelain Porcelain is a term correctly applied to the finest type of ceramic ware (china), having a translucent body and, if glazed, a transparent glaze also. It originated in China, where it is mentioned in books of the Han Dynasty as early as 203 to 220 BC. Chinese porcelains reached their peak of perfection in the Ming Dynasty during the fourteenth century. The base was a special clay called kaolin. Early European porcelains were attempted imitations of the hard Oriental porcelains so greatly admired in dishes and ornaments imported from the Far East.

The term 'porcelain' is applied loosely today in less glamorous fields. Enamelware pots and pans, as well as kitchen and bathroom fixtures, are frequently called porcelain. So-called porcelain enamel is a clay mixture, moulded in casts and baked. Enamelware is enamel, or glass, fused on steel at a high temperature. Vitreous china is made of fine china clay and is prepared like porcelain enamel.

See *China, Enamelware, Sink*, etc.

Pots and Pans Pots and pans made of cast iron require 'seasoning' before they are used to prevent rusting. Sometimes this is done at the factory. If you buy a pot or Dutch oven that is tagged 'preseasoned' you simply scour it, then wash it thoroughly in hot soapsuds, rinse and dry it. Grease the inside and the lid lightly with an unsalted fat and store. Grease it again lightly before putting food on to cook. This procedure, followed for the first month, will put your new pot in Grade-A working condition.

If your iron pot has not been 'pretreated' it probably has been given a thin coating of lacquer to prevent rust. This must be scoured off with scouring powder and a stiff brush. Then wash it in hot soapsuds, rinse and dry thoroughly. You are now ready to 'season' it. Coat the inside of the pot and cover generously with unsalted fat (lard, vegetable oils, or what have you) and heat it in a slow oven (or over a low fire) for several hours. During the heating process apply more fat now and then. Wipe off excess fat when the seasoning has been completed and you shouldn't have to scour it again. But grease it before and after using for the first few weeks.

Ordinary care from now on will call for soap and hot water, careful rinsing and drying. For a thorough cleaning (as when food has burned) boil it up with hot water to which a little washing soda has been added, or wash it in a soda solution. Afterward wash in hot suds, rinse, and dry carefully. Should rust occur, remove every trace with steel wool or scouring powder, wash, rinse, dry and re-season. If you are using a synthetic detergent, do not soak your ironware in it or the seasoning will be removed.

Don't put an iron pot away with its lid on. It will develop a musty odour if you do and is likely to accumulate moisture and rust. If storing iron utensils for a long period coat them with an un-salted oil, wrap them with paper and put them in a dry place. Or give them a coating of paraffin.

Avoid harsh abrasives, metal scrapers, and rough handling that could cause dents. Do not let gas flames lick up the sides and cause heat stains. Do not store foods in metal or enamelled cooking utensils because salt and acids damage some of them. Do not run cold water into a hot pan; such treatment can warp a metal pan and crack glass or earthenware. To remove stuck food, put cold water in the pan and let it stand until the food is soft. If food has burned, boil water in the pan. Add (except for aluminiumware, which it darkens) about two tea-spoons of baking soda per quart of water. For specific instructions, see *Aluminium, Copper, Steel - Stainless*, etc.

NON-STICK COOKWARE is mainly achieved by fluorocarbon resins such as 'Teflon', discovered at the du Pont laboratories. Sometimes silicones are used. Abrasive materials should not be used on either type. Instructions from du Pont for cookware with 'Teflon'-enamel linings follow:

PRE-TREATMENT: Wash the new utensil in hot suds, rinse, and wipe dry. Lightly grease the non-stick surfaces with cooking oil.

USE: Temperatures over 450°F cause discolouration; avoid them. Light greasing is recommended for pans used to bake foods containing sugar or fruit. This facilitates the removal of fragile cakes, encourages even browning, and improves flavour.

WASHING: Wash pans thoroughly after use; do not merely swish them under a tap. If there is a stubborn spot, use a nylon mesh dish pad or rubber scraper. Never use steel wool, metal sponges, or scouring powder. Thorough cleaning prevents the build-up of a greasy film which could impair the nonstick quality of the pan. 'Teflon'-lined cookware can go into the dishwasher, provided that such treatment will not damage the exterior. Uncoated parts of the pans can be cleaned by the usual method.

SCRATCHES do not impair the non-stick quality of the coating. Hairline scratches will not widen and the coating will not peel off. Only the appearance of the pan is affected. To avoid scratches, use metal accessories with a light touch or, better yet, use plastic utensils.

STAINS: Unless allowed to build up, do not impair the finish. Commercial preparations are offered on the market. If you use them, follow the directions on the label. The following home remedy often does the trick. Prepare a solution in these proportions; one cup of water, two tablespoons of baking soda and ½ cup of chlorine bleach. Put enough of this solution in the pan to cover the stain and boil it for five to ten minutes. Wash, rinse and dry the pan. Before using it again, wipe it with cooking oil. (This solution may lighten the colour of the lining. If it boils over, it may stain the outside of the pan.)

RE-FINISHING: Damaged 'Teflon' linings should be replaced only by a professional. (See also 'Teflon').

Pottery One of the two main classifications of ceramics. Pottery includes earthenware, stoneware, queensware, salt glaze, etc. The Anglo-Saxon earthenware, a soft pottery covered with glaze, finds its counterpart in delft (the Netherlands), faience (France) and majolica (Italy).

Glazed and partially glazed pottery can be hand-washed in warm, mild suds, but don't let it soak. Unglazed pottery can be dusted only.

Press Cloth See *Woollens*.

Pressure Cooker Wash your pressure cooker or canner after each use but do not immerse the cover in water to avoid damaging the dial gauge and possibly clogging the vents. Wipe the cover with a soapy cloth, and rinse it with a clean damp one. To clean the openings in the cover, draw a string or pipe cleaner through them. Carefully wash the gasket. Removable petcocks and safety valves should be washed, dried and replaced. For an occasional special cleaning, soak these parts in vinegar, then wash and dry them. Ball-and-socket arrangements should be cleaned now and then with silver polish.

If steam escapes from a source other than a weight-type gauge, examine the sealing edges of the vessel and the cover. If they are not smooth, rub them with a fine cleaning powder. Reversing the gasket sometimes helps, but if the gasket is worn or stretched get a new one from your dealer or manufacturer.

Should you remove the gauge from the cover, replace it carefully. A little plumber's paste (preferably with an oil or graphite base) on the threads will prevent steam leakage. Gauges that seem not to register accurately should be checked locally or packed carefully and sent with a letter to the maintenance department of the factory that made the cooker. If the gauge cannot be repaired, you can get a new one.

Canners should be stored clean and dry at the end of the season. Coat the threads of the thumbscrews with petroleum jelly ('Vaseline') or salt-free cooking oil to avoid rust. Place crumpled newspaper inside to absorb moisture. Wrap the cover with paper and invert it on the kettle.

Pressurized Cans Pressurized containers with push-button controls dispense their contents as a mist, spray, powder or foam. They depend for their activity upon compressed gases, which serve as propellants. Such cans should never be punctured, or thrown into a fire or incinerator. They should not be stored in any place where the temperature may reach 125°F – near radiators, stoves or in direct sunlight. Keep them out of the reach of children.

PVC (polyvinylchloride) To clean use a damp cloth or a cloth wrung out of soapy water.

'Pyrex' Trade name for heat-resistant glassware used in cooking. See *Glass*.

Quartz The term 'quartz' covers a range of lovely gems, all forms of native silica. In its crystallized form quartz will scratch glass and will not melt in the flames of a blowtorch.

Quartz may be clear and colourless, or it may be tinted in delicate colours. When colourless it is called 'rock crystal' or 'Lake George diamonds'. Pink quartz is known as rose quartz, purple or bluish violet as amethyst. There are also milk quartz (milk-white), smoky quartz (smoky yellow or brown), yellow (or false topaz), agate, onyx, etc. In Japan beautiful spheres of quartz several inches in diameter are found.

Apart from its value as a jewel, quartz has many uses, varying from making spectrum analyses to manufacturing sandpaper, glass and porcelain.

See *Jewellery*.

Quilts Cotton quilts that are well stitched and made of colourfast fabrics can be washed like blankets and do not require ironing, provided they are hung very straight on a taut line. They are heavy to handle when wet.

If you send them to a commercial laundry be sure that you select a reliable one and that your quilt is marked for special atten-

tion. Otherwise you may have a ruined heirloom. See *Blanket (Woollen)*.

Radiator Radiators are difficult to clean thoroughly, but this must be done regularly, especially during the heating season, to avoid dirt and stains on the walls behind and above them. Heat carries the dust up and spreads it over paint and wallpaper.

Some vacuum cleaners are provided with a device for cleaning radiators, which does a pretty fair job. The dust is sucked out; or you can reverse the action and blow it out and down onto a newspaper, dampened to make the dust cling. A good radiator brush however, does the most thoroughgoing job.

Radiators should be cleaned once a week during the heating season, less often during the summer.

Radiator Valve If you have steam heat and want to get the maximum in comfort and value from the fuel you burn, try this on your radiator valves. It is best to do it before the furnace is turned on for the season. Or you can do a few valves at a time.

First ascertain that the wooden knob on each radiator is turned to the off position. Then unscrew the valves. Place them in an enamelled kettle containing a solution of water and washing soda (or water and trisodium phosphate). Use about one tablespoon to each quart of water. Bring to the boil and boil for several minutes. Remove the valves from the kettle; shake the water out of each gently, rinse and return the valves to the radiators. Turn the knobs to on, and sit back to enjoy hearing them whistle and 'perk'.

Heating experts recommend a boiling up of this sort once a year, but few people seem to have heard of it. Often when you might think you need new valves, a cleaning is all that is required.

Petcocks on hot water radiators, incidentally, should be opened several times each heating season to draw off air which accumulates at the top. (Newer types do not require this.)

Raincoats Some raincoats are 'waterproof', others merely 'water-repellent'. To be actually waterproof, no water must come through the material, however sopping the rain (rubber, pliofilm). Water-repellent coats resist dampness and consist of a closely woven fabric, which has been treated with 'Zelan' or some other water-resisting formula. Some of these, including 'Zelan', retain their water-repellent properties in dry cleaning. Others must be reprocessed at the dry-cleaning plant. Unless otherwise specified on the label, always have raincoats dry-cleaned. Rainwear of synthetic materials can often be washed.

General good care includes the following pointers. Keep raincoats away from excessive heat and be sure that they are thoroughly dry and the fabric smooth before putting them away. Hang rubberized coats on a hook by means of the hanger sewed inside, not on a coat hanger. Mend breaks by taking a small piece of fabric from the hem or buckle end of the belt and securing it to the back of the break with rubber cement.

Clean plastic raincoats with a damp cloth and soap or mild detergent.

Rayon Rayon, the first synthetic textile fibre emerged from the test tube in Europe and appeared on the market there in 1902. It dates from laboratory attempts, begun as early as the seventeenth century, to create artificial silk. Chardonnet, a French scientist, was finally successful in producing a reasonable facsimile. Rayon today is sometimes called a semisynthetic, in contrast to newer fibres that are completely chemical. It is derived from cellulose, present in nearly all plant life. Wood pulp and cotton linters are mainly used.

Rayon textiles have many advantages. They are water-absorbent, nonstatic, and can be dyed with exceptional colourfastness in a wide variety of shades, from delicate pastels to brilliant hues. There are three main types of rayon: viscose, cuprammonium and Fortisan. While all are derived from cellulose, the methods used to produce them are different and the fibres which result are very different too.

Viscose rayon, produced under many trade names, is the original rayon. To make it, pure cellulose is converted into a thick, viscous solution by chemical treatment. The solution is pumped through a spinneret, a small metal disc with many tiny holes, into a hardening bath where the filaments coagulate. Each minute hole spins a filament. Viscose rayon is a versatile fibre, sturdy and equal to many tasks. It is soft to the touch, drapes well, and can be dyed in a wide range of colours that are very fast to light. Viscose is used for suitings, carpets, blankets, sports and dress fabrics, voiles, blends, knitted fabrics, velvet and plush. These rayons absorb and hold moisture, an advantage or disadvantage, depending on their use. They dry slowly, and are attacked by mildew and rot fungi, but not by insects.

Cuprammonium rayon is made from purified cellulose dissolved in a solution containing a copper and ammonia compound. It is similar to viscose, but its fibres are extremely soft, not quite as tough, and less resistant to heat. Cuprammonium rayon is used for lightweight dress fabrics, sheers, crêpes, marquisettes, voiles, gloves, hosiery and upholstery cloth. All rayon of this type is sold under the trade name 'Bemberg'.

'Fortisan' is the trade name of a rayon made from cellulose acetate yarn, saponified under high tension which converts it chemically to rayon. The yarn and cloth made of it are exceptionally strong, extremely resistant to stretch, yet soft to the touch. Its high strength makes possible lightweight, very tough fabrics, from filaments finer than silk. It is more resistant to heat than other rayons, and can be ironed at temperatures that normally scorch cottons. Rayon fabrics can be dry-cleaned or hand-washed, depending upon construction, finish and dyes. Look for the label. If hand-washed, treat them gently because the fibres tend to be weak when wet. If washing instructions are not given, or are incomplete, follow the directions given for acetates. See *Acetate* and *'Fortisan'*.

Records Tonal reproduction is impaired if records become smudged or dusty. Wash them with a soft cloth moistened with lukewarm water containing a mild detergent. Rinse them with a cloth squeezed out of clear lukewarm water and wipe dry with a fluff-free cotton or linen cloth.

Reed See *Furniture*.

Refrigerator Gas and electric refrigerators should be defrosted about every ten days or before the frost is more than a quarter of an inch thick on the coils. At this time the interior should be cleaned.

Make a note of the proper setting before turning the dial to 'off'. Wrap frozen foods in newspaper to place them in insulated bags. Defrosting can be accelerated by placing pans of hot water in the frozen food compartment or by using an electric defroster, available at hardware stores.

First empty the drip pan and remove all food from the shelves. Clean the inside with a solution of baking soda and warm water, using a soft cloth or sponge. Use two tablespoons of soda to a quart of water. After cleaning, wipe the surfaces dry with a clean, soft cloth. Clean the gasket (seal around the door) with warm water and soap or detergent. Rinse and wipe dry. Do not use harsh cleaning powders, steel wool or liquid cleaners on any part of your refrigerator.

Wash accessories with soap and warm water. Rinse in clear warm water and wipe dry. Remove vegetable and fruit containers and wash with warm water and soap or detergent. Use only soap or detergent and water on the ice

G

trays of the new models and take care not to scald them with boiling water. These trays are often coated with a special wax at the factory to make the removal of ice cubes easier. Scalding water and abrasives will remove the coating.

Clean the outside of the refrigerator about once a month, using a mild soap or detergent and water and a soft cloth or sponge. Manufacturers also recommend a special liquid cleaning wax, which cleans, protects and polishes the surface in one operation.

If your electric refrigerator has a finned-tube-type condenser, clean it about once a year, preferably in May before hot weather sets in. Remove the panel at the bottom of the refrigerator and clean the fins with a brush or vacuum cleaner attachment.

Electric refrigerators with an open-type mechanism require oiling and adjusting, not required of those with sealed units.

On gas refrigerators, to assure maximum efficiency, the burner compartment (usually at the bottom) should be cleaned occasionally and also the top louver assembly, on the top of the cabinet at the back. Use a vacuum cleaner attachment or a damp cloth. Special attention should be given to top louver since dust tends to accumulate on the underneath side where it is likely not to be noticed. Use a knife blade wrapped in cloth, or, for a really thorough job, remove the screws which hold the louver assembly and lift it out for cleaning. While this is out, clean the finned section underneath with a vacuum cleaner attachment. It is important, in gas refrigerators, that the top louver be unobstructed at all times so that air may flow underneath, through the burner compartment, up the back and out of the top louver.

Electric and gas refrigerators both are benefited by an occasional inspection by a serviceman.

Activated charcoal in a container will keep your refrigerator sweet by absorbing strong odours.

Registers Hot-air registers are dust catchers and distributors and should be cleaned once a week while the furnace is in operation. Lift out the grating, place it on a dampened newspaper and clean it with a brush or vacuum cleaner attachment. Clean the opening of the shaft also.

Reinforced Polyesters These rugged plastics invite outdoor use. In this group the plastic is combined with other materials which give it great strength.

Reinforced polyesters can be produced in all colours, transparent or opaque. They are very difficult to scratch and can be made as strong as needed. Such plastics resist the penetration of water and are not affected by freezing temperatures.

Reinforced polyesters are used for luggage, awnings, roofing, wall partitions, light panels, lamp shades, fishing rods and chairs. Since they vary in the chemicals they will stand, it is necessary to check the labels and instruction tags on merchandise.

Wash these plastics, when required, with warm water and soap or detergent. They are not damaged by cleaning fluids, but keep abrasives away. Do not place them near an open flame. See also *Plastics*.

Repp Fabric with heavy weft forming ribs from selvedge to selvedge. Many repps are all cotton but some are rayon and cotton. Wash according to material.

Rhinestone An artificial stone made of paste (a kind of fine and brilliant glass). Rhinestones were first made at Strasbourg and were named after the River Rhine. See *Jewellery.*

Ribbons Ribbons look like new, after laundering, if they are dipped in a gum arabic or gum tragacanth solution and stretched to dry over a smooth surface, such as the edge of the bathtub. Ribbons stretched thus do not have to be ironed.

See *Starch and Special Finishes* for directions for preparing gum arabic (page 186).

Rotary Ironer When the ironing has been completed and before the motor has been cut off, release the hot shoe from the roll so that it will not scorch the cover and padding.

The surface of the ironer shoe should be washed with a cloth squeezed out of suds. This will remove any traces of starch. Dry and rewax it, using paraffin or beeswax. Keep the muslin cover clean. To replace it, after laundering, move the shoe away from the roll and heat the shoe to normal ironing temperature. Unroll the undercover for about six inches and place one edge of the roll under it. Rewind the undercover back over the muslin cover and move the shoe against the roll. Iron the cover on, smoothing it with the palms of the hands. When the cover has been completely ironed on, stop the ironer. Pull up the drawstrings at each end, tie them securely and tuck them under the ends of the roll.

Air the roll padding every three months. To do this remove the muslin roll cover and unwind the undercover back to where it is attached to the padding and let it air for several hours in the open air and sunlight. (Do not loosen the padding from the roll for this operation.)

To avoid scratching the shoe, keep hooks and eyes, buttons, etc., toward the roll as much as possible. In ironing, use the full length of the roll as much as possible and iron small articles alternately at the ends. This tends to keep the padding firm and even and helps prevent the ends of the roll cover from being scorched.

If your ironer has been permanently lubricated at the factory, you will never have to oil it. Consult your dealer if you are uncertain about this.

'Rovana' 'Rovana' is a textile, which is described as a saran microtape. Combined with 'Verel' and rayon, 'Rovana' provides outstandingly fire-resistant material for hospital and home draperies and other items. These can be dry-cleaned, but tell your dry cleaner what the material is.

Washable 'Rovana' can be machine washed with a neutral (mild) soap or detergent and plenty of cool water. Rinse in cool water (high level), stopping the machine during draining and filling. Extract the rinse water by bringing the extractor immediately to full speed, then turning it off. Tumble dry for 20 to 30 minutes at a temperature between 140°F to 160°F, and remove the article immediately after drying. If these instructions are followed, 'Rovana' should not need ironing.

Rubber Articles made of natural rubber can be kept clean with soap and water. The addition of a little ammonia helps. Rinse them carefully and be sure they are perfectly dry before you store them. Or you can clean them with alcohol.

Rubber is damaged by heat, light, cleaning fluids, oil, grease, tar and copper. Heat, including sunlight (unless the rubber has been prepared to resist it), cracks and weakens rubber, making it sticky and inert. Grease, oil and tar, if left in contact long, are absorbed, causing the rubber to swell and weaken. Standard cleaning fluids can be used to remove grease, oil and tar, and small articles can be soaked in them, but not for more than two or three minutes. Rubber gloves, worn to protect the hands while polishing copper or brass, or when using copper filament scouring balls, become soft and sticky at first, then hard and brittle. (Gloves of synthetic rubber stand chemical cleaners and cleaning fluids better and are not damaged by oil or grease.) Wash and powder with talc both types after use.

Store rubber articles in a cool, dark place. Be sure they are clean and dry and, if they are to be folded, dust the surfaces that will touch with talcum powder or cornstarch. Blow a little air into hot water bottles, ice packs, neck collars, etc., replace the caps, and put them in boxes, preferably the ones they came in. Store rubber tubing loosely coiled and free of kinks.

Boots, rubbers and galoshes should be washed with water, or soap and water, to remove dirt and mud. Wipe them dry, or dry them in a cool, airy place. When you store them, stuff crumpled newspapers loosely inside to preserve their shape.

Sheets, raincoats and other articles or rubber-coated cloth can be spread on a table and scrubbed with warm suds and a soft brush Rinse them with a cloth wrung from plain warm water and hang them to dry in a cool, airy place. Avoid chlorine bleaches.

Cold and hot patches for mending rubber can be bought at department and hardware stores. See also *Garden Tools*, *Girdles*, *Rubber Tile*.

Rubber Tile Floors of rubber tile should be swept or dusted with an untreated mop or vacuum cleaner brush. Wash them with a synthetic detergent or mild soap and lukewarm water plus a little ammonia or other water softener. Proceed as for linoleum, cleaning a small area at a time with a soft cloth, sponge or mop, well wrung out. Rinse with clear, lukewarm water. Continue to an adjoining area until the surface has been cleaned.

For a very soiled floor, use your cleaner in a stronger dilution or use warm water and washing soda or trisodium phosphate. (One to two tablespoons to a pail of water.) Use steel wool or scouring powder on stubborn spots. Rinse well with a cloth, sponge or mop wrung out of clear warm water.

Paste waxes can be used on high-grade rubber tile, but may damage inexpensive rubber floors. If you are uncertain, use only self-polishing wax. Waxing is optional.

Ruby Strange as it may seem, this clear, rich red, highly prized jewel is a variety of corundum, that humble agent used for grinding and polishing gems. A ruby of good red colour ranks above the diamond in value. A fine gem of from one to three carats in weight sells for a price from three to ten times that of a diamond of similar weight and quality. The finest rubies (pigeon's blood) come from Upper Burma.

Synthetic rubies, first produced in 1894 by the French chemist Verneuil, have many of the characteristics of genuine rubies but the grain runs in curved, rather than straight, lines and the colour is more carmine. Such rubies are made by mixing, as a powder, the chemical elements of the true stone, then melting them under very intense heat. For the care of jewellery starring rubies see *Jewellery.*

Rug See *Carpets and Rugs.*

Rug Anchor Small rugs can be a safety hazard, especially on waxed floors, if precautions have not been taken to make skidproof. Manufacturers, recognizing this, often provide them with a rubberized backing, and paint-on adhesives. Also available are rubber or rubberized underlays. These may lose some of their adhesive quality after a while when used on waxed floors. If they seem discouraged and listless, wash them with a synthetic detergent or with warm soapy water containing a little ammonia, rinse them with warm water, and allow them to dry. They will then resume their anchoring duties efficiently.

Sailcloth Heavy, strong canvas, made from linen, cotton, jute and man-made fibres. Wash according to fibre. Test for colour fastness.

'Sanforized' A trade name for a special type of preshrinking.

Sapphire See *Quartz* and *Jewellery.*

'Saran' 'Saran' is a synthetic textile, classified as a vinylidene chloride, which is derived by chemical processes from salt and petroleum. It is a very durable fabric, used for upholstery, seat covers for cars, outdoor furniture, carpets, curtains, shoes, luggage and handbags.

'Saran' is available in many colours and in a wide array of patterns and weaves.

This fabric is very water-resistant and is not affected by age. Moths and mildew will not attack it. It is highly resistant to acids and alkalies (except ammonia) and to most other chemicals, including acetone and the common solvents. A rugged fabric, 'Saran' resists scuffing, tearing and snagging. While it will not stand great heat, it is self-extinguishing if ignited. Its colours are lasting, being built into the material.

'Saran' is easy to clean. Just wipe it with a damp cloth, or with a cloth wrung out of warm suds. If dirt or other matter has worked down into the weave and left a mark, use a good stiff brush, slightly dampened with soapsuds. Do not use too wet a cloth, or brush, in cleaning 'Saran' as the water may seep through the weave and wet the material underneath.

Under very dry atmospheric conditions 'Saran' may accumulate a static electrical charge, like fine pile rugs. To eliminate this simply wipe the surface with a cloth thoroughly saturated with a strong solution of a synthetic detergent. 'Saran' plastic film is useful as a protective wrapping for foods, linens, china and silver.

Sateen A hard-wearing fabric made from cotton, silk and cotton or rayon. It resembles satin except that the smooth grain runs across the material. Wash rayon and cotton sateens as for cotton and rayon. Sateen of silk and cotton mixture should be washed in warm, soapy water and handled gently. Use moderately hot iron.

Satin A type of weave in which warp predominates over weft, giving a smooth lustrous surface. It may be woven of silk, cotton, rayon,

Terylene or nylon; most satin dress fabrics today are made from acetate and from cotton.

Satin dress fabrics are washed according to fibre. Heavy furnishing satins should be dry-cleaned.

Screens See *Window Screens* and *Andirons*.

Sealers For surface protection and ease of maintenance, modern floors of various types are often finished with special preparations known as sealers. Sealers for wooden floors are more durable than varnish, shellac, and similar finishes because they penetrate the wood and do not tend to crack or peel. Other sealers are made for stone, cement, tile, marble, brick, etc. Such sealers are often applied to floors when they are laid, or they may be applied by home owners when renovating or refinishing floors. It is important to use the right type. For information about sealers consult a top specialist in flooring, or write to the manufacturer of your particular type of floor.

Seersucker (Plissé) Wash untreated seersuckers according to the directions given for white and coloured cottons. Ironing is not required, provided the garment is hung carefully. Smooth the hem and seams of dresses and hang them on rustproof coat hangers. Pad the shoulders with tissue paper for a fussy job; otherwise make sure the material is smooth and straight for drying. If you still want to iron it, iron when practically dry and on the wrong side. See also *Permanent Press*.

Septic Tank Septic tanks and cesspools are country arrangements for the disposal of sewage in areas not served by a municipal sewage system. They differ in construction but their basic idea is the same. Both depend, for satisfactory functioning, upon the action of bacteria upon waste matter. The main thing to know about these installations is that they require professional cleaning about every three years. This you had best *not* forget, or you may find yourself in serious trouble.

Shantung A Chinese plain weave fabric with slubs. Silk shantung is made from wild silk from the Tussah moth. Wash as silk, using final cold vinegar rinse. Iron with cool-to-warm iron on wrong side when *completely dry*.

Acetate and nylon shantungs are washed according to fibre.

Sharkskin Smooth fabric woven or knitted often made from acetate. To launder see *Acetate*. Do not iron over damp patches as this may cause watermarks.

Sheepskin To wash a sheepskin rug treat as nylon fur.

Shoes Your shoes will look better and last longer if you take these precautions: Be sure they fit when you buy them. Use shoe trees or toe cushions (for sandals). Keep the heels straight and wear rubbers when it's wet, or plastic protective covering.

Run-over heels not only look sloppy and make your feet ache but throw the whole shoe out of shape so that shoe trees could hardly be expected to remedy the damage. Going without rubbers when it rains makes the leather stretch and the soles bulge at the seams.

Shoes should be kept clean and polished with the proper dressing. Remove any oil or grease spots with cleaning fluid on a soft cloth and brush them well before polishing or dressing.

Wet leather shoes should be stuffed with paper to hold their shape while drying and should not be placed near heat. A little castor oil, rubbed onto the uppers and soles of slick leather shoes, after they have dried, will soften and recondition the leather. Castor oil is better than other leather conditioners for this purpose as it does not affect the finish and the shoes can be polished afterwards.

Suede shoes are brushed with a bristle, rubber or wire brush in a circular motion. Use wire brushes lightly or you may destroy the nap. After brushing carefully, smooth the nap in one direction. There are aerosol dressings which raise the nap, and other dressings containing dyes to restore colour. If oil or grease stains on suede do not yield to cleaning fluid, try mixing the fluid with fuller's earth or other absorbent, and letting the paste stand on the spot overnight.

Smooth leather shoes can be cleaned with saddle soap and shined with a polish of the same colour, lighter, or neutral. Patent leather is cleaned with a soft damp cloth and a mild soap. No waxes or polishes for patent leather; they tend to crack it.

White, rough leathers are first brushed with a soft, clean bristle brush, then cleaned with white shoe dressing. Brush off excess. Smooth white shoes are cleaned with a white cream dressing and a soft cloth. No brushes. Brown and white or black and white shoes present a problem. It is probably best to clean the white part first and, when that has dried, to tackle the rest, using a neutral cream.

For stains caused by shoe polish see *Stains*, page 154-5.

Shower Curtain Always spread out a wet shower curtain as smoothly as possible to dry. Watch for mildew or a musty odour. Special types are cleaned as follows:

Duck (light canvas) shower curtains are washed with hot soapy water like any other heavy cotton material. Dry them in the sun, if possible, and iron them, dampened, with a hot iron. If mildewed, use a chlorine bleach, rinse thoroughly and proceed as directed above. The newest duck curtains are water-resistant and mildewproof so look for the labels if you are buying new ones. To mildewproof cottons at home see directions given under *Mildew*, page 147.

Waterproof silk curtains are placed on a smooth flat surface and sponged with lukewarm suds, made with a mild detergent or soap. Rinse with clear lukewarm water and hang on the shower bar to dry.

Rubber curtains are washed in thick suds made of mild soap or detergent and lukewarm water. Be careful not to rub or squeeze the material together, but, rather, work it about gently in the water until clean. Rinse in cold water and hang on curtain hooks to dry.

Rubberized fabric curtains are washed like rubber ones. They may be pressed while damp with a warm (not hot) iron.

Plastic and plastic-coated curtains should be spread flat on a smooth surface and sponged with a damp cloth or mild suds. Rinse with clear, warm water and rehang to dry. Do not press. Some are machine washable. See *Plastic Sheeting*.

Water-resistant cotton, rayon and silk shower curtains can be washed in mild lukewarm suds. Rinse in water of the same temperature and press, while damp, with a warm iron.

(Since it is difficult to distinguish between the many fabrics used for shower curtains, you should always look for the label giving instructions and file it for reference.)

Silk The manufacture of silk, queen of all fabrics, was once a secret of the imperial house of ancient China. Legend says that in 2640 BC, the Empress Si-Ling-Chi accidentally dropped a cocoon into boiling water and discovered how to unreel silk. As time passed, silken fabrics became available to the humble and even the coolie had his pongee.

Today silk is again in the luxury class. Handle the silks that you have with care and they will be beautiful for a long time. Silk, reeled from the cocoons of delicate worms and adapted to a bewildering variety of exquisite and colourful weaves, is a strong and durable material.

Silks not known to be washable should be handled by a reliable dry cleaner. Hand-launder washable silks with lukewarm to cool water and an unbuilt synthetic detergent made for wool. Synthetic detergents are much better for silk than soap because silks are damaged by alkalies and even the purest soap is alkaline in reaction.

In washing silks do not rub the fabric but squeeze and work it about in the suds. Rubbing is likely to break the fibres and dull the finish. Rinse carefully in water of the same temperature, then remove excess moisture by squeezing and patting it between dry towels. To stiffen silks use gum arabic or gelatin. See *Starch and Special Finishes*, pages 186 and 187.

Do not wrinkle silks more than necessary. They may be difficult to press. Do not hang silks in the sun or place them near any source of artificial heat. But *do* dry them as quickly as possible. Rapid drying in front of an electric fan prevents the formation of water marks and aids in retaining the glossy finish. Exquisite bits of sheer silk, especially those whose colours are inclined to run, are sometimes dried by shaking them gently until of the proper dampness for ironing.

Silks should be uniformly damp when they are pressed. Iron them before they have dried completely for best results. (If allowed to dry, dampening may cause water spots.) If they are too wet when ironed, the material will be stiff and papery. Use a warm (never hot) iron and press on the wrong side, preferably with a piece of clean cheesecloth protecting the fabric. Silk scorches easily and too hot an iron will turn white silk yellow.

Pongee is a soft silk made from cocoons of wild silkworms. In Chinese the word means 'own loom'. Pongee has a rough, rather pleasing appearance in spite of its classification as a cheap silk. This fabric water-marks easily so be sure that the dampness is evenly distributed when you iron it and iron it on the wrong side. Or you can iron it dry. If ironed too wet, pongee becomes stiff.

Silver is commonly ranked next to gold among the precious metals, though other metals are rarer and more expensive than either. It is soft, white, lustrous and easily worked. For centuries silver has been cherished by women for tableware and enduring ornaments. Softly shining silver, good china and immaculate linen can make a feast of the simplest meal.

Sterling silver is a term used to specify that the metal contains at least 925 parts of silver to 75 parts of copper. The term is derived from an English penny, coined in the Middle Ages. 'Sterling' became the standard for lawful British coins. Pure silver is rarely used, as it is too soft.

There is no magic formula for keeping silver bright. Metallurgists have worked for years to produce a stainless silver, but without luck so far. So if you want your silver to look its best you will have to give it a reasonable amount of care.

Sterling silver should be used daily. Constant use gives it the deep mellow tone of fine antiques ... the 'patina' that is really a meshwork of very fine scratches. Wash your silver promptly after each use, using hot suds and a soft cloth. Rinse it in hot water and dry it immediately. If you follow this procedure, you will not have to polish it often. Flat silver should be rotated in daily use so that the finish will mellow uniformly. Keep it, preferably in a lined rack, in a special silver drawer. Dust ornamental pieces regularly and wash them once a week to keep them bright.

There are several methods of cleaning tarnished silver but hand rubbing with a prepared polish (liquid, powder or paste) is best. 'Dip shines' are tricky to use. They ruin some finishes and damage stainless steel knife blades as well as other materials if allowed to contact them. This is because they contain a very strong, corrosive acid. 'Dip shines' are heartily condemned by manufacturers of fine silver services. The electrolytic method is quick and easy but jewellers do not approve of it either because it kills the finish of silver. Every trace of oxidation is removed, leaving the pattern dead and the silver dull, white and

lustreless. Hand rubbing, on the other hand, gives silver a depth of lustre that is beautiful and desirable and leaves enough oxidation to bring out the beauty of its decoration.

When you polish your silver, take time to do it carefully. To protect your hands wear gloves if you like. Wash the silver first in hot soapsuds, then apply a reliable polish with a soft cloth, sponge, or chamois. Rub each piece briskly, but not hard, using even, straight strokes. Do not rub silver crosswise or with a rotary motion. A silver brush (made especially for this purpose) is useful for cleaning hard-to-reach crevices, chased surfaces and beaded edgings. After applying the polish, rub the silver with a clean soft flannel cloth or piece of chamois until it is clean and bright. Last of all wash each piece again carefully in hot suds to remove every trace of polish. Your brush will come in handy here, too, to ensure that no powder is left clinging to raised patterns. Polish left on silver causes it to tarnish again quickly.

Silver does not need to be polished each time it is cleaned. Often it is only necessary to wipe off the tarnish with your silver preparation.

Dull, or satin, finish silver becomes bright after many polishings. Reliable dealers are agreed that there is no satisfactory method of restoring satin finish at home, so it's back to the jeweller's with it if you want it dull again.

Gold linings, more often than not, are quickly rubbed out of jugs, bowls and salt dishes by energetic women who can't resist giving the inside a wipe. Keep your polish away from these delicate washes for the gold is soft, the lining thin, and it will vanish even with constant rubbing, polish or no. Gold linings can, of course, be restored by your jeweller.

Lacquered silver will not tarnish and, of course, requires no polishing. When you wash it, use lukewarm (never hot) suds made with a mild soap or detergent. Your jeweller can apply the lacquer, which is mainly suitable for large, ornamental pieces.

A finish which makes silver tarnishproof and resistant to damage from acids, salts, and other substances has been developed by Tiffany's, New York. This finish is applied at the factory and lasts several years. It is recommended for bowls, ash trays, candelabra, vases, trophies, and similar articles not subjected to abrasive treatment. It is not suitable for flatware or trays. Silver with this finish can be wiped clean with a damp cloth or washed like china. It will stand very hot water.

ELECTROLYTIC CLEANING: This method is presented with some misgivings because jewellers disapprove of it for the reasons already given and because I am in agreement with them. However, it is a time-saver and *is* completely harmless. Some may want to use it in spite of its shortcomings. The finish can be improved somewhat by polishing the silver a little after cleaning it. The electrolytic method calls for a porcelain pan in which a piece of aluminium foil has been placed, salt and baking soda.

Put into the pan one teaspoon of salt and one teaspoon of baking soda for each quart of water required. Bring the water to a boil, then put in the silver, making sure that it is is covered completely. Boil two or three minutes, or until the tarnish has disappeared. Remove the silver, wash it in hot suds, rinse carefully and dry with a soft cloth. Two teaspoons of washing soda or one teaspoon of trisodium phosphate per gallon of water can be substituted for the salt and baking soda combination. In this case boiling may not be necessary.

This method of silver cleaning involves an electrochemical reaction by which the tarnish (silver sulphide) is removed from the silver and deposited on the aluminium foil.

CAUTION: The electrolytic method should not be used on flat silver with hollow handles that may be fastened with cement. It should not be used on antique silver and is not desirable for hollow-ware.

STORING SILVER: Tarnish is caused by the action of certain gases in the air on the surface of silver. Therefore, if air is kept away, tarnish is diminished. Cloth and paper tissues, treated with silver nitrate, deter tarnish and are useful if silver is to be stored. Both may be purchased from your jeweller or at any department store. The cloth may be had in rolls or made up into bags and cases. Wrapping each piece of clean, bright silver in saran plastic film is almost as effective. It is self-sealing and you can easily identify the silver you want to bring out and use. Press out the air as you wrap. *Never* secure *any* wrapping with rubber bands. Rubber, a deadly enemy of silver, can corrode it in a few weeks through several layers of paper or cloth. When the corrosion lines cross etched patterns, the damage is permanent.

Other enemies of silver are table salt, eggs, olives, salad dressings, gas, sulphur, vinegar, fruit juices, perfumes and toilet water. Don't let any of these contact silver long. Sea air and leaking gas tarnish silver rapidly. Watch your fruit and flower bowls. Acids generated by decaying flowers, leaves, and fruits will etch into your silver, causing ugly little pit marks. So use an inner container, or change the water frequently on flowers in silver bowls and vases and do not keep them an instant after they begin to wilt. Watch your fruit bowl for decayed grapes and seeping juices that might cause damage if left in it too long.

Pearl, ivory and horn handles on silver knives or forks should not be allowed to soak in water. They usually are fastened with cement which might be loosened. No other care than ordinary washing is required of such handles, but do not put them in your dishwasher.

Silver Plate Silver-plated articles should not be confused with solid silver, or sterling silver. In silver plate a coating of silver has been been applied to another metal. The process used today is called 'electroplating'. The article to be plated is placed in a solution containing silver and, through an electro process, part of the silver is made to adhere to the surface. Sheffield plate, prior to about 1850, involved an altogether different method. A sheet of silver was fused to a copper ingot and the ingot was then rolled thin. Sometimes the silver was fused to both sides of the copper. This method was superseded by electroplating and Sheffield plate is no longer made.

The care of silver plate is the same as for solid silver, except that it should be polished, perhaps, with less energy. The plating is solid silver, softer than sterling.

Sink Clean the kitchen sink with soap and hot water after each use. If stained, use a mild scouring powder. Coarse abrasives damage the finish, making the sink more and more difficult to clean. Rinse with plenty of water, preferably hot. Wipe dry.

To whiten a sink, fill it with lukewarm water, add a little chlorine bleach and let it stand for a while. (Some cleaning powders contain chlorine.) Iron rust stains, if light, often can be removed by rubbing them with a cut lemon. If more stubborn, apply a 5 per cent solution of oxalic acid (poison) on a bit of cloth or paper. Rinse thoroughly after a few seconds as acids will eat into the porcelain finish.

For a sink so hopelessly stained that a new one seems the only solution try this formula. Mix cream of tartar and hydrogen peroxide (available at chemists) to a paste and scrub the sink with it, using a hand brush and plenty of elbow grease. The result will surprise you.

Stainless steel sinks seldom require more than washing with hot suds, rinsing and drying.

Sink taps are usually chromium – or nickel-plated. Clean them with soap and water, rinse and wipe dry. Scouring powders should never be used as they quickly wear off the plating.

See also *Drains, Steel – Stainless*, and *Monel Metal*.

Slate Slate is sometimes used for the hearth and facing of fireplaces. A little lemon oil, applied carefully after the slate has been washed and dried, makes it dark and lustrous. Be sure to wipe the slate with a clean cloth after applying the oil to remove every trace of excess polish. Do not use wax, because heat affects it.

For the care of slate tiles see *Stone Floors*.

Smocking In ironing, set the iron on the smocking gently, then fluff it up with your finger tips.

Spandex Spandex is a generic term for synthetic elastic fibres used in girdles and as a core for some stretch yarns. Trade names include 'Lycra', 'Spanzelle', and 'Nyrene'. Chlorine bleach yellows it. See *Girdles*.

Spectacles Opticians recommend washing glasses periodically with warm water and soap to remove the accumulation of oil that gets on to them from the skin. Use a soft brush to clean around the rims. Rinse and polish with a soft lintless cloth (non-fluffy), tissue paper or the specially treated papers sold for the purpose.

Spin Dryer See *Automatic Dryer*.

Sponge (n.) NATURAL SPONGES are the skeletons of odd little sea animals found adhering to rocks and shells under water, and to rocks about the shore when the tide is low. These are dried and bleached for commercial use.

Wash sponges in clean, soapy water. If very dirty, let them soak in soapy water to which ammonia has been added (one tablespoon per quart). Rinse thoroughly in clear water, squeeze out as much of the water as possible and dry in the shade. If used surgically, your sponge should be disinfected by boiling it for five or ten minutes. Sponges, when not in use, should be hung by a string run through them.

CELLULOSE SPONGES and sponge mops should be soaked carefully before using because they are brittle when dry. They are not harmed by ordinary cleaning soaps and powders but strong solutions and strong bleaches damage them.

Rinse cellulose sponges after each use, and to freshen them and prolong their life, put them in the washer with your clothes. Hang up your cellulose mop after you have washed it. Do not let it dry hard in the sun or near a radiator. Keep it moist between jobs for maximum service. Do not use it on rough surfaces.

Cellulose sponges can be bleached in a mild solution of household bleach, if necessary, but don't soak them too long. Rinse carefully afterwards. They can be sterilized by boiling.

Sponge and Foam Rubber mops and sponges should be washed in warm, mild suds and rinsed carefully. Store them in a cool, dry place. Strong chemicals are likely to damage them. Grease, oils, acids and petrol are all damaging to rubber.

Sponge Rubber Sponge rubber is made from crude rubber by a milling operation. Chemicals are added to the rubber to soften it and to permit the 'blowing of holes' in the rubber.

Stainless Steel See *Steel*.

Stairs If the stairway is covered, follow the directions given for the particular type of covering, such as *Linoleum, Rubber*, etc.

Stair carpets and pads should be taken up once a year for a good cleaning. Send them to a dry cleaner, or, if you want to do the job at home, follow these directions: Clean both sides of carpet and padding with the vacuum cleaner or a good stiff brush. Wash, if necessary, following the directions given under *Carpets and Rugs*. Hang outdoors to dry or air thoroughly. Replace the padding and then the carpet, turning it around so that wear will be distributed evenly.

he balustrade and rail of the stairway should be dusted like furniture. About once a month it should be cleaned and polished.

Steam Iron Steam irons are lighter than those that were first introduced and hold a better supply of water. Some are combination steam and dry irons, with and without detachable reservoirs. The following discussion of steam irons is based on information from *Mary Proctor's Ironing Book.*

A steam iron eliminates the need to sprinkle clothes, since the steam supplies the necessary moisture. It is ideal for pressing woollens, both heavy and light, and for ironing other heat-sensitive fabrics such as silk and the synthetics, nylon, rayon, 'Orlon', etc. The moisture produced by the iron helps safeguard these materials against 'invisible scorch' which so often shortens their life. Press all of these materials on the wrong side, unless you use a press cloth, to prevent shine. Exceptions to this rule are light-coloured wool crêpes, tweeds and flannels. In pressing woollens use a light stamping motion. Do not glide the iron over the material. And leave it slightly damp. Use an untreated press cloth for silks and synthetics. A chemically treated press cloth is excellent for woollens.

A steam iron gives good results on light cottons and linens, but dry ironing does a better job on the heavier cottons and on linen damask. However, these, too, can be steam ironed if time-saving is important. Dampen them a little first.

Velvet and felt hats, suede shoes and handbags may be given the steam beauty treatment with a steam iron. Set the dial for rayon and, with the iron placed on the board so that the tip overhangs, hold the hat in the steam and turn it around slowly. Steam the crown first, then brush it with a soft brush or rubber sponge to raise the the nap. Next do the brim. Suede and doeskin gloves and suede pocketbooks can be steamed the same way. Use a stretcher for the gloves and hold the leather about a half inch from the iron. When thoroughly steamed, brush up the nap.

CARE: Except for the special care required for their steam fixtures, the care of a steam iron is the same as for a dry one. Do not overfill the reservoir, and use the type of water – tap or distilled – recommended for your particular iron. If the opening of the sprinkler nozzle becomes stopped, insert a fine needle in the centre hole to clear it.

When the ironing is finished, and while the iron is still hot, empty the water reservoir and let the iron cool in an upright position on its heel rest. Wrap the cord around the handle when the iron has cooled and store it in the same position.

Steel TEMPERED: The enemies of tempered steel (knives, spatulas, egg beaters, etc.) are acids, which, corrode the metal, and moisture, which causes rust. Keep steel spotless with scouring powder. Wash tempered steel immediately after use to prevent stains and dry meticulously to prevent rust.

STAINLESS: Stainless steel is an iron alloy containing chromium. It seldom requires more attention than washing in hot suds, rinsing and drying. Stainless steel is rustproof, but salt and acids in foods can cause pit marks if left in contact too long. If spots do appear, clean the utensil with fine steel wool or steel wool and a fine scouring powder. Polish with a soft cloth. Special cleaners are made for stainless steel cooking utensils.

In using stainless steel pans, do not let gas flames lick up the sides and cause heat stains. These cannot be removed.

Stainless steel tableware, increasingly popular, should be washed promptly to avoid pitting from salts and acids in foods. It never tarnishes, but too much detergent in electric dishwashers sometimes films it, giving it a dull appearance. To remove this film use a good silver polish. *Do not* use steel wool on stainless steel tableware.

VANADIUM: Vanadium steel is a stainless steel containing from two-tenths to 4 per cent of vanadium, a light grey metal that increases the toughness and tensile strength of the steel. Spatulas, pancake turners, knives and ladles are often made of vanadium steel.

Steel Wool pads that have begun to rust should be discarded, because small bits that pierce the skin can cause infection. Rust retardants are sometimes added to pads treated with soap to prolong their safe use – or you can put the pad in a cup of soda water. Use about three tablespoons of baking soda in a cup of water. The steel wool will then not rust.

Stone Floors Stones used for flooring – quarry tile, bluestone, slate, flagstone, magnesite – are porous and so is the concrete in which they are usually set. When washed with soap-type cleaners, a scum forms on the concrete which cannot be completely rinsed away. Washing soda can be used to clean them, or a synthetic detergent. Such floors are usually protected with a cement sealer and waxed to provide gloss. Self-polishing wax is recommended, but polishing waxes can be used. See also *Marble*.

Stove See *Gas Cooker, Electric Cooker*, etc.

Straw Hats Keep them well brushed and they will be damaged less if caught in the rain. To clean them, wipe with a cloth dipped in warm suds, made with a synthetic detergent or soap. Rinse with a cloth wrung out of plain water. Do not get a straw hat too wet or it may shrink.

Limp straws can be stiffened by brushing them over with a light coat of clear shellac, diluted with an equal amount of alcohol. To brighten the colour and renew the gloss of dark straws, rub them with a dark cloth dampened with alcohol, diluted with one quarter the amount of water, then polish them lightly with a piece of dark-coloured velvet.

Stretch Clothing Most of the stretch clothing now on the market is made with stretch-textured nylon or polyester fibres. Stretch-textured means that the fibres are heat set in corkscrew coils that resemble miniature steel springs. When extended and released, they return to their original form. Prior to weaving, these heat-set yarns are untwisted. When a fabric made with them is stretched, it too returns to its original dimensions. Sometimes the elastomeric fibre 'Spandex' is used.

By combining these fibres with others – cotton, wool, silk, synthetics – almost any fabric or weave can be made stretchable. The stretch can be longitudinal, horizontal, or both.

Stretch clothing is washed or dry-cleaned according to the material of which it is made. Washable stretch clothing requires no special techniques. It can be pressed with either a dry or steam iron at the rayon or synthetic setting (275°F to 300°F). Some stretch clothing, such as baby wear, never needs ironing.

Suede An undressed leather, with a nappy, velvet surface. Large suede garments such as coats should be sent to a dry cleaner. For cleaning accessories such as shoes and handbags, see *Shoes*.

Sun Lamp The manufacturer's directions for your particular lamp should be followed carefully, but here are some basic instructions. Dust the reflector frequently to keep it clean and polish it occasionally with a suitable metal polish. Clean the bulb in mercury arc lamps about once a month (when the bulb is cold and the lamp disconnected), using a clean cloth moistened with spirit. Do not use soap and water and do not handle it or oil will be left on the glass.

Surah A fine twill fabric, made sometimes in silk but more often in Tricel. It was once called 'Foulard'. Wash according to material.

Swan's-Down Swan's-down is made in a variety of soft raised fibres. Wash in soapflakes and warm water well lathered. Immerse the swan's-down and swish it gently. Rinse in warm water. Hang to dry, shaking frequently.

Sweaters (Synthetic) Sweaters made of the various synthetic fibres differ in what they will stand, and instructions on the hang tags should always be followed. All can, of course, be dry-cleaned or washed, according to preference. Hand-washing is nearly always recommended as best, but most of them can also be machine-laundered. (Do *not* machine-wash sweaters with delicate trimmings such as beads and sequins.)

Safe for all synthetics is lukewarm water with soap and a softener, or detergent. Squeeze the sweater gently through the suds; never rub or twist it. Rinse it thoroughly in lukewarm water, and for a soft, fluffy texture, add a fabric conditioner such as 'Comfort' or 'Stergene' to the final rinse, following the directions on the box. Squeeze out excess water and, preferably, lay the sweater flat to dry.

'Orlon' acrylic and nylon sweaters are preferably washed by hand in lukewarm water with a synthetic detergent. Squeeze the suds gently through them. Rinse *thoroughly* in lukewarm water and use a fabric conditioner in the last rinse for best results. Roll in a towel to remove excess moisture.

Dry flat. If you wash the sweaters by machine, omit the final spin-dry cycle, remove them dripping wet and dry as for hand washing. No blocking is necessary. If you are going to use a dryer, let the sweaters go through the spin-dry cycle. Dry at a low temperature setting for about 20 minutes and remove immediately.

'Orlon' sweaters containing special acrylic fibres (labelled 'Sayelle') can be machine washed in warm water with a detergent. (If washed by machine, they must be dried by machine. Use the regular setting.) If the sweaters are washed by hand, rinse them thoroughly in cold water. Squeeze out excess water gently. Roll in a towel and squeeze again. Spread flat, bunch into shape, and allow to dry. Avoid stretching. Do not place on hangers. Such knitwear must be dried thoroughly to ensure automatic blocking. If stretched during washing or wearing, wet thoroughly, squeeze, and tumble dry to reshape.

'Dacron' knits are usually washable. (Check the hang tag.) In a machine, use warm water and standard detergents. Do not spin or wring. Gently squeeze out excess water and tumble dry at a medium temperature setting. Or hand wash the knits in warm water and let them drip dry on rustproof hangers.

Sweaters (Wool) Unless you are very expert, measure your sweater before washing it the first time. The best way to do this is to lay it flat on a large piece of plain wrapping paper and draw a line around it. Later you will pin your sweater to this pattern.

Preferably, hand-wash all sweaters made of untreated wool. Use plenty of lukewarm water (95° to 105°F) and an unbuilt synthetic detergent, or a detergent made especially for woollens such as 'Woolite' and 'Woolfoam'. Synthetic detergents are better than soap for woollens because they are free of alkalies, which damage wool, and do not require water softeners, which also are alkaline.

The soak-wash method recommended for blankets is very effective and safe for woollen sweaters. First moisten with lukewarm water and detergent any especially soiled spots. A soft little brush comes in handy here. Then lay the sweater in your detergent solution and let it soak for 10 or 15 minutes, turning it once or twice. (Do not rub, scrub, or twist it. The less handling wool receives, the better.) Rinse twice by the same soak method, then gently squeeze out excess water and roll the sweater in a Turkish towel and knead it gently. For heavy sports sweaters use two towels, one folded and placed inside, to help absorb the moisture.

If you are using a pattern, place this on a Turkish towel or cotton pad and pin the sweater down, patting and easing it into its original shape. Dry in a warm, airy place, away from heat and sunlight. When the sweater is almost dry, turn it occasionally to speed the process. Woollens are best dried quickly.

If untreated, wool sweaters are to be machine washed, follow this procedure after pretreating spots. Soak for five minutes in a cool detergent solution, then extract the water. Soak-rinse twice for five minutes, extracting the water after each rinse. *Do not agitate the washer during washing and rinsing.* Remove and dry flat as described for hand washing.

Instructions for sweaters made

of the new machine washable wool yarns vary according to the treatment given them by the manufacturer. Some treated woollens can stand hot water. Your guide is the hang tag.

Woollen sweaters may be pressed lightly with a warm iron, if desired. Use a dampened press cloth and take care not to press them absolutely dry or they will lose their fluffy, nubby look. After pressing, allow them to air, then fold them neatly and place them in a drawer. Do not use hangers, especially for hand-knits, if you want them to keep their shape. See also *Pilling.*

Synthetic When this term is used it means that the product is not a natural one, but one that has been built up of various chemical elements in imitation of the genuine product. Synthesis, in chemistry, is the exact opposite of analysis. In analysis, the chemist takes a compound to pieces to determine the elements that compose it. In synthesis, he builds it back again.

We hear a great deal of synthetic products today: flavourings used in cooking, plastics, cloth and even synthetic jewels.

Synthetic Textiles – WHAT THEY ARE Synthetic textiles are textiles woven from man-made fibres in contrast to those woven from natural fibres such as cotton, linen, wool and silk. The synthetic fabrics on the market today were developed in chemical laboratories from raw materials such as wood, cotton linters, coal, glass, limestone and various plastics. Years of painstaking research lie behind each one.

By a special technique, which the chemist calls 'polymerization', the molecules of the compound are bunted around until thousands are linked end to end in giant molecules known as polymers. The resulting compound is then 'extruded', which means that it is directed, or forced, through tiny holes, or spinnerets, to form an almost invisible filament. The filament is stretched, twisted and plied into thread for weaving.

Rayon was the first synthetic textile. It is derived from cotton linters and wood pulp. Nylon, 'Orlon' and 'Dynel' are others. In making today's fabrics, synthetics are combined with synthetics, as well as with natural fibres, to give them various desired qualities, such as wrinkle resistance, increased strength, softness, body or drape.

Each synthetic has its individual characteristics, which qualify it for specific jobs, and each differs from the others in the treatment it will stand. In many instances, the synthetics are better than natural fibres. Often they are cheaper to produce. But to get your money's worth from them in pleasure and service, you will have to know how to care for them.

Always look for the identifying label when you buy synthetic materials and follow the manufacturer's instructions for laundering or dry cleaning. Then file the label, marked so you will know what garment it came with, in case you need to refer to it later.

Synthetic textiles produced for home use fall into these classifications: glass, rayon, acetate, nylon, acrylic, modacrylic, polyester, spandex, olefin and saran. Each class is listed in this book as well as the more important trade names such as 'Orlon', 'Dacron', 'Acrilan' and 'Kodel'. Under law the exact fibre content of clothing and yard goods must be stated.

H

For special information and for cleaning instructions look up both the generic and trade names of the textile. For no-iron synthetics see *Drip Dry*.

Taffeta Plain closely woven material made from filament yarn in e.g.: Nylon, Acetate, Triacatete. See these fibres for laundering.

Tapestry A fabric, often hand-loomed, in which the woof of coloured threads is added to the warp in such a way as to produce a pattern. Have tapestries dry-cleaned.

Tarlatan A transparent muslin, stiffened to make underskirts, etc. Dry clean.

Tatting Tatting is a type of knotted lace, hand-made with a shuttle. Press it into shape with your fingers and set the iron down on it gently to dry it out.

Teacloths See they are dry before putting them in the laundry basket as they may mildew. Wash in hot suds and, if necessary, very mild bleach. Knitted and gauze cotton tea towels have a high absorbency.

For dishes and glassware use linen or cotton and linen, non-fluffy cloth.

Teapot ALUMINIUM: Fill with water, add two tablespoons 'borax', boil, then wash in the ordinary way.

CHINA: To remove tarnish, wipe inside of teapot with cloth dipped in bicarbonate of soda. Then wash in hot detergent suds, *or* fill pot with hot water and a little soda, leave overnight. Brush inside spout with bottle brush. Rinse in hot water.

CHROMIUM: Clean inside with cloth moistened in vinegar and dipped in salt. Rinse pot in very hot water. Rinse with boiling water before using.

SILVER: To prevent mustiness place sliver of wood across top so that the top does not close when the pot is not in use – or leave two lumps of sugar in the pot.

Remove tarnish stains with hot water and 'borax'. One teaspoonful of 'borax' to one pint of hot water, leave for an hour or so then clean with cloth and a brush for the spout. Finish by washing in warm soapy water and rinsing thoroughly.

'Teflon' 'Teflon' is the du Pont trade name for an unusual plastic which was discovered accidentally in 1938. Scientists working with refrigeration gases found a white waxy solid in a supposedly empty cylinder. Tested, the material would not yield to conventional solvents and was unaffected by extremes of temperature. Further tests revealed other outstanding qualities and identified the mysterious substance as a fluorocarbon resin.

The key unit is a minute particle containing myriads of carbon and fluorine atoms tightly bonded together. This togetherness tames the fluorine, an element so active that, alone, it will burn water and concrete. United with carbon it produces an organic material which is singularly inert. Fluorocarbon polymers resist attack by corrosive chemicals, retain their strength in extremes of heat and cold, provide superior electrical insulation, and are so slippery that practically nothing adheres to them.

'Teflon' played a vital role during World War II, then entered peacetime industries and the space programme. Bakers and sweet makers began to utilize its non-stick qualities in the 1950s, and the 'Teflon'-coated frying pan appeared in 1961.

Much of today's cookware – glass, porcelain and metal – is

made slick and pretty with 'Teflon'-enamel finishes in a range of colours. There are 'Teflon' tools, both coated and moulded, to go with them. The 'Teflon'-coated steam iron has made its debut, as well as stoves with removable 'Teflon'-coated oven panels, racks, griddles and drip catchers.

For cleaning and care see *Pots and Pans.*

Telephone Don't forget to dust the telephone when you are doing the other furniture. If gummy, clean it with a damp cloth and soap. After use, replace the receiver carefully or your friends will get a busy signal and party liners will suspect you of listening in.

Television Set Clean the face 'glass' with a clean soft cloth wrung out of mild soapsuds. Rinse it with a cloth wrung out of clear water, and wipe it dry with another cloth. *Never* use cleaning fluids or chemical cleaners: these can severely damage the glass. Do not use furniture polish on the face glass or spatter such polishes on it. They often contain solvents that are damaging. Gritty or harsh dusters alone can cause scratches.

To maintain the finish of the cabinet use a fine furniture polish. Do not place rubber articles or articles likely to contain harmful chemicals on top of your television cabinet and do not drape it with a cover. Cloths or scarves that hang down behind obstruct the holes designed to ventilate the tubes and keep them from overheating. In placing your set, for this same reason, make sure that air can circulate freely between it and the wall. Do not place your set near any device that might overheat the chassis or damage the cabinet.

Terra Cotta Terra cotta floors are composed of glazed clay tiles of a red or red-yellow colour. They are non-porous, but because they are set in concrete, such floors are often sealed. They can be waxed, if desired. Self-polishing wax is recommended because it is less slippery than polishing waxes. See also *Sealers.*

Terrazzo Terrazzo flooring is made by mixing marble chips with cement. When hard, the mixture is ground down smooth and polished. Terrazzo is often made in blocks, separated by metal strips. This allows for contraction and expansion of the blocks under temperature changes. Allow a newly laid terrazzo floor to set for one week before washing it. At this time a marble sealer, such as Tri-Seal, can be applied, if desired. (See *Marble.*)

Sweep terrazzo with a soft broom or clean it with the floor brush of your vacuum cleaner. Mop it occasionally with clear water or light suds made with a mild synthetic detergent. (Soap leaves a scum on marble, acids dissolve it.) Self-polishing wax is generally recommended for terrazzo floors because it is less slippery than polishing wax. If you prefer another type of wax, check the instructions on the container to see if it is suitable for terrazzo.

Varnish and lacquer should never be used to seal terrazzo because they discolour it.

Terry Cloth Wash bath and beach robes made of terry cloth like any other cotton material. Shake them out lightly and hang them to dry on rustproof hangers or tumble dry. When dry, fluff them out again and fold carefully. No starch. No ironing. Fabric softener if desired.

Terylene A polyester fibre. See *Polyester.*

Thermos Bottle See *Vacuum Flask*.

Ties Washing a tie sometimes does it more good than dry cleaning. Make a thick suds with lukewarm water and an unbuilt synthetic detergent. Wash the tie carefully; do not rub or twist it out of shape. Use a soft brush on badly soiled places. Rinse carefully in lukewarm water. Roll and squeeze to extract excess water. Starch the tie lightly, shape it carefully and hang it over a rod to dry. Press the tie before it is completely dry. To do this, cut a piece of cardboard in the shape and size of the larger half of the tie and slip it inside.

Press first on the wrong side, then on the right, using a press cloth. The cardboard keeps the tie from being marked by the seams. When the tie has been pressed carefully on both sides, remove the cardboard and press the edges. A steam iron is excellent for this pressing job.

Tile GLAZED CERAMIC TILES usually need only to be wiped with a clean, damp cloth or sponge. However, if soap, grease or dirt has caused a cloudy film or slight discolouration of the surface, use trisodium phosphate or a packaged water softener such as washing soda or 'Oakite'. One teaspoonful in a pail of water should do the trick. If heavily soiled, sprinkle a little softener on a moist cloth and wipe the tiles clean. Rinse and wipe dry with a clean soft cloth.

Cleansing powders also can be used, but must be carefully rinsed away. Do not use acid solutions on tile; they also damage it.

UNGLAZED CERAMIC TILES: Used for floors, can be scrubbed, mopped, or wiped clean easily with water containing trisodium phosphate, washing soda or other softener. Often a moist cloth or sponge is sufficient. If very soiled, scouring powders may be used.

Afterwards of course, you will have to rinse carefully to remove traces of the powder. Wipe dry.

Cellulose sponges and mops are ideal for tile because they never leave ravellings on the cement in which the tiles are set.

Tile installations which are adjacent to oiled or waxed floors often acquire a scummy appearance, owing to wax being tracked into them. This dirt or scum can be removed and the tiles restored to their original freshness by the generous use of scouring powder applied with a wet cloth or steel wool.

If *stains* on your tile floor do not

yield to trisodium phosphate or to scouring powders, try these remedies.

PAINT spattered on tile should be wiped up immediately and the spot scoured. For old or stubborn paint stains several methods are suggested by tile experts and it will be a toss-up as to which works best for the stain on your tile.

All chemicals suggested can be bought in small quantities at chemists or, in larger amounts from chemical supply houses. The cheapest grade, known as the commercial grade, will do.

Buy at your hardware or paint store a commercial bleaching compound called 'Tile Bleach'. Following directions on the container, attempt to remove the stains from a small area, experimentally. A good paint remover will sometimes work. Again test it on a small inconspicuous area.

A third suggestion for removing a paint stain is to saturate a thick, white cloth, or layer of cotton batting, with hydrogen peroxide and place it over the stain. Place a second cloth, moistened with ammonia water, over the first to hasten the bleaching action. Repeat the operation if required.

Method four is somewhat involved. Cut a piece of white cotton flannel, larger than the stain, and saturate it with one part acetone and one part amylacetate (highly inflammable). Place this over the stain and cover with a piece of glass, marble or dry porous tile. If the cloth becomes dry, saturate it again and re-cover as before. The solvent may spread the stain, in which case the second cloth should be larger.

A fifth suggestion for paint stains is to obtain and mix the following chemicals: trisodium phosphate (one part), sodium perborate (one part). Prepare a strong soap solution with hot water and add to the dry ingredients to form a thick paste. Cover the stain with this paste and let it stand until dry. Repeat if required, re-moistening the same powder with soap solution. Alternating this treatment with the hydrogen peroxide treatment sometimes hurries the job along. (And the moral of that is: Don't spill paint on tile.)

For INKSTAINS, try method five, described for paint stains.

Grouting (mortar or cement) that has become stained or discoloured is practically impossible to restore. You can try scouring powders or rubbing the joint lightly with folded sandpaper, or swabbing with a weak acid solution. Tile Bleach, paint remover and hydrogen peroxide might also be helpful.

Wax is not recommended as a finish for ceramic tiles.

Tin Tin is a metal which approaches silver in whiteness and lustre. It is easily worked and can take a high polish. Tin resists oxidation but is corroded by acids. It is used in many alloys and as a coating on iron.

Tin piepans, tart moulds, bread pans and other kitchen accessories should be washed in soap and water, rinsed and dried thoroughly to avoid rust. You aren't supposed to keep tin utensils bright and shining. They heat better when they have become darkened. Besides, if you scrub tinware with scouring powders you will remove the tin. It's just a plating. Remove burned foods from tin vessels by boiling them up for three to five minutes (no more!) in water to which a little baking soda has been added.

To remove rust from tinware rub it with a piece of cut raw potato that has been dipped in a mild abrasive. To remove accumulations of grease, wash the utensil in a solution of hot water and washing soda. Use one fourth of a cup of soda to one quart of water.

Decorative tinware can be coated with clear lacquer or with hard wax to protect the finish. Lacquer is best if the tinware is to be used outdoors.

Toaster See *Electric Appliances.*

Toilet Before adding a cleaner or disinfectant, flush the toilet to wet the sides of the bowl. Sprinkle the cleaner on the wet surfaces and in the water. Let it stand for a few minutes, then clean the bowl with a toilet brush or swab. If stains remain, sprinkle on more cleaner and let it stand for at least an hour, preferably overnight, and again brush or swab. Repeat if necessary. Such stains are usually caused by hard water and do not appear if the toilet is cleaned regularly.

For cleaning, preferably use a standard commercial preparation and follow the directions on the label exactly. Do not *ever* try to improve their action by adding any other cleaning or bleaching agents. Toxic gases could be released. Store bowl cleaners carefully; many are poisonous. Do not use them for stains in sinks or bathrubs; they damage the finish. Clean the outside of the bowl, the rim and the seat with hot soapsuds or a mild scouring powder. Rinse and wipe dry to avoid streaks.

Toilet bowl brushes should be washed promptly after use in hot soapsuds, rinsed thoroughly and hung to dry. Use paper towelling for the rim and outside of the toilet and discard them.

Tole Tole is painted metal, used most often for lamp bases and trays. See *Lamp – Electric.*

Tools If you like to potter about with tools, perhaps you ought to know the fundamentals for their care. Rust, next to the borrower, is their worst enemy. If a spot appears, remove it promptly with fine emery cloth. To prevent rust wipe tools now and then with a cloth moistened with any good oil. Olive oil is perfect; Vaseline is all right. Linseed oil is worse than none for metal, but it is good for wooden handles.

Store sharp tools so that the cutting edges won't be damaged ... planes on their sides, chisels in racks, etc.

See also pages 145 and 154.

Tucks Iron vertical tucks lengthwise. Iron rows of tucks from the top down, in sections.

Turkish Towels Wash Turkish towels like any other cotton material. Fluff them with a vigorous shake and hang them straight on the line (or tumble dry). Stretch woven borders gently. When dry, give them another good shake and fold them neatly. No starch. No ironing.

Typewriter Clean the platen (large rubber roller) and the little rubber rollers that feed in the paper by wiping them periodically with a clean cloth, moistened with alcohol. This will keep them free of ink, and resilient. Some platens are removable. This makes it possible to brush out easily the inevitable accumulation of dust and erasings.

Type can be cleaned with alcohol or cleaning fluid. Slip a blotter or folded paper under the type bars and scrub the type with a stiff-bristled typewriter brush. The paper will absorb any excess fluid. A doughy compound also is available at typewriter stores for this purpose and (very easy to use) a cleaner that is sprayed on.

Once a month oil the carriage rails. To do this move the carriage over to the extreme left and place *one* drop of typewriter oil on the rails. Do *not* oil the type bars.

To remove old ribbons move the carriage to the extreme left and snip the ribbon in two. Lift off both spools. Save one spool for the left side and put the new ribbon (already on a spool) on the right. Stick a straightened paper clip or hairpin through the hole in the middle of the left spool and spin it over a wastebasket, letting the old ribbon go into the basket.

PRECAUTION: When making erasures move the carriage over so that erasings will drop out of the machine. If using a portable, replace the lid after use to safeguard it against dust. Cover larger models with a dust jacket. When your typewriter is not in use the paper release lever should be down, or in the release position. Constant pressure on the paper feed rolls tends to flatten them and make them less efficient. Brush out dust and erasings regularly.

Umbrella Never mind old wives' tales. Open up your wet umbrella when you come in out of the rain and give it a chance to dry decently to avoid streaks. If a rib slips out of place you can cement it in easily, using one of those handy tubes of quick-drying household cement that you can buy in hardware stores.

There are umbrella specialists in every city who will supply new handles, new covers and make any sort of repair, so don't run to buy a new one at the first sign of trouble.

Upholstery See *Furniture – Upholstered* and *Vinyl Upholstery*.

Urea See *Melamine and Urea*.

Urethane Urethane foam, polyfoam, or 'plastic' foam is used for package cushioning, rug underlays, sometimes for furniture cushioning and mattresses. It is a plastic material, not comparable to foam rubber. Small items are washable.

Vacuum Cleaner Pamper your vacuum cleaner. If you don't keep it clean and in good working order it will get even with you by making a joke of your house-cleaning efforts. Just dumping the bag, or container regularly is not enough.

Before you start on a floor pick up pins, buttons and other objects that might make it choke. Move it slowly in straight, even strokes, lengthwise of the rug, and go over each section at least seven times. Avoid swishing the wand like a broom if your machine is of that type.

Disposable paper bags have largely eliminated the need to empty dust bags. If you still use a cloth bag, turn it upside down on a newspaper, hold the mouth firmly in place (use your feet) and gently shake out the dirt. This is Rule One. But remember that the air you use in the suction process may be filtered through the bag and that, if the pores of the fabric are clogged with dust, your machine will operate less efficiently. Rub the sides of the bag together gently to loosen embedded dirt. Now and then turn it inside out and give it a good brushing with a stiff whisk broom. (Outdoors, of course.) This will be a good time to check on its condition. Hold it to the light and inspect it for rips and tears. If you find any, it's time to invest in a new bag. Never wash a dust bag.

If your vacuum cleaner has a cloth container for dust, empty it after using, wash the container with soap and water, rinse and dry it, then return it to the cleaner.

Vacuum off all hair and fluff from the brushes. If the brushes become worn get new ones or treat them to new bristles. Wipe off other attachments before storing them.

Filters used on some types of vacuum cleaners need replacing every six months. In between they should be removed now and then and vacuumed.

Upright vacuum cleaners should be inverted for cleaning. Remove hair and threads. A little rubber belt usually is used to secure this roll and care must be taken that it is replaced correctly when the roll is put back into place. And be sure the belt itself is in good condition. It is a good idea to keep a few on hand so that you can replace a belt that is cracked or loose. Buy the kind that is made for your particular machine.

Many women put the various attachments of their vacuum cleaners on a shelf or in a drawer and forget all about them.

This is partly because it is a bother to carry them from room to room. Some of the newer models have solved this particular problem by devising ways for them to ride pickaback.

The attachments are great labour-savers and enable you to do a really thorough job. The little duster will whisk dirt and dust from lampshades, the insides of drawers, from mouldings, the crevices of brick fireplaces, from hard-to-reach corners and carved surfaces. The floor brush will also dust the walls, gobbling webs, spiders and even hornets.

Not only stuffed furniture but draperies, curtains, mattresses, blankets, coats and hats can be cleaned with the upholstery attachment. An enterprising salesman once told me that this part would even remove fleas from a dog, but, since none was available, we were unable to test the theory and the possible canine reaction. The spray attachment can be used for spraying rug shampoos, liquid wax, insecticides and mothproofing compounds.

Vacuum Flask Clean the inside of a vacuum bottle with hot water and synthetic detergent, or with water and baking soda. Toss in torn bits of paper for mild abrasive action if desirable. Rinse the bottle thoroughly, wipe the outside with a damp cloth, and place it upside down to dry. To keep the bottle fresh, leave it uncapped until used again. Never immerse the entire bottle in water, to avoid seepage into the metal barrel. Occasionally, unscrew the metal shoulder of the case and wipe the interior dry to prevent the possible formation of rust.

The inner container of a vacuum bottle is made of rather fragile glass and should not be subjected to sudden changes of temperature. Cool it before pouring in iced beverages and warm it before filling it with liquids that are hot. Do not use it for carbonated beverages. Fill your bottle to a level just below the stopper.

Stoppers vary. Some snap on, some slide into place when the top is replaced, others twist in. If a cork is used it can be sterilized and sweetened by boiling. If the stopper is a twist-in type, be gentle to avoid breakage. The glass inner bottle, however, is replaceable.

Vanadium A metal added to steel to make it more flexible and tougher. See *Steel – Vanadium*.

Vase Look up the material of which the vase is made.

Velcro Cockleburs gave Swiss inventor George de Mestral his inspiration for the newest in fasteners, trademarked Velcro. Velcro consists of two woven nylon tapes – one covered with hundreds of tiny loops and the other with hooks – that lock securely when pressed together and are peeled open lengthwise. The tape can be cut to size in patches and lengths, and can be stitched, glued, or stapled to cloth, metal, wood, or plastics, to form closures.

Velcro can be substituted for zippers, buttons, snaps, toggles, and hooks and eyes on clothing. It can do things that zippers can't do – fasten down a square, for instance, and provide adjustable fasteners by varying the amount of overlap. This is a boon for such items as brassières, wrap-around dresses and housecoats, skirts and petticoats, nappies and reversible belts.

Experiments have determined that only half a pound of pressure is needed to peel the tapes apart, while a 16-pound yank is required to open them sideways. This means they won't pop open under stress.

Velcro is washable and dry cleanable. Bleaches do not hurt it and it does not melt or fuse under normal pressing temperatures. But close the fastener before washing to avoid pickup of lint, fuzz and threads, and during pressing to minimize the danger of breaking the little hooks.

Vellum Vellum is a fine grade of parchment made from the skins of lambs, kids, or very young goats. See *Parchment*.

Velon Velon is a saran vinylidene chloride monofilament (!) used mainly in webbing for outdoor furniture, automobile seat covers, insect screens and venetian blind tape. It is cleaned by wiping with soapy water; the furniture can be hosed down. The monofilament is nonabsorbent with excellent chemical, weather and mildew resistance. Its colours tend to darken a little with prolonged exposure to the sun.

Velour A heavy-pile fabric in cotton, silk, rayon or other man-made fibres. Velours are now often made in acrylic fibres, including knitted types. Nylon brushed knitted velours are laminated to a locknit in nylon or acetate for curtains, and there are similar upholstery velours in laminated nylon. Treat according to manufacturer's instructions. It is usually advisable to have it dry-cleaned.

Velvet Washable velvets and velveteens are handled like corduroy. The label on the garment should be your guide in determining whether the material will stand water. Those that are nonwashable should be sent to a dry cleaner. If the nap is merely crushed, you can fluff it by steaming it over the spout of a tea-kettle.

To steam velvet follow these directions. Tie a piece of muslin or several layers of cheesecloth

over the spout of the kettle. When the water is boiling rapidly pass the crushed velvet back and forth through the steam, making certain that the steam goes from the wrong to the right side. Velvet is never pressed. Let the material dry thoroughly before wearing it.

For laundering washable velvets see *Corduroy*.

Venetian Blinds To dust, drop the blind to its full length, tilt to full-light position and dust with a divided venetian blind brush which does several blades at a time. Or brush the blades flat and dust them with the round dusting brush of your vacuum cleaner. Turn the other way and dust the reverse side.

To wash painted or plastic blinds use a sponge or soft cloth, wrung out in suds made of a mild detergent or a good paint-cleaning solution (Oakite, washing soda), washing one slat at a time ... both sides. Rinse and dry carefully. Some venetian blind cleaners wax as they clean.

If the blinds are of natural wood finish, clean them with liquid wax, one slat at a time, changing the cloth as it becomes soiled. Rub up with a soft cloth.

Tapes can be scrubbed with a brush or upholstery cleaner, or with dry-cleaning fluid. If you want to wash them you will have to take the blind down, unknot the cord at the bottom, remove the tacks which secure the tapes and slip them off the slats. Measure the tapes before washing them, then stretch them to their proper length while they are drying.

Venetian blind tape and cord can be bought by the yard, if you wish to renew them. Be sure to measure carefully the distance between the cross-tapes if you want the blinds to be the same length. Better yet, take a sample with you. Replacing tapes is a tedious job and is to be recommended only if you are handy at such operations and anxious to save money. Otherwise you can have them redone professionally.

Waxing blinds of painted or natural wood makes them easier to clean and prevents spotting. A hard-finish wax is best, or use a wax spray containing silicones. If the blinds are to be repainted, remove the wax first by wiping each slat carefully with turpentine.

Verel Manufactured in America. Verel is the trade name for a modacrylic fibre spun from an acetone preparation. It is a soft, resilient, low temperature fibre, highly resistant to acids, alkalies and other chemicals. It will not support flames and is resistant to damage from sunlight, age, mildew, moths and other insects, and rot. These qualities suggested carpeting as a prime role for the new fibre.

According to its producers, tests have disclosed that Verel carpeting is equal to wool for wear (second only to nylon), with higher strength and stretch and better elastic recovery. In addition it is readily dyeable in both dull and light lustres in a range of bright and pastel colours.

Verel fibres are smooth, and shed dust and dirt easily. They are easily shampooed, and most ordinary stains can be removed with a soft cloth or sponge and a detergent solution or cleaning fluid. Do not use acetone for spot removal.

Vinyl Vinyl plastics are made from such raw materials as coal, limestone, natural gas, petroleum and brine. The first vinyl plastic was made by the French scientist Regnault more than 100 years ago.

Vinyls may be rigid, semi-rigid, film, sheeting or a coating. They may be of any colour or colourless – transparent, translucent, or opaque. Sturdy, long wearing, and resistant to abrasion, they are hard to tear if flexible. They resist the penetration of water, but must be guarded against high heat from oven or flame. Special types are made for outdoor use.

Flexible vinyls appear in the home as upholstery, raincoats, curtains, garment bags, packaging material, inflated toys, jackets, boots, pants for babies, dresses, sunhats, bikinis, skirts, men's vests, walking shorts and trousers. Rigid vinyls are used for gramophone records, roll flooring and floor tiles.

Vinyl film can be bent back and forth many times without sustaining breaks or tears, and rigid vinyls will return to their original shape after a blow, but sharp knocks should be avoided.

Such plastics are not harmed by common chemicals, resist acids, alcohol and stains from food, ink and dirt. They have a low absorption rate. They are fire-resistant – some types stop burning as soon as the flame is removed, while others actually snuff out fire. Vinyls are light in weight and their colours will withstand long exposure to the sun without fading.

All of these qualities recommend them for upholstery. Vinyl film can be stamped in dainty patterns, and the material can be hemmed, tucked, pleated and seamed by heat. When closely boxed, vinyls may develop a slight (not unpleasant) odour but this disappears with airing.

Hand-wash vinyl plastics with warm water and soap or synthetic detergent. Keep hot dishes and burning cigarettes away and, in cleaning, do not use carbon tetrachloride, ammonia, nail polish remover, acetone, or abrasives. Some vinyl products have a tendency to stick to, mar, or discolour lacquered surfaces when in close contact under certain conditions. If you are using moth or insect sprays, be careful not to spatter vinyl surfaces.

Vinyl Plastic Floors are nonslip and easy on the feet. They resist abrasion, acid, grease and alkalies. They are washed with warm water and either a soap or detergent. Waxing is optional. Either self-polishing or polishing waxes can be used, but self-polishing waxes are preferred.

Vinyl Upholstery needs only wiping with a damp cloth, but it can be washed when necessary with warm water and mild soap. Sponge a good-sized area and let the soapy solution remain for a minute or two, then rinse with a damp sponge. If the soil is not removed, rub it again or scrub it lightly with a soft-bristled brush.

Common stains can be removed as follows: chewing gum – scrape off as much as possible and remove the residue with naphtha, kerosene, or lighter fluid; paint and shoe polish – wipe up immediately and remove the rest with turpentine (do *not* use brush cleaner or paint remover); tar, asphalt, road oil – remove immediately with turpentine or lighter fluid to avoid a permanent stain; ink – wipe away immediately with water or alcohol; nail polish and remover – to minimize the damage, blot carefully or daub up instantly (wiping spreads the damage).

Viscose Rayon See *Rayon*.

Viyella Trade name for a wool and cotton fabric made in England. Viyella is 55 per cent wool and 45 per cent cotton. It washes almost like cotton and doesn't shrink. Wash with warm suds made with soap or a synthetic detergent. Iron on either the right or wrong side with the temperature setting on 'wool'.

Voile A fine sheer material made from high twist yarn. In cotton or viscose or nylon or polyester. Launder in hand-hot suds; rinse well, roll in Turkish towel. Iron with cool iron while slightly damp when nylon or Terylene. For cotton or rayon use a warm to moderate iron.

Vycron This is the trade name for a polyester fibre made from a polymerized resin. Vycron is used for suitings, dress fabrics and raincoats of the wash-and-wear type, and for upholstery. It dyes well and the fabrics have excellent colourfastness. They are wrinkle-resistant, pill-resistant and very strong. Consult the label as to whether to wash or dry-clean. Washable Vycron should be ironed at a temperature of 300°F (lower than silk). See *Synthetic Textiles*.

Wallpaper See *Walls and Ceilings*.

Walls and Ceilings Some bright day, when your energy is high, it may strike you suddenly that your walls need cleaning. Assemble your ammunition, clear the decks and go into action while the mood is upon you. Whatever the wall, your first step is to turn back the rugs (or take them out), push the furniture to the middle of the floor and cover it, and take down the pictures.

For *painted walls* you will need: a wall brush, either hand or vacuum, or cloth-covered broom; two sponges; two pails, one for your washing mixture and one for rinsing; a good mild soap or a chemical cleaner. (See *Paint Cleaners* for information about preparations suitable for flat and enamel paint – page 181.)

Your first step is to dust the walls. Cobwebs and dust threads are attached by one end and hang down. They will be removed most readily if you dust from the bottom of the wall up. After dusting carefully begin washing, again from the bottom up. The reason for this is that if dirty water runs down over the soiled part it leaves streaks that are hard to remove. Squeeze your sponge or cloth as dry as possible and clean a small area (not more than three square feet) at a time, using a circular motion. Rinse with a sponge squeezed out of clear water and wipe the area dry. Proceed to the space adjoining this and repeat, taking care to overlap the edges of the area just cleaned. Continue until the wall has been finished.

NOTE: If you are using soap and water, you should add 'Borax' to the suds to soften it and make the job easier. Use one tablespoon of 'Borax' per quart of water and add it to the rinse water too. Scouring powders damage paint so do not use them unless the walls are extremely dirty and a new paint job is indicated. A little whiting, or a mild scouring powder, will usually remove scuff marks. And, of course, remember to change the water in your pails as soon as it becomes dirty or you will frustrate your efforts. If you are using a commercial paint cleaner, follow the directions exactly. Too much can damage, or even remove, the paint.

If you are cleaning a painted wall with the idea of repainting it, give it a final wash with turpentine. This will remove any greasy film and help bind the paint to the wall.

Walls finished with *calcimine* and similar washes cannot be cleaned. They must be redone. Paints which have an oil base, though they are mixed with water, can be cleaned but are difficult. See *Whitewash*.

PAPERED WALLS: You may not know whether the paper on your walls is washable, but even if it is so labelled it is a good idea to test it in an inconspicuous place before proceeding with an all-over job. Squeeze a sponge out of clear, lukewarm water and rub very lightly. Use as little water as possible to avoid soaking the paper off the wall. If the pattern doesn't blur and the test is otherwise successful, go ahead with the washing, working from the bottom of the wall up. Few papers are really washable.

For thin papers clear warm water with no soap is recommended. Strokes should be overlapped and gently patted dry.

Do not rub. For the heavier washable papers use a suds made of mild white soap. Apply with a soft sponge, squeezed out of the suds, and wash a small area at a time, proceeding with a very light touch. Rinse with a sponge squeezed out of clear water. Pat dry with a clean soft cloth.

Non-washable papers can be cleaned with a commercial cleaner that looks like a lump of dough and can be bought in paint and hardware stores. Follow the directions on the container. Or you can use any of the following: art gum; the inside of a loaf of stale bread, preferably rye; wheat bran sewed in a bag or pipe clay. Overlap your strokes and proceed with great care or the wall will look streaky.

STAINS ON WALLPAPER: Grease spots should be removed from wallpaper promptly. Make a paste by mixing fuller's earth, French chalk or other absorbent powder with cleaning fluid. Test an inconspicuous place to make sure the colours won't bleed, then smooth the mixture on the spot. Allow it to dry thoroughly, then brush it off. For a bad spot two or three applications may be necessary. To remove crayon marks, try sponging them lightly with a soft cloth moistened with cleaning fluid. (Test first.) It may be necessary to repeat the sponging a number of times. Washable papers may be given a final soap and water treatment. If the cleaning fluid leaves a ring on non-washable wallpaper, try the fuller's earth poultice described for grease stains. Ink spilled on wallpaper should be blotted up promptly. Be careful not to smear it. Apply fuller's earth or French chalk. Brush off the absorbent as quickly as it takes up the ink. This may not remove the stain completely. Try ink eradicator (obtainable at stationers) to finish the job, but remember that it is likely to remove the colour, too.

Clean light smudges and pencil marks with art gum. Brush off food stains as well as possible and sponge any greasy marks that remain with cleaning fluid, or apply a poultice made with it, as described for grease stains.

Wallpapers that have been lacquered can be washed safely with warm suds. Rinse and wipe dry. Wall waxes, available at paint and wallpaper stores, also make cleaning easier. Spots on these can be wiped off with a damp cloth.

WOOD-PANELLED WALLS: If waxed, require little attention other than dusting. If they become soiled, or begin to look dry, clean them with liquid wax, and rub to a soft polish. Varnished or shellacked wood panelling that is not waxed can be cleaned with a polish made by mixing half a cup of turpentine with a cup of boiled linseed oil (see *Linseed Oil*) and about a tablespoon of vinegar. Apply sparingly. Let it stand for 15 minutes, then rub until no smudge is left by a clean, dry finger.

FABRIC-COATED WALLS should be cleaned according to the directions provided by the manufacturer for the covering. If you do not know who manufactured the covering, ask for a cleaner made especially for this type of wall.

See also *Mildew*, page 147.

Wash Basin See *Bath*.

Washing Machine Whatever its make, the consideration you give your washing machine will help determine its length of life and the job it does on your clothes. Over-loading strains the motor, and the clothes are not properly washed. Too much soap or detergent spreads a blanket of suds and makes soil removal difficult. If your machine has a lint trap, clean it often. These are primary rules.

In using your particular machine you should follow the manufacturer's directions for best results. If yours have been lost, write to the manufacturer, giving the model number which is stamped somewhere on the washer. The directions which follow are for general care.

AUTOMATIC WASHERS: When washing is completed, turn off both taps to eliminate pressure on the hoses. Occasionally wipe the exterior with a clean damp sponge or cloth. Use of an appliance wax is optional. If you use it, do not apply it to plastic parts.

During normal use, the inside of a front-loading (tumbler) washer is self-cleaning. Occasionally remove the agitator from top-loading washers and clean the washer basket underneath. Wipe out the inside of the agitator. Also wipe the metal tube. Automatic washers are permanently lubricated at the factory and never need oiling.

If the machine has been used for starching or tinting, it will need special attention. Washing a load of clothes after starching will remove any excess starch from the basket. Or start the washer at the final rinse and let it complete the cycle. To remove traces of dye, use detergent and chlorine bleach. For top-loading washers use one cup of detergent and one cup of bleach; for front-loading washers use ½ cup of detergent and ½ cup of bleach. Start at wash and complete the cycle. Wipe off any dye that may have spilled on the exterior with a diluted bleach solution and rinse well with a clean damp sponge. If the rubber around the door remains discoloured, wipe it with a diluted bleach solution and rinse thoroughly. The clothes guard of top-loading washers may be permanently tinted.

NON-AUTOMATIC washers should be cleaned when the last load has been removed. Lift out the washing mechanism (unless directions say not to), wash and dry it. Remove any hardwater deposit from the tub, using soapsuds on a cloth dipped in a strong solution of water softener. Rinse the tub and wipe it dry. (Never use an abrasive.) Clean lint and loose threads from the drain screen or trap. Drain off any remaining water by lowering the hose. Replace the washing mechanism in the tub, preferably leaving it off the shaft. Disconnect the electric cord. Release pressure on the wringer rollers because if left compressed they are likely to become flattened, and the rubber may stick and tear. Always leave the rollers clean and dry.

It is a good idea to have a washer checked periodically. You will be wise if you select a service mechanic accredited by the manufacturer of your particular machine.

Watch A watch should be cleaned and oiled regularly ... men's watches every 12 or 18 months, small wrist watches every eight months. The tiny watch on your wrist needs more frequent attention because it works harder (31,000,000 ticks a year) and is constructed more delicately. It will warn you when the time for overhauling is overdue by refusing to run. Even the best oil thickens with time and the delicate mainspring of a small watch cannot overcome the resistance of congealed oil. A large watch, on the other hand, because of its more powerful mainspring, will keep on running for a while after almost all of the lubrication has disappeared, just as a car will, and with equally disastrous results.

Men's pocket watches should be wound once a day, preferably in the morning and at the same hour. Small wrist watches will give their best service if they are wound both at night and in the morning. This practice keeps the mainspring taut and helps overcome damage from the many shifts of position a wrist watch experiences.

Many persons injure their watches, especially small wrist watches, in setting them. The winder should never be pulled out, because there is always the danger that it will break off or come out altogether. The proper way to set any watch is to place the thumb nail and middle finger nail just below the winder and *press* them together. This forces the winder out just far enough to permit the setting of the hands, after which it should be snapped back into position.

A FEW 'DON'TS': Don't open the back of your watch; moisture and dust are harmful. Don't fail to remove your wrist watch before washing your hands. Should your watch become accidentally wet, send it to your jeweller promptly to prevent rust and a large repair bill. Don't wind your watch too tight; you may break the mainspring. A loose hold on the stem acts as a safety valve.

Water Colour Paintings cannot be cleaned.

Water Heater Have your hot-water heater cleaned and serviced once a year by your fuel company when the heating system is checked and cleaned. The burner, flue and chimney should receive attention and the water should be drained to remove any sediment.

Automatic gas and electric heaters require little or no attention, once they are correctly installed. If the water is hard, it may be necessary to have the heating element checked occasionally and the lime deposit removed.

Water heaters are of many types ... oil, coal, wood, etc. Cleaning and caring for them properly is a job for a capable service mechanic, not for the homemaker or inexperienced household mechanic.

For average use the setting on the thermostat control should be about 140°F. Higher temperatures put extra wear and tear on the tank and plumbing lines are a hazard to small children. If, however, your water heater is linked with a hot water heating system, the thermostat control may have to be set much higher in the winter to secure adequate heat. Ask your fuel service mechanic about this matter.

Water-Repellent Finish Follow the washing, or dry-cleaning instructions on the labels of garments with water-repellent finishes. Some stand up under repeated washing and dry cleaning. Others are removed, but can be restored by your dry cleaner. If the garment is washable, follow instructions for the fabric of which the garment is made. See also *Raincoats*, *Zelan* and *Silicones* (page 183).

Whitewash Whitewashed surfaces cannot be cleaned; they must be given a fresh coating. Whitewash formulas vary. For instance, you would use different mixtures for inside and outside jobs and a

special blend for walls that are inclined to be damp. The following recipe is for average inside use.

Mix thoroughly one pound of powdered glue and one gallon of water. In another container mix 20 pounds of hydrated lime with two gallons of water, stirring carefully until all lumps have been eliminated. Combine the two mixtures and mix until very smooth. Thin with water to a suitable consistency and apply with a whitewash brush.

Wincey A lightweight fabric similar to flannel but finer. Originally it had a wool weft and cotton warp but may now be in wool mixture yarns. Wash in hand-hot water; use moderately hot iron while damp.

Winceyette A soft slightly raised fabric similar to a flannelette but lighter in weight. Originally cotton or cotton and wool blend but now also in rayon blends. Wash as for wool and rayon.

Wicker Wicker furniture and wicker baskets are made of osiers, rattan twigs, or thin, flexible strips of wood. Unless finished with a paint or varnish damaged by water, they should get an occasional wetting to keep them from becoming dry or brittle.

See *Furniture – Bamboo*.

Windows Aerosol sprays take the fuss out of window washing and reduce the amount of equipment that must be carried about. You spray the cleaner on, then wipe the glass clean with soft paper towels or with window wipes. Because they are so convenient to use and because they keep the hands out of water, many women consider them well worth the extra cost.

Otherwise, many simple home mixtures will clean windows. Professionals, who polish off a hundred a day, are adamant in their view that clear, cool water is best.

If you are doing the job yourself, use an aerosol cleaner, plain water or water containing vinegar, washing soda, 'Borax', spirit, ammonia, or trisodium phosphate. Use about a tablespoon of ammonia or vinegar for each quart of water, about two teaspoons of borax or kerosene, one to two teaspoons of washing soda or trisodium phosphate, and about a quarter of a cup of alcohol per quart of water. The spirit mixture is recommended if windows are to be washed during freezing weather. Alkaline solutions (soda, ammonia) and solutions containing alcohol should be handled carefully because they damage painted, lacquered and varnished surfaces.

Follow this procedure if you are using a liquid mixture of the homemade variety. Dip your chamois, sponge or soft lintless cloth into the water and squeeze it as dry as possible. Wash the top, the bottom, then the middle, of the pane. If the window is very dirty, rinse and repeat. Polish immediately with a clean, damp chamois or paper towels. Change the washing water as soon as it becomes dirty.

Rubber squeegees are useful for large windows. Hold the squeegee firmly, stroke downward, and wipe the edge after each stroke. Some squeegees have long, hollow handles into which the cleaning solution can be poured, an additional boon to the hasty or bored as it eliminates dunking and splashing about with a brush on large expanses like sun porches.

A FEW 'DON'TS': Don't scrub dirty glass with a dry cloth; you will scratch the panes. Don't work on windows when the sun is shining on them; they dry too fast and show streaks. *Don't* use soap, *ever*; the panes will be smeared and the smears are hard to remove. Don't 'sit out' a window to clean it; you might lose your balance, and lorry drivers will wave to you. Clean the outside by raising and lowering the sashes.

Window Blinds Some window blinds are washable, while others are not. If yours are the washable variety, clean them this way: take them down, lifting the slotted end of the roller first, then pulling the other end out of the socket. Spread the blind on a flat surface and scrub it with a stiff lather, using a cloth or brush. Wash a small section at a time and overlap the strokes. Care must be taken not to get the fabric too wet. Rinse with a clean damp cloth. Hang and allow to dry thoroughly before re-rolling.

If your blind is stubborn about re-rolling, or refuses pointblank to do so, the spring in the slot end of the roller probably needs rewinding. Use a pair of pliers, or your fingers, but don't wind it too tightly or your blind will become vicious. An easier way is to remove the shade (or just lift the slotted end of it) while partly unrolled, roll it up and replace it. This amounts to rewinding.

Non-washable blinds can be

cleaned with oatmeal, with a commercial cleaner or with art gum. If the blind is beyond satisfactory cleaning, take the roller to a window-blind man and have it redone. No need to toss away a good roller. Blinds that are worn or stained at the bottom can be removed from the rollers and turned. Hem the 'top' and tack the 'bottom' to the roller.

Window Screens Dirty screens shut out sunlight and soil windowpanes when it rains. Brush them now and then with a hand brush, or with the dusting brush of your vacuum cleaner. For a thorough job (as before putting them up) brush them on both sides with kerosene, after dusting, using a small paintbrush. Wipe carefully with a clean, soft cloth to remove any surplus. This treatment also helps prevent the formation of rust on iron screens.

Spar varnish applied to copper screens will prevent the unsightly greenish-grey stains caused by water trickling down from the mesh on to painted frames.

Window Sills Clean your window sills according to the finish (paint, varnish, lacquer), then wax them to prevent damage from moisture. Hard wax, well rubbed in and carefully polished, is best. (This wax coating must be removed when woodwork is to be repainted. Just wipe it off with turpentine.)

'Wintuk' 'Wintuk' is the trade name for a new 'Orlon' acrylic fibre by du Pont, engineered for knitwear. It looks and feels like fine Shetland, merino, or lambs' wool; it dyes well, is light in weight and absorbent. 'Wintuk' sweaters can be washed by hand or machine and do not need to be blocked. For instructions see *Sweaters (Synthetic)*.

Woodwork WOODEN FLOORS: For the proper care of a wooden floor it is helpful to know whether the finish is lacquer, shellac, varnish or sealer. However, if wax has been applied to any of these finishes, the routine cleaning and polishing procedure is the same for all.

WAXED FLOORS: Waxed floors should be dusted with the brush attachment of the vacuum cleaner, a soft brush, or an untreated mop. An oiled mop damages the finish. They should be polished monthly with a weighted buffer or electric polisher, which can be rented in most towns if you do not own one. At this time worn spots can be rewaxed. Re-wax the entire floor twice a year. Use liquid or paste wax, according to your personal preference. Liquid and paste polishing waxes are identical in composition, except that liquid wax contains more solvent. They are considered best for wood.

If a waxed floor has been well cared for it is not necessary to remove the old coat before applying more. A good method is to go over the floor first with liquid wax (sometimes called 'cleaning wax'). Apply the wax to a small area at a time and wipe it carefully with a clean dry cloth. Change cloths as they become soiled. The solvent in the wax removes the soil and a fine film of wax remains on the floor. Let it dry the length of time stipulated on the container, then buff. If desired, paste wax can now be applied. This will give a beautiful and lasting finish. Fine floors are often given a second and even a third coating of hard wax.

Interim care of a waxed floor includes prompt removal of spots with liquid wax (a damp cloth if the spot is sugary), rewaxing and polishing. Spilled water should be wiped up instantly. Scratches should be treated like spots.

WORD OF WARNING: In waxing a floor it is better to use too little than too much wax. Apply it with a slightly dampened pad of cheese-cloth (wax inside) in a very thin layer. Too much wax will make the floor sticky and difficult to polish to a hard finish.

OILED FLOORS: Oiled floors and woodwork are dusted with an oiled cloth or mop and washed, when required, with suds made of mild soap. Rinse thoroughly with a cloth or mop wrung out of clear water, wetting the surface as little as possible. Dry thoroughly with a clean soft cloth. Cover a small portion of the floor at a time and proceed in this way until the task has been finished. When completely dry, apply a fresh coating of warm oil. (Those with a paraffin or linseed oil base are best.) The oil may be applied with a cloth or a mop and should be rubbed in thoroughly. Any excess oil should be wiped up carefully to avoid a dustcatching, slippery surface.

If a wax finish is to be substituted for an oil finish, clean the floor carefully with liquid wax, then apply paste wax and buff.

GLOSS LACQUERS: Gloss lacquers give floors a durable finish and are resistant to heat and water. They can be washed with a mop wrung out of mild lukewarm suds and rinsed with clear water. They do not have to be waxed, but may be, if desired. If unwaxed, dust with a treated mop. Lacquered floors can be patched. They can be re-coated, after cleaning, without removing the old lacquer. Lacquer can be applied to a shellacked floor, but not to a painted or varnished surface.

VARNISHED FLOORS: Varnished floors can be waxed, if desired. If not waxed, they can be dusted with a treated mop. Unless the varnish is waterproof, these floors should not be washed unless it is absolutely necessary. Wash waterproof varnish like lacquer. Wash other kinds, a very small area at a time, using the greatest care not to let the water stand. Use mild suds, a cloth well wrung out. Rinse and dry each small segment quickly. Varnished floors can be patched but it is very difficult to make a good job of it.

SHELLACKED FLOORS: Shellacked floors are ruined by water and should never be washed. Unless kept protected constantly with wax they spot, crack and wear away easily. They cannot be patched satisfactorily and water whitens them.

SEALED FLOORS: Sealed floors are usually waxed. These finishes penetrate the wood, do not scratch easily and can be patched. Properly applied, they give a beautiful and lasting finish which can be washed as described for lacquered surfaces.

PAINTED FLOORS: Painted floors can be washed with soapsuds made from a mild soap, or oil soap, or with one of the materials discussed under *Paint Cleaners*. Use a cloth or sponge and as little water as possible, clean a small area at a time, rinse and wipe dry. Painted floors are often waxed to make cleaning easier. For glossy enamel paint use plain hot water or hot water containing one teaspoon of washing soda per gallon of water. Rub gently. Stubborn spots on the painted surface may be rubbed lightly with whiting or a very mild scouring powder.

UNFINISHED WOOD FLOORS: Unfinished wood floors are difficult to keep clean and are not often found in homes. They can be swept with a broom or vacuum cleaner brush, and can be washed. For such floors detergents are better than soap. Use as little water as possible so as not to raise the grain and scour bad spots with a brush and scouring powder. Rinse carefully. A little chlorine bleach added to the rinse water will whiten the wood.

Woodenware Wood absorbs water and is cracked or warped easily if it remains long in contact with it. Woodenware such as pastry boards, rolling pins, salad bowls and salad sets should be cleaned promptly after use. Wipe them with cold water, wash quickly in lukewarm suds, rinse with cold water and dry immediately.

Do not soak woodenware in water or put it in an electric washer. Do not stand it on edge to dry. Do not stack or store individual salad bowls until they are thoroughly dry. Do not heat or chill wooden bowls. This care applies to finished as well as to unfinished woodenware.

Salad bowls are often finished with waterproof varnish, but many gourmets prefer them to be unfinished on the inside so that seasonings will be absorbed. Or they season the interior by rubbing it with olive oil.

Wooden Work Surface A wooden work surface that is extremely durable can be had by treating the wood with boiled linseed oil. First remove any existing finish down to the clean, bare wood. Heat the boiled linseed oil (you buy it as *boiled* linseed) in a double boiler or by putting it in a cup and placing the cup in boiling water. Linseed oil, raw or boiled, is highly

flammable and should never be placed over an open flame. Apply the hot oil to the surface, then rub it down with steel wool. Repeat this treatment twice (three coatings), allowing a full day each time between applications.

Such a surface can be cleaned by wiping it quickly with lukewarm water or mild suds. Re-oil occasionally.

Woollens (Treated) Machine washable woollens – available as clothing and yard goods – are produced by grafting a very thin chemical coating onto the fibres of wool yarn or fabrics. The U.S. Department of Agriculture, which originated the treatment, calls this the Wurlan process, but Wurlanized woollens also appear under trade names.

Wurlanized woollen dresses, sweaters, shirts and socks look like other woollens but do not shrink, mat, or pill when they are machine washed. In an advanced test stage are blends of Wurlanized wool with cotton and rayon that have been treated for durable press. The best qualities of each fibre seem to be combined. This will mean durable-press, part-wool, garments and permanently pleated skirts.

Instructions for machine washable woollens vary because of differences in techniques used by the manufacturer. Look for hang tags giving washing and drying instructions when you buy them. Directions for yard goods are usually given on the end of the bolt. The manufacturer is the best authority for his particular fabric. If the article is marked Wurlanized, it can be machine washed like cotton. If the process has been modified, the instructions usually say to use warm water and a mild soap or detergent in a short-cycle wash. Some of these woollens can be put into an automatic dryer; others cannot. Here too, follow the manufacturer's instructions. If directions are missing, ask the buyer of the department of the store where you bought the garment for washing and drying instructions.

Woollens Washable woollens and wool blends can be handled successfully at home if a few simple rules are followed. Careless treatment will cause them to shrink, mat, pill and roughen, and they can never be restored.

Wool fibres are damaged by alkalies in soaps and water softeners, by water that is too hot, by sudden changes in the temperature of the water, by chlorine (household) bleaches, by rubbing, twisting, or just too much handling when they are wet. A peroxy bleach can be used on white woollens.

For washing woollens use a mild synthetic detergent. By mild we mean 'unbuilt', containing no alkaline softeners. (See *Synthetic Detergents*.) Some of these are made especially for wool (Woolite, Wool Foam, Wool Wash).

If you use them, read and follow the directions given. The water used should be cool or lukewarm. Hot water shrinks wool and makes white wool yellow. If you are not sure just how warm 'lukewarm' is, test it with a thermometer; the reading should be about 100°F. Wool absorbs a great deal of water, so be sure to prepare an abundance of suds. Be certain too that the detergent is dissolved completely.

Before placing the garment in the water, pretreat spots, because they might not show when wet. Moisten them with lukewarm water, apply a little detergent, and brush them lightly with a soft brush. Sometimes a brief soak in the detergent solution (five to ten minutes), during which the garment is turned once or twice, will clean it. At any rate, handle it as little as possible. Drain off the wash water and soak-rinse it twice. Squeeze it very gently, roll it in a Turkish towel to absorb excess water, and hang it to dry in a warm airy place – away from sunlight or any source of artificial heat. Or lay it flat on a towel or pad.

Woollens should be steam pressed, never actually ironed. Use a steam iron if you have one, following the instructions given for wool. Or use an ordinary iron (not too hot) and a press cloth. A chemically treated press cloth will give practically professional results; heavy muslin will do, if you haven't a treated one.

Some experts advocate using two muslin press cloths. If you are pressing the right side of the material, the first cloth goes over the material dry and the second, moistened uniformly, is placed on top of the first. Press by setting the iron down carefully on the press cloth, lifting it and setting it down again, until the entire surface has been pressed. Do not lean heavily on the iron; it is not necessary and it marks the cloth. Now lift the press cloths and gently shake or beat out the steam from the wool, using the palm of the hand. Some moisture should always be contained in wool after pressing if it is to have a fresh look. Hang the garment carefully on a hanger with the fastenings closed, to finish drying.

Fabrics of unusual weave should be pressed on the reverse side. In this case the first press cloth is placed under the material and the second, dampened, on top of it.

Chemically treated press cloths are available at any good store dealing in housewares. Such cloths should never be washed or drycleaned. Brush them off well, wipe them with a wet sponge and then iron them dry on a clean paper or piece of cloth. Follow the simple directions supplied with these timesavers in using them. See also *Blanket* and *Sweaters (Wool)*.

Worsted Worsted, named after the parish of Worsted in Norfolk. Worsteds are made from wool which has been combed to remove short fibres and spun on parallel and the result is a smooth, even yarn.

Today the word 'Worsted' often refers to a method of spinning. Polyester/wool blends, 100 per cent nylon for hand knitting and jerseys are spun on the worsted system.

Wrought Iron Wrought iron, used for lamp stands and other ornamental pieces, is a purer form of iron than cast iron and resists rust. It can be polished with liquid wax to increase its rust resistance and make dusting easier, or you can keep it painted with a good paint, made especially for iron. Such paint is available in both flat and glossy finish.

Should rust appear on wrought

iron, remove it with steel wool and paraffin. If very badly rusted, soak it for a time in paraffin, then rub it with steel wool.

Zefran This is the trade name for an acrylic fibre belonging to the Orlon-Croslan-Acrilan family. Depending upon dyes, construction and finish, it is washed or drycleaned. Look to the label.

Zefran and its blends can be drycleaned by standard methods. For washable Zefran use cool-to-warm water (not over 150°F) and ordinary laundry soaps or detergents. Hand-washing and drip drying are preferred. If tumble dried, the heat of the dryer should be from 160°F to 170°F. Remove the garment from the dryer immediately and place it on a hanger. Touch up with an iron (low setting), if desired. See also *Acrylic Textiles* and *Drip Dry*.

Zelan Zelan is the trade-name for a coating applied to fabrics to make them water-repellent. It also makes them resistant to perspiration and non-oily spots. Such fabrics are used notably for raincoats, snowsuits and ski jackets.

Non-oily spots can be removed from Zelan-coated fabrics by sponging them with a damp cloth. Grease and oil spots can be removed safely with cleaning fluid. Dryclean Zelan-coated fabrics in pure fluid, without soap.

Zinc Zinc is a hard, brittle, bluish-white metal, sometimes seen as a covering for work surfaces. Regular washing with hot soapsuds will keep a zinc surface clean. If required, a mild scouring powder can be used. Tarnished zinc can be brightened by rubbing with vinegar or lemon juice, diluted with a little water. Let the acid remain on the surface for several minutes, then rinse with clear water and polish.

Zipper It took fifty years to perfect this gadget, which is based on the principle of the hook and eye. Remember this steadfastly if you get into trouble with one.

Close zippers before washing or pressing a garment, and when it is going to a dry cleaner, and they will be less likely to get out of commission. The trouble spot is usually at the bottom of the zipper. During rough treatment the ends of the 'track' (or whatever) are loosened and the thing goes haywire.

A zipper made of two metals can be a hazard to clothing, warns the U.S. Department of Agriculture. Aluminium in the track and copper or nickel-plated copper in the slide can act as electrodes. Salt in liquid starch (or minerals in water used for dampening) serves as the carrier of a tiny electric current in the cloth. A small amount of acid is formed, and brown spots or holes appear when a hot iron is used. Zippers of one metal and nylon zippers pose no such problem. No-iron materials sidestep it. But too hot an iron may melt a nylon zipper.

If a zipper has run off the track and the usual jiggering fails to restore it, better spare your nerves and take it to an expert. Good dry cleaners understand these gadgets and can make repairs. Or you can get a new zipper if the situation is hopeless.

Should a zipper jam, with you inside the garment, don't panic. Call for help, if necessary, but remember that there is usually a way out without shears.

How to remove stains and marks

ABSORBENTS
Oatmeal
Cornflour
Powdered chalk
Talcum powder
Fuller's earth
French chalk

BLEACHES
Chlorine bleach
Hydrogen peroxide
Sodium perborate
Colour remover

OTHER CHEMICALS
Acetic acid (10 per cent) or white vinegar (5 per cent acetic acid)
Ammonia*
Iodine*
Oxalic acid
Sodium thiosulphate ('Hypo')

SOLVENTS FOR NON-GREASY STAINS
Acetone*
Amyl acetate (chemically pure)*
White Spirit (inflammable)*

CLEANING FLUIDS FOR GREASE
Non-flammable Carbon tetrachloride
Perchloroethylene*
Trichloroethane*
Trichloroethylene*
Inflammable Usually trade-marked petroleum naphtha mixtures

WASHING AGENTS AND ACCESSORIES
Absorbent cotton or cloth, paper towels and tissues
Glass rod
Liquid synthetic detergent
Medicine dropper or small syringe
Soaps

Chemicals on this list can be bought at the chemist. Other materials are available at a grocery or hardware store. Keep inflammable solvents tightly stoppered and away from sources of heat.

*poisonous.

GREASY STAINS: On *washable* materials such stains may, or may not, be removed by hand or machine laundering. You will save yourself trouble if you pretreat them first by rubbing in a detergent. Or rub liquid detergent into stains that appear after washing and then rinse them with hot water. Often, however, a grease solvent (cleaning fluid) will be needed. This will remove the spot equally well after the article has been laundered. Let the material dry and sponge it repeatedly if necessary. Fabrics with special finishes often tend to hold greasy stains and persistent effort is required to remove them.

If a yellow stain remains after the solvent has been used on old or heat-set stains, use a sodium perborate or chlorine bleach, or hydrogen peroxide. On materials for which it is safe, the strong sodium perborate bleach is usually the most effective.

Sponge *non-washable* materials repeatedly with cleaning fluid, allowing them to dry between applications, or use an absorbent. (See page 169.) If a yellow stain remains, use one of the bleaches described for washable materials.

For the black oil often found on beaches try eucalyptus oil. Place a pad underneath, then work the eucalyptus oil into the stain on the wrong side with cotton wool and rub gently.   Repeat if necessary.

NON-GREASY STAINS: On *washable* materials, some of these stains are removed by laundering while others are set. Play safe. Always sponge such stains promptly with cool water. This simple treatment will remove many of them. Or soak them in cool water for 30 minutes or more. Some may need to be soaked overnight. After sponging or soaking, work undiluted liquid detergent into the stain and rinse. An enzyme detergent may do the trick. See *Enzymes*. If the stain remains, you will have to use a bleach. Old stains and stains that have been ironed are in the difficult-to-impossible category.

On *non-washable* materials, sponge the stain with cool water or put a sponge under it and squirt cool water through the cloth with a small syringe or medicine dropper. If this does not remove the stain, work detergent into it and rinse. A final sponging with spirit helps to remove the detergent, and the fabric dries faster. Dilute the alcohol with two parts of water for acetate; test colours to see if it is safe for dyes. If the detergent treatment does not remove the stain, you will have to try a bleach.

COMBINATION STAINS: (Greasy and non-greasy mixtures). Treat the stain first for the non-greasy portion, using cool water and detergent as described in the two preceding paragraphs. Rinse the spot thoroughly and let the material dry. Then sponge the remaining greasy part of the stain with cleaning fluid. Let the cloth dry and repeat if necessary. A bleach is sometimes necessary to remove all traces.

See *Cleaning Fluids* and *Sponge* (v) for instructions and precautions. See *Absorbent*. See *Chlorine Bleach*, *Hydrogen Peroxide* and *Sodium Perborate Bleach*, for using bleaches. See *Enzymes* for 'biological' stains. All are in Section 4 of this book.

Acid Acids do not usually stain white fabrics, but if very strong they may weaken or destroy textile fibres, especially cotton and linen. On coloured materials they are apt to change the colour of the dye. Spilled acids, therefore, should be removed at once.

Rinse the material thoroughly with cold water to remove as much of the acid as possible. Next sponge it with ammonia (one tablespoon to a cup of water) or with baking soda dissolved in water (one tablespoon to a cup of water), to neutralize the remaining acid. Rinse well with water.

Alkalies such as ammonia and baking soda combine with the acid to form what is known in chemistry as a 'salt'. The acid is then said to have been neutralized, a process that usually restores the original colour. Care must be taken, however, that the spot has been neutralized completely; otherwise the discolouration may reappear.

If the acid spot is light, or the material water-spots easily, dampen the stain and hold it over an open bottle of ammonia. The fumes should neutralize the acid and restore the colour. Should the colour be affected by the ammonia, sponge the stain quickly with white vinegar, or acetic acid diluted with one part of water. Rinse with water.

Adhesive Tape Sponge with cleaning fluid.

Aircraft Cement Use acetone on all fabrics except acetate, Arnel, Dynel and Verel. Chemically pure amyl acetate can be used on materials damaged by acetone, but if the cement contained acetone, the material may be damaged already. Test acetone first on any delicately coloured fabric; it affects some dyes.

Alcohol Stains are caused by spilled drinks, medicines, skin lotions and perfumes. Since alcohol dissolves many finishes, you have a real problem. When accidents occur, wipe up the spilled liquid instantly and rub the spot vigorously with the palm of your hand or with a cloth moistened with an oil polish. For old stains use rottenstone or powdered pumice, mixed to a thin paste with raw or boiled linseed oil. Rub lightly in the direction of the grain. Wipe with a cloth dampened with plain linseed oil. Repeat as many times as necessary, then polish. Sometimes refinishing is necessary

One method is to sponge the stain with white spirit. For acetates dilute the spirit with two parts of water. If a trace remains, use a sodium perborate or chlorine bleach, or hydrogen peroxide. Alcohol in these beverages sometimes makes dyes run and fade; there is no remedy for this damage.

See also *Wine*.

Alkalis Alkalis can damage fabrics and alter colours. Silk and wool are especially sensitive to them.

Damage will vary with the strength of the alkali. Rinse or sponge the spot promptly with cold water. This is usually sufficient for mild alkalis such as ammonia or washing soda. However, if the colour has been altered, to be absolutely safe, neutralize the spot by applying a mild acid. Any of the following treatments will do:

Squeeze lemon juice on to the stain and let it remain until it loses its bright yellow colour.

Apply white vinegar.

Apply a few drops of 10 per cent acetic acid solution.

The acid treatment should be followed with a thorough rinsing or sponging with cool water.

Anti-perspirant Wash or sponge stains caused by anti-perspirants with warm water and liquid detergent. Rinse carefully. If the stain is not completely removed, use a chlorine or sodium perborate bleach, or hydrogen peroxide. Rinse. Some anti-perspirants contain aluminium salts which are acidic in nature and may damage the fabric or colour. It is sometimes possible to restore colours by sponging them with ammonia. (Dilute the ammonia with an equal amount of water for use on silk or wool.) Sponge or rinse thoroughly with plain water. CAUTION: Never iron or press cloth that is stained with an anti-perspirant. The heat of the iron may destroy the stained portion of the garment.

Apple See *Fruit and Berry.*

Argyrol A fresh stain can usually be washed out with water and detergent. If not removed, dampen the stain with water, and apply a few drops of iodine with a glass rod. Let it stand for a few minutes, then apply sodium thiosulphate (a few crystals dissolved in half a cup of water). Rinse or sponge with water. This method is good for all fabrics. If stains on silk and wool are not treated promptly, a yellow or brown discolouration will remain.

Asphalt See *Tar.*

Asphalt Paint See *Tar.*

Beer See *Alcoholic Stains.*

Beetroot Follow the directions for non-greasy stains, page 137.

Berry See *Fruit and Berry*

Blood Soak or rub *washable* materials in cold water until the stain is almost gone, then wash with warm water and a detergent. To old or stubborn stains apply a few drops of ammonia and wash again with detergent.

On *non-washable* materials sponge the stain with cold or lukewarm water. Sponging with a little hydrogen peroxide will usually remove any final traces of stain. If not, use a sodium perborate or chlorine bleach, depending on the material. Blood stains that have been set by heat are very difficult to remove, but on cottons and linens a warm solution of trisodium phosphate will usually remove such stains.

For blood stains on thick materials such as carpets and rugs, use an absorbent mixed to a paste with cold water. (See *Absorbent.*) Spread the paste thickly on the stain, let it dry, then brush it off. Repeat until the stain is gone. An enzyme detergent may also be used. See *Enzymes,* page 177.

Bloom The grey discolouration that sometimes appears on highly polished furniture often, disappears when the furniture is wiped with a soft cloth that has been wrung out of warm water containing a little vinegar. (One tablespoon of vinegar to one quart of water.) Wipe dry with a clean, soft cloth. An application of liquid wax often will accomplish the same result. Polish afterwards.

Blueing Wash the stain with plenty of plain cold water or allow the article to soak in it – overnight, if necessary. If traces remain, launder in warm water with a detergent, rubbing the stain vigorously.

Burns If very light, sometimes disappear when rubbed with your usual polish. If not, use rottenstone or finely powdered pumice, mixed to a thin paste with raw or boiled linseed oil. Rub in the direction of the grain. Wipe with another cloth moistened with plain linseed. Repeat a number of times, if necessary. Polish. If the burn is too deep to be corrected by this method, the furniture will have to be treated professionally. However, the treatment described for deep scratches may improve the appearance of the burn.

Butter Ordinary laundering will remove butter stains from washable fabrics. Sponge non-washables with cleaning fluid. An absorbent can also be used on delicate fabrics. Dust it on. Let it remain until the fat has been absorbed. Brush it off. Repeat if the spot has not been removed completely.

Candle Wax With a dull knife scrape away as much of the wax as possible. Place the stain between two pieces of white blotting paper (paper towels, facial tissues) and press with a warm iron. Use fresh paper as the wax is absorbed. Sponge final traces of the stain with cleaning fluid. A quick method on fabrics that will stand it is to pour boiling water through the stain. Dry, and remove final traces with cleaning fluid.

On furniture, scrape away using stiff card, smooth stick or fingernail. Wash off the remainder with a damp, soapy cloth. Polish.

If a dye stain remains from coloured wax, sponge it with alcohol diluted with two parts of water. Then rinse or sponge with water.

Carbon Paper Work undiluted liquid detergent into the stain and then rinse. If the stain is stubborn put a few drops of ammonia on it and re-treat with detergent. Rinse and repeat if necessary.

Carrot Follow directions for non-greasy stains.

Casein Glue See *Glue and Mucilage, Adhesives.*

Catsup and Ketchup Follow the directions for non-greasy stains.

Cellulose Tape Sponge with alcohol. Test colours first. Dilute with two parts of water for use on acetates.

Checked Varnish (fine, criss-crossed lines on furniture caused by excessive heat or a poor grade of finish) cannot be corrected. The surface must be refinished. Careful polishing will make it look a little better.

Cherry See *Fruit and Berry.*

Chewing Gum Choose one of the following methods:

If water does not spot the material, rub the gummy portion with a piece of ice and scrape, or rub the gum out of the fabric. This method is very good for carpets and other heavy materials.

Saturate the stain with cleaning fluid, repeating applications as necessary. If a sugar stain remains, sponge it off with water. This method is good for all fabrics and can be used when the material will not wash.

Chlorine Resin finishes are often applied to cottons, linens, and rayons to convert them to drip dry, or to give them crease resistance, sheen, crispness, and durable embossed or sculptured designs. If chlorine bleaches are used on such materials they are likely to be weakened and yellowed. This is because the resins in some finishes absorb and retain the chlorine in the bleach.

If you have inadvertently used a

chlorine bleach on an article with such a finish, rinse it immediately and thoroughly with water. After rinsing, soak it for half an hour or longer in warm water containing sodium thiosulphate. (Use one teaspoon for each quart of water.) For fabrics that will stand it, make the water hot.

Even more effective treatment for white or completely colourfast fabrics is to use a colour remover, following the directions on the package.

On some materials the yellow chlorine stains do not appear until the material is ironed. Ironing before the chlorine is removed weakens the fibres.

Chocolate Follow the directions for combination stains, page 137.

Cocktail See *Alcoholic Stains*.

Cocoa Follow the directions for non-greasy stains, page 137.

Cod-Liver Oil Fresh cod-liver oil stains can be removed easily from any fabric by sponging the material with cleaning fluid. Washables can be laundered in the usual way afterwards, or put liquid detergent on the stain while it is still fresh. Rub lightly between the hands, rinse carefully in water, then wash.

Cod-liver oil stains are almost colourless when they are fresh. When they are old they are light brown in colour and almost impossible to remove even with bleaches, especially if the material has been washed and ironed, or pressed.

If bleaching is desirable see *Sodium Perborate Bleach, Chlorine Bleach, Hydrogen Peroxide* for instructions. (Section 4.)

Coffee and Tea To remove fresh tea and coffee stains containing cream from washable materials, follow the directions for combination stains, page 137. If cream is *not* involved, follow the directions for non-greasy stains, page 137, or stretch the stained fabric over a bowl, fasten it with a rubber band, and pour boiling water on the stain from a height of two or three feet. Launder afterwards in the usual way. If a trace of stain remains, bleach the fabric in the sun or use a chemical bleach. (Do not use this boiling water method on heat-sensitive textiles.)

Cosmetics (All Types) Apply a liquid detergent directly to the stain if the material is *washable*, or dampen the stain and rub synthetic detergent or soap into it until thick suds are formed. When the outline of the stain is gone, rinse thoroughly. Repeat as many times as necessary. Sometimes it helps to let the fabric dry between treatments.

Sponge *non-washable* materials with cleaning fluid repeatedly until no more colour can be removed. If a trace remains, work synthetic detergent into it and rinse.

Crayon Follow the directions for cosmetics.

Cream Sponge non-washables with cleaning fluid. When the solvent has evaporated, sponge carefully with cool water. Rinse washable materials with cool or lukewarm water, then launder.

Cream Sauce Launder washables with warm water and soap or detergent. Sponge non-washables with warm water. Allow to dry, then sponge with cleaning fluid.

Cream Soup See *Cream Sauce*.

Curry See *Turmeric*.

Dandelion See *Grass, Flowers, Foliage*.

Deodorant See *Anti-perspirant*.

Duplicating Sponge with spirit (diluted with two parts of water for acetate). If not removed, rub in liquid detergent and rinse. Repeat if necessary. A bleach is sometimes needed. Rinse after using all bleaches.

Dyes Follow the directions for non-greasy stains, page 137. For fresh stains, a long soak in detergent suds often does the trick. If a bleach is needed, use a chlorine bleach if the material will stand it, or a colour remover.

Egg Scrape off as much as you can with a dull knife, then sponge the spot with cold water, or soak the article in it. If the material is washable, launder in the usual way. An enzyme detergent may be used. See page 177. If non-washable, allow it to dry after sponging with water, then sponge with cleaning fluid.

CAUTION: Never use hot water on an egg stain: it will set it.

Eye Shadow See *Cosmetics*.

Face Powder See *Cosmetics*.

Fingernail Polish See *Lacquer*.

Fish Oil Follow the directions for cod-liver oil.

Fish Slime Soak the stain in a solution made by adding half a cup of salt to two quarts of water. Or sponge the stain with this solution. Rinse with plain water and wash with warm water and soap. Or follow the instructions for non-greasy stains on page 137.

Flypaper Sponge with cleaning fluid.

Washable materials may then be laundered.

Food Colouring Follow the directions for non-greasy stains, page 137.

Fruit and Berry Follow the directions given on page 137 for non-greasy stains. Or, if the material will stand it, stretch the stained part over a bowl, secure it, and pour boiling water on it from a height of one to three feet.

Always sponge fresh stains promptly with cool water before they have time to become set. Some, such as citrus, are invisible when dry; ageing or heating turns them yellow and they are hard to remove. Never use soap and water first on fruit stains. It may set them. Ironing makes matters worse.

Furniture Polish Treat it like a grease stain, page 137. If wood stain is included follow the directions under *Paint*.

Glue and Mucilage, Adhesives For *casein glue* follow the directions for non-greasy stains, page 137. Apply liquid detergent promptly to stains caused by *plastic glue*, rub and wash. If plastic glue hardens it is not always possible to remove it, but on materials that will stand such treatment, try soaking them in hot vinegar or acetic acid, maintained at or near the boiling point until the glue dissolves. This may take fifteen minutes or longer. Rinse finally with water. For *household cement* and *model aircraft cement* see *Aircraft Cement*. For all other glues and for mucilage, follow the directions for non-greasy stains, page 137, but soak in hot water instead of cool. See also *Rubber Cement*.

Grape See *Fruit and Berry*.

Graphite See *Pencil*.

Grass, Flowers, Foliage Sponging with white spirit will remove most plant stains from washable and non-washable textiles. Dilute it with two parts of water for acetate, and always test colours first to see if they are affected. Or work liquid detergent into such stains on washable materials and rinse. If a stain remains, use a mild sodium perborate or chlorine bleach, or hydrogen peroxide. Detergents and bleaches also can be used on non-washable materials, but always try the alcohol treatment first.

Gravy Soak gravy stains on washable materials in cold water to dissolve the starch, or use an enzyme detergent (see page 177), then wash. If a stain remains when the fabric is dry, sponge it off with cleaning fluid.

Sponge stains on non-washable materials with cool water. Then sponge with cleaning fluid or apply an absorbent.

Grease and Oil Treat fresh oil or grease stains promptly according to the material. For stains caused by axle grease, road oil, etc. see *Tar*. Otherwise, follow the directions given for greasy stains, page 137.

For stains on fine materials or those that will not wash use either cleaning fluid or an absorbent. Cover the spot with the absorbent and let it remain until it becomes gummy. Brush it off. Repeat this process several times, if necessary.

For oil and grease stains on carpets use a coarse absorbent such as corn meal.

Spots containing grime or metal filings yield to treatment more readily if they are rubbed first with Vaseline. Sponge afterwards with cleaning fluid or work the stain around in a small bowl of it.

Heat Marks A cloth dampened with camphor oil, peppermint oil or turpentine will often remove white marks caused by hot dishes, etc. Rub lightly. Another method is to use finely powdered rottenstone or pumice, mixed to a light paste with linseed oil. If you do not have rottenstone or pumice on hand, try cigar ash. Rub lightly in the direction of the grain, wipe with a cloth dipped in plain linseed oil, then polish.

Ice Cream Follow the directions given for combination stains, page 137.

Ink, Ballpoint Since some types will wash out, while others will be set by washing, test first by making a mark on a similar material. If the stain will not wash out of your sample you will need to use acetone or amyl acetate. Use chemically pure amyl acetate on acetate, Arnel, Dynel and Verel; acetone on other fabrics. Sponge the stain repeatedly. For a stubborn stain, apply the solvent, then water, then a bleach. Repeat as many times as necessary.

Ink, Drawing (INDIA, BLACK): Go to work at once on these stains because if they dry they are very difficult to remove. If the material is washable, put an absorbent pad or sponge under the stain and force cool water through it with a small syringe or medicine dropper. This will remove loose pigment and prevent the stain from spreading. Wash repeatedly with liquid detergent, then soak the stained article for several hours in warm water containing ammonia (one to four tablespoons for each quart of water). Dried stains may require overnight soaking.

Another method, which works on some stains, is to apply ammonia directly to the stain (after removing loose pigment as described), work in liquid detergent, rinse, and repeat if necessary.

On non-washable materials, after forcing water through the stain to remove loose pigment, sponge the stain with water and ammonia (one tablespoon per cup). Rinse with plain water. If this does not remove the stain, moisten it with ammonia, then work in liquid detergent. Rinse and repeat if necessary. If the ammonia affects colours, sponge the material first with water, then with white vinegar. Rinse carefully.

For *coloured drawing inks* follow the directions for non-greasy stains on page 137. If a bleach is needed, colour remover will be the best if it does not fade the dyes. If a test shows it is not safe, select another bleach.

FOR FURNITURE: After quickly blotting up as much as you can, apply a dampened cloth to the spot and press it down firmly. Turn the cloth to a clean place and again press it against the stain.

Repeat as many times as necessary. Do not rub the ink in. Ink washes off some surfaces easily. Old ink stains that have penetrated the wood call for professional treatment, though you might try the rottenstone-linseed-oil treatment described for burn and heat marks.

MARKING INK: There are two common types of marking, or indelible, ink: those with an organic dye (usually aniline black) as a base, and those containing silver nitrate.

Directions for aniline black inks usually say not to iron articles marked with it until after they have been washed. If directions for using the ink say that articles marked with it must be placed in the sun, or pressed with a warm iron before being washed, the ink is probably of the silver nitrate type.

To remove stains from silver nitrate inks, follow the directions given under *Silver Nitrate*. Aniline black inks are impossible to remove after they have dried.

MIMEOGRAPHING AND PRINTING INKS: Mimeographing and printing inks, when fresh, can often be removed by the method given for greasy stains, page 137 or by sponging them with turpentine. Treat stubborn stains like paint stains, pages 151–2.

WRITING INKS: Writing inks vary in chemical composition so no general rule can be laid down for removing them. For materials that will wash, try first the methods outlined for non-greasy stains on page 137. If a bleach is needed it may be necessary to try more than one kind. Use a chlorine bleach first on materials that are not damaged by it. For others try sodium perborate or hydrogen peroxide. The strong treatment of any of these bleaches may be needed, a process which may leave faded areas on some coloured fabrics. Certain inks require colour remover; others yield to oxalic acid. If a yellow stain remains after bleaching, treat it as an iron rust. (See *Iron Rust*.)

For non-washable materials, first blot up small stains with an absorbent material such as facial tissue, or cover the stain quickly with an absorbent powder to soak up excess ink and keep the stain from spreading. Then follow the directions given for washable materials or, especially on rugs, continue the absorbent treatment. Keep removing the stained absorbent powder and applying more until no more ink is absorbed. Then mix some of the powder with water (or half water and half spirit) to form a paste and put it on the stain. Allow the paste to dry, brush it off. Repeat a number of times if necessary.

Iodine Iodine makes a brown or yellow stain on unstarched materials and deep blue or black on those that have been starched. Ironing turns the stain dark brown.

Fresh iodine stains on fabrics can be removed by the following simple method. Moisten the stain with water and place it in the sun, on a warm radiator, or in steam from a kettle. The stain will be gone in a few minutes. Sometimes an iodine stain will yield to a detergent after a long soak in cool water.

Materials injured by water may be sponged with white spirit. (Dilute it with two parts of water for acetate.) Or place a pad of cotton soaked with alcohol on the stain, keeping it wet with alcohol for several hours.

Iodine stains, old or new, on any fabric not damaged by water, can be removed easily with a sodium thiosulphate solution. Dissolve a tablespoon of crystals in pint of water and either sponge the spot with the solution or dip the stained article into it. Rinse carefully. This chemical does not usually damage colours, but test first. It is harmless to all fabrics.

Iron Rust Iron rust stains can be removed from washable white fabrics by any of the methods which follow. If the stain is on a coloured material, test your bleach first in some inconspicuous place, such as an inside seam, to determine its effect on the dye. Iron rust stains are almost impossible to remove from materials that must be dry-cleaned.

Lemon juice will remove iron rust stains from the most delicate cottons and linens without injuring the cloth. Moisten the stain with water, squeeze lemon juice directly onto it and hold it in the steam from a kettle for a few minutes. Rinse with water and repeat as many times as necessary. Another method is to sprinkle salt on the stain, add lemon juice and dry in the sun. Repeat if necessary.

Oxalic acid (poison) can be used for iron stains as follows. Spread the stained material over a bowl of boiling water. Apply a few drops of oxalic acid solution (one tablespoon of crystals to one cup of water) to the stain. Rinse quickly by dipping in the hot water. Repeat until the stain disappears. Or sprinkle oxalic acid crystals directly on the stain, then apply very hot water. *Do not use this method on nylon.* It is very important, when oxalic acid is used, that the material be carefully and thoroughly rinsed. If not, the fabric will be destroyed. Ammonium bifluoride (one tablespoon in

K

a cup of hot water) is an excellent rust remover which may be obtained from your chemist. Soak or sponge the material with the solution. (This may take up to ten minutes.) Rinse carefully.

Still another method is to boil the stained article in a solution of water and cream of tartar. Use four teaspoons of cream of tartar to each pint of water. Boil until the stain is removed, then rinse in plenty of water.

Lacquer Stains caused by lacquer, including fingernail polish, can be removed from all fabrics except acetate, Arnel, Dynel and Verel, by sponging with acetone. Use chemically pure amyl acetate for fabrics that will not stand acetone. Nail polish remover may also be used but it may contain acetone. Test before using it on materials damaged by acetone.

Lead See *Metallic Stains*.

Lead Pencil See *Pencil*.

Leather Stains caused by leather rubbing against a textile are difficult to remove, since they probably contain tannin. If the material is washable, try liquid detergent, applying it directly to the stain. Rub and repeat. Final traces can be bleached with sodium perborate or hydrogen peroxide.

Leg Lotion Let the lotion dry, then brush off as much as possible. Sponge washable materials with cleaning fluid, then wash.

Sponge non-washables with cleaning fluid, or use an absorbent.

Linseed Oil Sponge the stain with cleaning fluid, then use liquid detergent or put the detergent directly on the stain and rub the fabric between the hands to loosen the stain. Wash in warm suds. Rinse thoroughly.

Lipstick See *Cosmetics*.

Liquor See *Alcoholic Stains, Wine*.

Mascara See *Cosmetics*.

Mayonnaise and Salad Dressings See combination stains, page 137.

Meat Juice Follow the directions for combination stains, page 137.

Medicine Medicines are composed of such a variety of substances that no single method can be given for stains caused by them. Instructions for iodine, argyrol, mercurochrome and silver nitrate are given under special headings. The instructions which follow are general and should prove helpful for other types.

Gummy medicines often respond to the treatment for tar stains. Rub in Vaseline or lard to soften the stain, then sponge with cleaning fluid. Or dip the stain into the solvent and rub the fabric between the hands. Rinse in the solvent, or launder the material if it is washable.

Medicines in a base of sugar syrup, such as cough medicines, can usually be washed out with soap and water, or sponged off non-washable. Those dissolved in alcohol (tinctures) can sometimes be removed by sponging with white spirit. Dilute the spirit with two parts of water for use on acetate.

Prescriptions for swabbing sore throats often include silver nitrate. See *Silver Nitrate*.

For medicines containing iron, follow the directions for *Iron Rust*. Treat those containing colouring matter as dyes. See page 142.

Mercurochrome   Mercurochrome stains should be treated as promptly as possible because they are very difficult to remove when old.

Soak washable materials overnight in a warm detergent solution containing ammonia (four tablespoons per quart of water). Sponge non-washable fabrics with spirit. (Dilute the spirit with two parts of water for use on acetate. Test coloured materials before using.)

If a stain remains, place a pad of cotton saturated with alcohol on the stain and keep the pad wet until the stain is gone. (An hour or more.)

On coloured materials that will not stand alcohol, wet the stain with liquid detergent, add a drop of ammonia with a medicine dropper, then rinse with water. Repeat if necessary.

Merthiolate Follow the directions given for *Mercurochrome*.

Metallic Stains Stains on fabrics caused by contact with tarnished brass, copper, tin and other metals can be dissolved by applying white vinegar, lemon juice, acetic acid, or oxalic acid. (Look up in Section 4.) Rinse with water. Should the acid change the colour of a dyed material, sponge with mild ammonia water or a baking soda solution. Do not use bleaches on these stains; they may cause damage.

Metaphen Follow the directions for *Mercurochrome*.

Mildew Spores of moulds, always present in the air, are the cause of mildew. In warm humid weather they flourish on any substance that can provide the simple nutrients they require. They grow on textiles, leather, wood and paper – especially in places that are poorly ventilated and lighted – causing stains, discolouration and eventual destruction. A musty unpleasant odour advertises their presence.

TO PREVENT mildew keep your home clean, well ventilated, and dry. Grease and dirt provide food for developing moulds. Even mildew-resistant fabrics such as Acrilan, Dacron, nylon and Orlon may be attacked if allowed to lie around damp and soiled.

In humid weather ventilate your house when the air outside is drier than the air inside. Cool air holds less moisture than warm air, so take advantage of cool nights for a thorough airing. The moisture will be absorbed and carried outdoors. (An electric fan will help.) Cupboards and dresser drawers may be left open periodically to discourage the accumulation of moisture and to freshen the air. Make sure that clothing in cupboards is hung loosely so that the air can circulate around it, and put articles especially susceptible to mildew (shoes, luggage) on a shelf instead of on the floor. A small electric light burned continuously in a closet will often provide sufficient heat to prevent mildew.

Sometimes, especially if a house has been closed, a brief heating will be needed to rid it of mildew-inducing dampness. Use a stove, furnace, or electric heater, then open the doors and windows to let out the moisture-laden air.

ELECTRIC DE-HUMIDIFIERS may prove a worthwhile investment for rooms where moisture condensation is a serious problem. They draw in the damp air, condensing the moisture it contains on refrigerated coils.

CHEMICAL MOISTURE ABSORBERS are also available. Silica gel, activated alumina and calcium chloride absorb moisture from the air and are sold for this purpose in some chemists, department stores, and by building supply dealers – often under trade names.

Silica gel and activated alumina granules absorb half their weight of water, feel dry even when saturated, are harmless to fabrics, and can be dried out and used again.

These chemicals are placed in small cloth bags which are suspended in clothes cupboards, or placed in a pan on a shelf or on the floor. They may also be sprinkled between layers of clothing in chests or trunks. Keep the doors shut and the chests closed. To dry the granules put them in a pan and heat them for several hours in a vented oven (300°F). Silica gel is sometimes treated with a colour indicator so that it changes from blue to pink as it absorbs moisture.

Calcium chloride is available in granular form and in specialized products consisting of porous clay-like materials soaked with the chemical. The specialized products are placed in cloth bags which are hung in closets or other damp areas. They can be dried in an oven and re-used. Granular calcium chloride holds twice its weight in water but gradually liquefies as it absorbs moisture. It damages clothing and household textiles if allowed to contact them, producing holes. To use it place the granulated chemical on a rust-proof screen, supported in an enamelware container. Place the container (uncovered) on the floor of the cupboard and keep the door shut. When the granules liquefy, add fresh chemical.

MUSTY ODOURS in a basement or shower stall indicate mould growth. Eliminate the odour and forestall damage. Usually thorough heating and drying will take care of the problem but special treatment may be required.

Sprinkle earthen floors in musty cellars with chloride of lime, available at groceries. Let it remain until the odour is gone, then sweep it up. Scrub cement floors, tiled walls, and tiled floors with a solution of chlorine bleach. Use one half to one cup of bleach to each gallon of water. Rinse with clear water and wipe the surface as dry as possible, leaving the windows open to complete the process. WARNING: On plastic and asphalt tile, work quickly to avoid a spotted surface.

Also useful in eliminating musty odours are low-pressure aerosol sprays which contain a fungi-toxic (mildew-inhibiting) chemical. Not all room sprays contain a fungicide, so read the labels carefully when making a selection. In using such sprays follow the manufacturer's directions exactly.

Wax-emulsion and silicone water-repellent sprays help keep moisture out of textiles and discourage mould growth. They are used on draperies, loose covers, golf bags, mattresses, and similar articles. Even more satisfactory as a protection against mould growth are special mildew-resistant finishes. Such a finish is often given to shower curtains, awnings, tents and sails by the manufacturer. If not, you can provide it rather easily yourself. Chemicals required are available at chemists, hardware stores and ships' suppliers.

For canvas chairs, sails, awnings, and other heavy fabrics used outdoors, two copper treatments – copper naphthenate and copper-8-quinolinolate – are especially recommended. Brush, dip, or spray the material, following exactly the directions given on the package. These products give fabrics a green tint, may stiffen them, and have a distinctive odour. Another copper treatment – copper cupferron – is also effective. It leaves a slight odour and imparts an off-white tint.

For shower curtains, draperies, blankets, seat covers and other items not exposed to weathering there are fungicides which are odourless and colourless. They make use of such chemicals as zinc naphthenate, quaternary ammonium napthenate, dichlorophenol and salicylanilide. Fungicide products which may include these compounds are available in low-pressure aerosol containers. Some also contain a wax or silicone resin that makes the fabric water-repellent as well as mildew-resistant. Or an insecticide may be included to provide protection against moths. In using commercial sprays always read and follow exactly the instructions given on the container. Such sprays should not be applied to clothing unless recommended by the manufacturer. Their vapours should not be inhaled, and precautions should be taken not to spatter them on plastic or asphalt tile.

An inexpensive home treatment for fabrics makes use of soap and copper sulphate. Fabrics treated are tinted a light blue-green, but the formula is suitable for many cotton articles. First dip the article in hot soapsuds (do *not* use a synthetic detergent) made of soft, or softened water and a mild soap. Soak it until it is thoroughly wet, then remove it without rinsing and put it at once into a hot solution of copper sulphate. Use one-and-a-half ounces of copper sulphate to one gallon of water. Soak the article for about 15 minutes in this solution, stirring and turning it about, then wring it out and hang it to dry. It is the combination of soap and copper sulphate that makes this treatment effective, so be sure to use strong suds.

WARNING: Copper sulphate, obtained at chemists, is poisonous. Store it where children cannot reach it. If kitchen utensils are used, wash them thoroughly afterward.

Clothing and household fabrics, leather, wood and books require special care when threatened with mildew damage. Don't let damp or wet clothing lie around. Don't place damp soiled clothing in the clothes' hamper; dry it out first. Don't leave washcloths and shower curtains bunched together; spread them out to dry. Don't sprinkle for ironing more articles than you can finish in one day. Don't store clothing or other textiles if they are not perfectly clean. Dirt invites trouble, so have them dry-cleaned or launder them.

In laundering clothing and household textiles for storage do not use starch unless it contains a mould inhibitor. If cottons have a musty odour, add dilute chlorine bleach as directed on the container – unless the cotton has a wrinkle-resistant resin finish.

During hot humid weather keep a wary eye on clothing stored in closets, especially items in garment bags. Unless stored with a mildew inhibitor they may be attacked. A closed bag, dampness, and hot summer days provide ideal growing conditions for moulds.

Two volatile chemicals provide vapours which inhibit mould growth and can be used to protect stored fabrics. Para crystals (paradichlorobenzene), widely used for moth control, also deter mould. Scatter them through the folds of garments stored in boxes, drawers or chests, or hang bags of the crystals at the top of garment bags. Use a pound of crystals for a 100-cubic-foot space and exclude air as effectively as you can. Para crystals damage some plastics, so avoid using plastic hangers and remove plastic buttons, buckles and ornaments. The other chemical used to inhibit mould on stored clothing is paraformaldehyde. It is sold at some chemists in powder form, sometimes in cloth bags of various sizes. Use two ounces for each 100 cubic feet of space. CAUTION: Paraformaldehyde is poisonous. Do not inhale the fumes; keep it away from children.

Low-pressure aerosol sprays, already described, are also useful in closed areas. Spray thoroughly until wet the interior surfaces of cupboards or storage containers paying special attention to cracks and crevices. Re-spray when necessary. PRECAUTION: Do not inhale the mist from the spray or use it near a flame.

If clothing or household fabrics show spots of mildew they should be treated immediately to avoid serious damage. Brush off surface growth – outdoors, if possible, to avoid scattering spores – and air and sun them thoroughly. Send non-washable clothing to a dry cleaner and launder washables promptly with plenty of hot suds. Rinse and dry in the sun. If a stain remains use a bleach.

UPHOLSTERED FURNITURE, mattresses and rugs that show mildew should be brushed thoroughly, outdoors if possible, or cleaned with a vacuum attachment. Sun and air the article if you can or dry it with an electric heater and a fan. If mildew remains, sponge the article lightly with thick suds made with soap or detergent and wipe with a clean, damp cloth to remove the suds. Or sponge the article with spirit diluted with an equal amount of water. Use as little of the solution as possible and dry thoroughly. Sponge rugs and carpets with suds or rug shampoo; rinse with a sponge squeezed out of clear water and dry. Fungicide sprays also can be used. If mould has grown inside upholstered furniture, send it to a reliable dry-cleaning or storage company to be thoroughly dried and fumigated. This will kill moulds that are present but will not protect against future attacks.

LEATHER can be protected against mildew by sponging it with a one per cent solution in spirit of any of the following chemicals: dichlorophene, salicylanilide, thymol, paranitrophenol. Let your chemist make the solution for you. Commercial products are also available at some shoe and luggage stores. Before using, test a small area of the leather to be sure that the colour will not be altered. (Paranitrophenol should not be used on white or light-coloured leather.) Treat shoes inside and out and repeat as needed. Some shoe dressings contain a fungicide to prevent mould growth and wax or a silicone resin to protect against perspiration and wet weather.

If stored during hot humid weather, shoes, jackets, luggage and other leather articles should be protected with paradichlorobenzene or paraformaldehyde. Wrap and seal. (Do not use paradichlorobenzene on luggage with plastic fittings.) Fungicide sprays can also be used. Spray until the surface is thoroughly wet. When dry, wrap and store in airtight containers.

To remove mildew from leather wipe it with alcohol diluted with an equal amount of water and dry in a current of air. If mildew remains, wash it with thick suds of saddle soap, a mild soap, or soap containing a germicide or fungicide. Rinse it with a damp cloth and dry it in an airy place. Shoes and luggage can then be waxed.

INTERIOR WOODWORK seldom mildews, especially if it is painted. If affected, scrub it with a mild alkali such as washing soda or trisodium phosphate (Oakite), using four to six tablespoons to a gallon of water. Mildew-resistant paints can then be applied, if desired.

BOOKS AND PAPERS should be kept as dry as possible during damp weather to prevent mildew damage. A small electric light, kept burning continuously in a closed bookcase, is often sufficient. Or hang bags containing one of the volatile inhibitors, paradichlorobenzene or paraformaldehyde, in closed bookcases. Papers can be dusted with paraformaldehyde, then wrapped tightly.

WARNING: Paraformaldehyde is poisonous and should be used carefully and sparingly. It is highly irritating to some people. Fungicide sprays may also be used to protect papers. Re-spray frequently unless they are in a closed container. In areas where mildew is a chronic problem, book covers can be protected by applying a clear shellac or thin varnish to which 2 to 3 per cent of salicylanilide or dichlorophene has been added. (Test colours before using.)

If books or papers already show mildew damage, wipe off the loose mould with a clean soft cloth. (Dry before wiping if the paper is damp.) To dry wallpaper heat the room slowly several hours or days to dry the plaster as well as the paper. Avoid cracking the plaster by applying too much heat. If the mildewed paper is washable, follow the directions under *Walls* (page 124). Remaining stains can some-times be bleached with ink eradicator, but colours will be bleached also.

If books are damp spread them fanwise to dry, or dust talcum powder or cornstarch between the leaves to take up the moisture. Let it remain for several hours, then brush it off.

Milk Follow the directions for non-greasy stains on page 137.

Mimeograph Correction Fluid Follow directions given for *Lacquer*.

Mucilage See *Glue and Mucilage, Adhesives*.

Mucus Follow the directions given for fish slime.

Mud When the mud has dried completely, brush it off. Sometimes this is all the treatment needed. If a trace remains, follow the directions for non-greasy stains, page 137.

Mustard On washable materials apply liquid detergent to the dampened stain, then rinse. If the stain is not removed, place the article in a hot detergent solution and let it remain for several hours or overnight. If the stain still shows, use a bleach. Sodium perborate is often the best. See *Sodium Perborate Bleach* in Section 4.

Sponge stains on non-washable materials with spirit. Dilute the spirit with two parts of water before using on acetate. Test your fabric first for colour damage.

If the colours will not stand spirit, or if the stain is not completely removed, follow the instructions for washable materials but do not soak.

Mustard stains are practically impossible to remove from plastic materials.

Nail Polish See *Lacquer*.

Oil Follow the directions for greasy stains, page 137.

Paint Oil paint and varnish stains can

be removed quite readily while they are fresh, but are almost impossible to remove if the paint has hardened.

Very fresh paint stains on washable materials can often be removed by prompt laundering. Rub liquid detergent or laundry soap directly into the stain and wash.

If the stain is only partially removed by washing, or has dried, sponge it repeatedly with turpentine or other solvent until as much as possible of the paint or varnish has been removed. Then, while the stain is still wet with the solvent, work liquid detergent into it thoroughly, place the article in hot water, and let it soak overnight. Careful washing after this treatment will remove most paint stains. If not, repeat the treatment.

Paints today are mixed with a variety of solvents and your clue to the one that may be best for your particular stain lies in the manufacturer's directions for thinning the paint. For turpentine paints, use turpentine as a solvent. White spirit will remove most stains caused by shellac. (Dilute with two parts of water for acetate; test colours first.) For aluminium paint, trichloroethylene (see *Cleaning Fluids*) may be better than turpentine, but do not use it on Arnel or Kodel. Acetone is effective for lacquers, but should not be used on acetate, Arnel, Dynel or Verel. (On these use chemically pure amyl acetate.) Water paints usually wash out. Or sponge them with turpentine or cleaning fluid.

The solvents mentioned in the foregoing paragraphs can be used to soften paint and varnish stains on washable materials prior to treatment with a detergent. They can also be used to sponge stains from non-washable fabrics. On such materials it may sometimes be necessary to place a pad of cotton moistened with solvent directly on the stain to loosen it. For stubborn stains, keep the moistened pad on the stain for half-an-hour or longer. Then, if necessary, put a drop or two of liquid detergent on the stain and work it in with the edge of a spoon. Alternate this treatment with solvent and detergent until the stain disappears. If spirit is safe for the dye, remove the detergent from the cloth by sponging the stain with it. Otherwise rinse by sponging with plain water.

Commercial products designed for cleaning paintbrushes are good for paint stains too. Follow the directions on the container.

Water colour paints usually wash out. Sponge materials that will not wash with cleaning fluid or turpentine. Or sponge first with glycerine, then with warm water. See also *Lacquer*.

FOR FURNITURE: Wipe off fresh paint spatters with a cloth dampened with liquid wax or turpentine, or use soap and water. Polish. Soften old spots first with linseed oil. Daub it on and let it stay a while. Scrape away the softened paint carefully, then rub off remaining traces with a cloth moistened with linseed oil and rottenstone, mixed to a thin paste.

Wipe with plain linseed oil and polish.

Paraffin Follow the directions given for candle wax.

Peach and Pear See *Fruit and Berry*.

Pencil Pencil marks can often be removed from cloth with a soft eraser. If not erasable, work detergent into the stain and rinse. For stubborn marks, put a few drops of ammonia on the stain, follow with detergent, and repeat until the mark is gone.

Sponge stains caused by indelible pencil with white spirit, diluted for acetate with two parts of water. If a stain remains, rub detergent into it, wash and rinse. Repeat if necessary. A sodium perborate or chlorine bleach, or hydrogen peroxide, may be required.

Perfume To remove stains caused by perfume, follow the instructions for alcoholic stains. To avoid, apply perfume to the skin, not to clothing.

Perspiration Perspiration tends to weaken textile fibres if allowed to remain on fabrics and to alter or fade the colour of dyes. Always wash or sponge off as promptly as possible, using warm water containing a detergent. (Silk is especially sensitive.) Enzyme detergents work well on perspiration. See page 177.

If colours have been changed by perspiration it is sometimes possible to restore them. Sponge fresh stains with ammonia or hold them in the fumes from an open bottle of ammonia. On old stains try vinegar. Rinse carefully with water. If oily traces remain when the fabric has dried, sponge them with cleaning fluid. Cleaning fluids alone will not remove perspiration stains; they must be dissolved with water.

Yellow stains that remain after the treatment with detergent may require use of a sodium perborate or chlorine bleach, or hydrogen peroxide. The strong sodium perborate bleach is often the most effective for fabrics that will stand it.

Should perspiration odour cling to washable materials after they have been laundered, soak them for an hour or more in warm water containing three or four tablespoons of salt for each quart of water.

Always remove perspiration stains before ironing. Ironing such a stain will weaken the fabric.

Pitch See *Tar*.

Plastic Plastic hangers and buttons, softened by heat or mothproofing agents, sometimes cause stains on cloth with which they are in contact. They can be removed with amyl acetate or trichloroethylene. (Do not use on Arnel or Kodel.) Test coloured fabrics first to be sure the dyes will not bleed. If sponging the stain with solvent does not remove the plastic, cover the stain with a pad wet with solvent and leave the pad on the stain until the plastic has been softened. Then sponge repeatedly with a fresh pad, moistened with solvent, until all traces of the plastic have been removed.

Plum See *Fruit and Berry*.

Printer's Ink See *Ink*, page 144.

Raspberry See *Fruit and Berry*.

Resins Resins and resinous substances can be removed from textiles by means of solvents. Sponge with cleaning fluid, turpentine or white spirit. Dilute the spirit with two parts of water for use on acetate. (Test coloured fabrics first if using spirit.) Rinse by sponging with plain water, or launder.

Rouge See *Cosmetics*.

Rubber Cement Scrape or rub off

the gummy part of the stain, then sponge it with cleaning fluid.

Running Colours See *Dyes*.

Rust Preparations to prevent the formation of rust on iron and steel can be bought at hardware stores. Rust removers also are available. IMPORTANT TO REMEMBER: If oxidation (rust formation) has begun, no matter how slight the degree, it will continue under any coating. So be sure the surface to be protected is both bright and thoroughly dry before filming it over. To remove oxidation, scour with an abrasive or steel wool. Kerosene helps, too.

Rust stains in bathtubs and sinks can be prevented by eliminating leaky taps. For the removal of rust stains from plumbing fixtures see *Bath*.

Salad Dressings Follow the directions for combination stains on page 137.

Sauces Follow the directions for combination stains on page 137.

Scorch To remove light scorch stains from washable materials, follow the directions for non-greasy stains on page 137.

Light scorch stains on non-washable materials can be removed by sponging the fabric with hydrogen peroxide. The strong treatment may be necessary. (Test first for colourfastness.) Rinse afterwards with plain water.

Scorch stains are almost impossible to remove from silk or woollen materials. Brushing scorched spots on thick woollens lightly with emery cloth or very fine sandpaper may improve their appearance. Scorch stains cannot be removed if the fibres of the cloth have been burned.

Scratches If light, often disappear when the furniture is carefully waxed or polished. Using your usual mixture, rub an extra amount into the scratch. If the scratch still shows, try rubbing it with a piece of walnut. This will darken the stain. Be careful to rub the walnut directly into the scratch so as not to darken the surrounding wood excessively. Another method is to rub, or brush, a little turpentine into the scratch. Let it dry, then polish. A quality of turpentine is that it can penetrate the finish and restore the colour of the original stain. Don't use too much; it might soften the finish.

Deep scratches must be filled in carefully, a job that usually calls for a professional furniture man. If you want to try it yourself, this is how it is done. Wrap very fine steel wool around the pointed end of a manicure stick and smooth the scratch carefully. Brush away all the particles, then apply turpentine, or a matching stain, very carefully, using a fine-tipped water colour brush. When this has dried thoroughly, apply a thin coating of white shellac to the scratch, being careful not to spill it over. Let this dry completely and apply a second coating. Repeat the coatings, letting each one dry thoroughly, until the scratch has been filled. Polish carefully.

Shellac Sponge the stain with spirit or soak the stained material in it. Dilute the spirit with two parts of water for acetate and test before using on colours. If spirit makes the dyes bleed, try turpentine.

Shoe Polish Because shoe polishes vary in their ingredients it may be necessary to try more than one method in attempting to remove stains caused by them.

Try first the method described under cosmetics. If the stain is not removed, try next sponging it with spirit. (Test coloured materials first to be sure the dyes will not bleed. Dilute the spirit with two parts of water for acetate.)

For stains not removed by spirit, try sponging with cleaning fluid or turpentine. If turpentine is used, sponge afterwards with a warm detergent solution or spirit to remove the turpentine.

For traces of stain that still remain after these treatments, use a sodium perborate or chlorine bleach, or hydrogen peroxide. If safe for the fabric, the strong sodium perborate bleach is probably the most effective.

Silver Nitrate Stains caused by silver nitrate can often be removed by sponging promptly with cool water, and then washing. If a stain remains, put a few drops of iodine on it and let it stand for a few minutes. Then sponge with a solution of sodium thiosulphate. Use one teaspoon of sodium thiosulphate to one cup of water. Rinse, or sponge with plain water. This chemical can be used on any fabric. It is important to treat promptly stains on silk or wool because otherwise a brownish stain will be left on the cloth.

Smoke and Soot Follow the instructions for cosmetics. An absorbent is sometimes effective.

Soap When soap has not been rinsed thoroughly from a laundered article, ironing sometimes causes a stain resembling iron rust or scorch. This discolouration will come out if the garment is re-washed. Rinse thoroughly this time.

Soft Drinks When soft drinks are spilled, always sponge them off immediately with plain cool water. If they are allowed to dry they are sometimes invisible, but turn yellow with age or when ironed, and are then difficult to remove.

To remove stains caused by soft drinks, follow the directions for non-greasy stains on page 137.

Soup Treat it as a combination stain, page 137.

Stove Polish If the material is washable, apply liquid detergent directly to the stain and rub it in thoroughly. On materials injured by water, first use an absorbent, then cleaning fluid. Sprinkle the absorbent on the stain, work it into the fabric, and brush it off when it becomes soiled. Apply fresh absorbent and repeat until most of the stain is gone. Then sponge with cleaning fluid, or immerse the stain in it and rub it gently or brush it with a small soft brush.

Strawberry See *Fruit and Berry*.

Sugar Syrup Stains caused by sugar syrups are no problem on washable materials. Laundering removes them. Sponge non-washables with warm water.

Sweets and Chocolate Routine laundering usually removes sweet spots from washable materials. If the fabric is not washable, sponge the spots with plain warm water. For chocolate stains and stains from coloured sweets, see *Chocolate* and *Dyes*.

Syrup See *Medicine* and *Sugar Syrup*.

Tar Stains caused by tar and such tar-like substances as road oil, axle grease, asphalt, asphalt paint and pitch are similar and certain solvents are effective for them all. However, they are not easily removed, especially from cotton materials.

Scrape off as much of the substance as possible, then follow the directions for greasy stains on page 137. If traces remain, sponge with turpentine. Washables may then be laundered.

For stains on carpets or rugs use this method: scrape off as much as possible with a dull knife, then sponge with a cloth soaked with cleaning fluid. Use a light, upward, brushing motion so that the stain will be rubbed out of the rug rather than into it. Change your cloth when it becomes soiled and continue until the stain is gone.

Tea See *Coffee and Tea*.

Tin Foil See *Metallic Stains*.

Tobacco. Follow the directions under *Grass, Flowers and Foliage*.

Tomato Juice Follow the directions for non-greasy stains, page 137.

Transfer Patterns Follow instructions for greasy stains, page 137.

Turmeric Turmeric is a spice used in curry powder, prepared mustard and often in pickles. It produces a bright yellow stain, which is especially difficult to remove from cotton materials.

For fresh stains on white washable materials, try soaking the article in a diluted solution of ammonia water or white spirit. If the material is not washable, sponge the stain with these agents. Test coloured materials first to see if spirit affects the dye and dilute it with two parts of water for acetate. Rinse with water.

If the stain still shows after this treatment, and for old stains, use a bleach.

NOTE: Coloured materials should be tested in an inconspicuous place, such as an inside seam, before being subjected to bleaches.

Typewriter Ribbon Use method described for carbon paper.

Unknown If greasy, treat as a grease stain, page 137. Otherwise, follow the directions for non-greasy stains on page 137. See also *Yellowing*.

Urine Follow the directions for non-greasy stains on page 137.

If colours have been changed, sponge the stain with ammonia. See *Ammonia*, page 170.

If ammonia does not help, sponge with acetic acid (page 169) or white vinegar.

If a bleach is required, follow the directions for *Medicine* and *Yellowing*.

Varnish See *Paint*.

Vaseline Use the method given for greasy stains, page 137.

Vegetable Follow the directions for non-greasy stains, page 137.

Vinegar If vinegar has changed the colour of a fabric, use the treatment for acid stains, page 138.

Vomit Follow the directions for fish slime.

Walnut (Black) The husks of black walnuts cause a dark brown stain that is extremely difficult, if not impossible, to remove once it has become set. Very fresh stains can be removed from materials that will stand the treatment by boiling the article in strong soapsuds. Use a half-inch cube of laundry soap for each cup of water. Old stains will leave a grey colour, which may yield to a strong chlorine or sodium perborate bleach.

Stains on non-washable materials cannot be removed by home methods. Try a dry cleaner.

Water marks A well-waxed surface is a safeguard against water marks. Should a waxed surface show marks from a misplaced water glass or vase, remove the old wax by wiping the surface generously with liquid wax. Wipe with a dry cloth and polish. Apply extra coatings of wax, if desired, to build up protection.

On other surfaces a little peppermint oil or camphor oil on a damp cloth, or a cloth wrung out of warm water containing a few drops of ammonia, will often remove such marks. If not, rub the stain carefully but lightly, in the direction of the grain, with rottenstone or finely powdered pumice, mixed to a thin paste with raw or boiled linseed oil. Wipe with a cloth moistened with plain linseed oil. Polish.

Water-Spots Materials that water-spot usually contain sizing or other finishing agents. The water dislodges part of these substances and causes them to be rearranged and deposited in a ring. Fabrics most likely to water-spot are taffeta, moire and other crisp silk and rayon materials.

To remove such spots dampen the entire garment by sponging it with water or by shaking it in steam from a kettle (not too close to the spout.) Press the garment while it is damp.

Sometimes water-spots can be eliminated by scratching the fabric lightly with the fingernail, or by rubbing it with a clean, stiff brush. Or try rubbing the material gently between the hands.

Wax (Floor, Furniture) Follow the directions for greasy stains, page 137.

White Sauce Treat as a combination stain, page 137.

Wine See *Alcoholic Stains*. A quick method for materials that will stand it, is to stretch the stained portion over a bowl and secure it with a rubber band or string. Sprinkle salt on the stain, then pour boiling water on it from a height of one to three feet. Use care to avoid being splashed.

Fresh stains on non-washable materials can sometimes be removed with an absorbent. Alternatively, sponge them with spirit. (Dilute with two parts of water for acetate.)

Yellowing Yellow or brown stains sometimes appear on clothing and household linens that are stored. For these, and for all yellow and brown stains of unknown origin, try the following treatments in the order given until the stain has disappeared.

1. Wash the article.
2. Use a mild treatment of a chlorine or sodium perborate bleach, or hydrogen peroxide.
3. Use the oxalic acid treatment described for *Iron Rust* stains.
4. Use a strong chlorine or sodium perborate bleach.

For bleaching directions see *Chlorine Bleach*, page 173 *Sodium Perborate Bleach*, page 185, *Hydrogen Peroxide*, page 178.

For removal of yellow stains caused by chlorine bleach on resin-treated fabrics see *Chlorine*, page 140.

NOTE: Brown stains on stored linens are caused by particles of iron in hard water which eventually rust. Always use soft, or softened, wash and rinse water for linens that are to be stored.

Control of Household Pests

Ants In fighting ants remember that you are dealing with a tough, highly organized insect army, whose infiltration tactics have been perfected since prehistoric times. A simple classification of the many ant species might be: those that crave sweet things and those that like grease.

Many weapons have been trained on ants that invade the home. Some were not effective, others were deadly poisons which brought tragedy. Usually effective are sprays containing Malathion. They have a killing power which lasts for days, or longer. Apply the spray generously behind and beneath skirtings when possible, around sinks and window sills, and in cracks and crannies that serve as ant runways. Give special treatment to table legs and the undersides of furniture.

If, by watching the invaders, you can locate the nest from which the ants are launching their raids, so much the better for you and the worse for them. If the nest is indoors douse it with spray, preferably oil based. (But never use oil-based spray in the garden; it damages plants.) A product called 'Nippon' (from household stores and, originally, from Japan) works quite well. It is not a spray, you just pour a few drops on to a piece of wood or a flat stone and the unfortunate ants will seek it out with enthusiasm. 'Nippon' is non-poisonous to humans and household pets.

Ants dislike the smell of paraffin and naphthalene and camphor, but so, probably do you. However, as these substances are not killers but only repellents, their use is a humane way of dealing with the problem. See *Insecticides*, for precautions, pages 178–180.

Bats If bats have shown an interest in sharing your attic they will usually leave if you sprinkle the floors and window sills with naphthalene or paradichlorobenzene crystals, available at chemists.

When you are sure that all the bats have left, clean the attic thoroughly, then cover all openings through which they could return with sheet metal or ¼ inch mesh hardware cloth.

If this method does not work, or if the bats are between the walls, take your problem to a professional exterminator. Bats are usually harmless but they are subject to rabies. They also create an unpleasant odour.

Bedbugs Bedbugs are brown, wingless insects, varying in size from one eighth to one quarter of an inch. They are flat and oval, and emit a disagreeable odour that frequently advertises their presence. Bedbugs hide in the daytime and emerge to bite sleeping people.

Brown and black spots on walls and skirtings indicate where these insects hide. In the early stages of an infestation they are found under the tufts and in the seams of mattresses. Later they spread to crevices in bedsteads and, if allowed to multiply, become established behind window and door frames, skirtings, picture mouldings, furniture, loose wallpaper and in cracks in the plaster. An effective spray should be applied in all possible hiding places.

To destroy bedbugs use a household surface spray containing malathion, DDT, lindane, or pyrethrum. (However, some bedbugs have developed resistance to DDT.) One application of DDT, or malathion may take care of the problem. Spray the slats, springs and frames of beds so that they are thoroughly wet. Spray, but do not soak, mattresses, paying particular attention to seams and tufts. WARNING: do not spray mattresses with an insecticide containing more than 1 per cent of malathion; a higher concentration is not safe. If the container does not give the appropriate information ask your dealer to find out for you or get in touch with the manufacturer direct. Also spray skirtings and cracks in the walls and floor boards. If insects are seen several weeks after treatment, spray again. See also *Insecticides* for precautions.

Book Lice Insects that feed on microscopic moulds that grow on furniture, wallpaper and other house furnishings. They thrive in rooms that have been closed or poorly ventilated. Rout them by spraying infested places with 5 per cent DDT oil spray. Book lice (psocids) do not bite people.

Carpet Beetle Rare in these islands but when spotted they are often confused with moths. There are three or four species of carpet beetle – a destructive pest – but the common variety is a reddish-brown creature, somewhat fuzzy in appearance and about one quarter of an inch long. Like clothes moths, they are harmless in the adult, or winged form. They flit from flower to flower, imbibing nectar, then in at the open window and the trouble begins.

Carpet beetles deposit their eggs near pleasant sources of food supply for their larvae, such as rugs, hair mattresses and cushions, feather pillows and fur. The eggs hatch and the larvae munch voraciously.

Carpet beetles are hardier than clothes moths and much more active. They may quickly infest an entire house yet many women do not recognize them and blame the damage they do on moths. Certain insecticides will control both moths and carpet beetles. For instructions see *Moths – Clothes*.

Centipede The house centipede is non-poisonous, seldom bites people, does not damage food or clothing, and destroys other insects, but I have known grown men to quail before it. The thing has altogether too many legs, its antennae are longer than would seem necessary and it goes too fast. To see it scooting along, its legs rippling in fantastic locomotion, gives one creepy sensations along the spine. The same goes for the millipede, which has a trimmer figure but many more legs.

You can destroy both pests by spraying them with a household surface spray containing DDT. Spray openings and cracks around doors, windows, skirtings and pipes. See *Insecticides* for precautions.

Cockroaches Here is a bit of information, totally irrelevant to your problem, which may or may not interest you. In scientific circles the cockroach is regarded as a minor miracle, since it has come down to us, practically unchanged by evolution, from the Coal Age, 300 million years ago. Specimens have been found in ancient geological strata that are almost identical to the creature that haunts crevices and sometimes carries disease.

Cockroaches hide during the day and forage at night. They eat food, garbage, starch, glue, fabrics and paper. Switch on a light suddenly in a dark room and they will reveal their hiding place.

Good housekeeping and the use of a suitable insecticide will usually control cockroaches in the home. In hotels or boarding houses, drastic over-all treatment by a professional exterminator is usually necessary. Take the problem to the management.

To destroy the cockroaches, apply a household surface spray or dust, after thoroughly cleaning the areas to be treated. If the infestation is severe, spray first and when the spray has dried apply the dust, blowing it into cracks and openings.

Insecticides containing malathion will control all kinds of cockroach. Household surface sprays in pressurized cans are the easiest to use. Apply enough to moisten the surface thoroughly without running or dripping. Useful as an auxiliary weapon is an air spray (aerosol) containing pyrethrum. It is not recommended as a roach killer but it will penetrate cracks and other hard-to-reach places and drive the insects into the open where surface sprays or dusts can destroy them.

Treat with insecticide all places where roaches may hide: areas under the kitchen sink and draining board; behind the refrigerator, stove and washing machine; cracks around and beneath cupboards and cabinets, especially in the upper corners; around pipes and conduits; behind loose skirtings, mouldings, and door and window frames; on the undersides of tables and chairs, and on pantry shelve and bookshelves.

To avoid contamination of food by the insecticide, remove all food, dishes, and utensils from cabinets, cupboards and pantry shelves before spraying them. Remove and empty drawers, spray them on the outside. The inside, if thoroughly cleaned, does not need to be treated.

Crickets A cricket on the hearth may be poetic, but crickets in droves are a menace. They eat holes in fabrics and are not particular about the kind. Field crickets enter the house when the weather becomes cool and seek cosy corners near fireplaces, radiators, in kitchens and warm basements. House crickets breed in dumps and swarm to nearby houses.

To prevent crickets from entering the house, close all openings and tighten windows, doors and screens. To destroy an infestation, use a household surface spray containing DDT or malathion. Apply it around skirtings, in cupboards and in cracks where insects might hide. Dusts containing these insecticides can also be used. See *Insecticides*, for precautions.

Firebrats See *Silverfish and Firebrats*.

Fleas Flea escapees from dogs and cats sometimes cause infestations in homes. To correct the situation, first clean the rooms and all upholstered furniture carefully with a vacuum cleaner, then use a household surface spray containing DDT or malathion. Be sure the spray you choose does not stain if you plan to use it on rugs, carpets or upholstered furniture.

Apply the spray to skirtings, cracks in the floor, rugs, carpets, furniture and to places where your pet likes to sleep. It may be necessary to spray again in about a week.

To destroy fleas at their source, treat your pets too. A dust containing malathion is effective and safe. Rub it into the fur to the skin. A dust containing DDT may be used on dogs over two months old, but never on cats, who lick off the insecticide when cleaning themselves.

If possible, treat your pet out of doors since the fleas will try to leave him within a few minutes of the application. The insecticides will increase the activity of the fleas and may cause your pet to feel uncomfortable for a few minutes. See *Insecticides* for precautions.

Fly See *House Fly.*

Gnat See *House Fly.*

Hornets See *Wasps and Hornets.*

House Fly House flies breed in filth and spread the germs of a dozen or more diseases to animals and people. The first line of defence is sanitation – the elimination of their breeding places.

Keep garbage and other refuse tightly covered – never let it accumulate in the open. On the farm, dispose of manure promptly. Keep screen doors and windows in good repair. (The doors should swing outward.) Fourteen-mesh screens are adequate for flies: 16-mesh will keep out additional pests. Use copper, aluminium, bronze, plastic, or rust-resisting alloys for screens in humid climates. Galvanized screens will serve where the weather is dry.

To kill flies quickly inside a house, use an insecticide in a space or aerosol spray. Be sure the label says the spray is for flying insects and follow exactly the directions given. See *Insecticides* for precautions.

Insects Cleanliness is the first line of defence against household pests.

Insects thrive on food spilled on pantry shelves and in the cracks and crevices of cabinets, walls and floor boards. Out-of-the-way places – behind refrigerators, stoves, washers, and around pipes and toilets – serve as hideouts for breeding. Scrub these places regularly with hot water and soap or detergent.

Store all foods in tightly closed containers and avoid buying dry foods in packages that have breaks in them. Do not leave cardboard cartons used for food or other materials in the kitchen or basement; hitch-hiking insects such as cockroaches and silverfish may lurk in their crevices. Dispose of garbage promptly. Do not let waste materials of any sort accumulate; they provide hiding places for insects.

To frustrate prospective invaders, seal cracks and openings where insects could enter your home – around washbasins, toilets, pipes, electric conduits, baseboards and floorboards.

When an insecticide is needed, first scrub all the areas to be treated. Some insecticides are better than others for specific insects and for that reason instructions are given under separate headings, such as *Ants*, *Moths*, *Crickets*. If you cannot identify the insect that is plaguing you, take or send a sample to the appropriate section of the Ministry of Agriculture; alternatively your local Council office may be able to help.

Mice Block all entrances; store loose foods in jars and tins; keep garbage and trash closely covered in metal cans.

Mice enter the house through small holes around pipes, through defective or ill-fitting cellar screens

L

and under loosely hung doors. Autumn is the time to be especially on guard because cold weather drives them from the fields to the shelter and abundant food supply of your home. If the infestation is. extremely serious, you can call in a professional exterminator. Otherwise, lay in a good supply of spring traps, and bait them carefully. Set your traps night after night until victory has been achieved. Peanut butter smeared on the trigger of the trap is one of the best baits. Other good ones are cake, bacon, flour, cut meats, cheese, and soft sweets such as gumdrops and milk chocolate. Place the traps at right angles to walls between objects, or near holes and damaged materials, so that the mice will intercept the triggers. Rolled oats or dry cereals, sprinkled around baited traps, sometimes help. Trapshy characters can sometimes be outwitted by concealing the entire trap with rolled oats, cereal, or flour. If you prefer to use poisoned baits, buy a kind recommended for this specific purpose and follow the directions on the container exactly. The least hazardous are the anticoagulants e.g. 'Rodine's Warfarin' by Rentokil. Several weeks may be required to achieve control by means of them. Be careful not to let them contaminate food. Safeguard children and pets by placing the bait in protected stations, behind a board nailed to a wall, inside a sealed cigar box with a mouse-sized hole, etc. Dispose of dead mice promptly and safely.

Other rodenticides give faster results than the anticoagulants but they are extremely poisonous and should be used only by a professional exterminator.

Mites Mites are small, often very minute, arachnids which occasionally become household pests. Those that bite cause swelling, itching and sometimes fever, but seldom transmit diseases.

Mites that bite include bird and rodent mites, certain food mites, and chiggers, which breed outdoors and enter the home only on clothing. Clover mites, which sometimes invade homes, are harmless but leave bright red spots when crushed.

Rodent and bird mites can breed in a home where rats, mice, or pet birds are present. Bird coops and wild birds' nests near a chimney, window, or ventilator are other sources of bird mites. Food mites breed in cheese, grains, etc.

To destroy mites, treat infested areas with a household surface spray containing malathion, then turn your attention to their source. (See *Rats, Mice*.) If the source is birds, destroy nests near house openings and clean up bird cages or chicken coops and spray them with malathion. If food is infested, destroy it. Clean the food shelves carefully, then spray them with an insecticide containing not more than 2 per cent malathion. When the spray has dried, cover the shelves with fresh paper or foil. Replace the food and keep it covered. See *Insecticides* for precautions.

Mosquito To destroy mosquitoes inside the home, use an aerosol spray designed for flying insects. Release of the aerosol for a few seconds will quickly kill all mosquitoes in an average-sized room. Best results are obtained if the doors and windows are closed during the treatment and kept closed for five to ten minutes afterward. (Do not spray a room with people or pets in it.)

Sometimes an outdoor clean-up is indicated. Old tin cans, bird-baths, discarded tyres, clogged rain gutters, and other containers of stagnant water provide ideal breeding places for mosquitoes.

Fish ponds and ornamental pools that contain 'wigglers' (larvae) can be sprayed with a very light mist of a pyrethrum oil solution. Apply no more than one ounce of the spray to each 100 square feet of water. This will kill the mosquito larvae without harming the fish and plants. See also *Insecticides*, page 178.

Moths – CLOTHES: Two important organs of thought, *The New Yorker* and *House and Garden*, have at different times, advanced the fascinating theory that there is some connection between marriage and moths. Correlated with this theory is the vague implication that women bring them, since bachelors apparently, do *not* have them. But let's not go blaming each other. The problem is: What to do? Consider first three circumstances.

1. You have moths and have them badly. The best thing to do is to call in a reliable exterminator. His services may be expensive, but it will pay you in the end because moth damage can run easily into a good many pounds.

2. You think you haven't any, but your sweaters, upholstery and coats seem to be wearing in the darnedest places or sprouting holes beyond all reason. You had better wake up and *do* something. The larvae are there!

3. You have never had moths that you know of, but you have accumulation of blankets, sweaters and other impedimenta to store. Don't be lulled by a false sense of security; rather be on guard to defend your woollies against possible invasion.

Your enemy is a small moth no more than three-eighths of an inch from antenna to tail, and the larva (worm) is white with a brownish head. May and June are the months when the clothes moth flits normally, but we have encouraged him with steam-heated homes until he is practically a year-round foe. Moth larvae like woollens best, especially spotted and soiled woollens. If very hungry they become less particular and even attack cottons. Furs and feathers are ambrosia to them. Rayon and other synthetics are moth-resistant unless mixed with wool or spotted with food.

The moth hazard is minimized by good housekeeping tactics. Rugs that are vacuumed regularly and clothing that is well cared for and properly stored are not likely to be attacked.

Use your vacuum cleaner brushes to keep cracks in the floors and baseboards free of fluff and dust where moths can breed. Never let old sweaters or bits of woollen cloth lie around in boxes, corners, drawers, or on shelves. They are often a source of infestation. Remove spots from clothing and keep woollens well brushed. Store only clean clothing. Either have it dry-cleaned or brush it carefully and hang it in the sun. Hot sunlight destroys moth life, but it must reach every part of the garment and this is difficult to arrange, what with pockets and seams providing ideal hiding places. Dry cleaning also kills moth life. Neither treatment, however, guarantees the fabric against a future invasion. Mothproof your clean woollens, or let the dry cleaner do it for you.

Clothes moths frequently share their food sources with carpet beetles which often go undetected while the damage they do is blamed on moths. DDT will control moths but not carpet beetles; other insecticides will take care of both. (See *Carpet Beetle* for description.)

If you have noticed moths or carpet beetles in your home, your first step should be to spray all places over which insects are likely to crawl. Use a household surface spray, recommended by your local household store. Spray the edges of wall-to-wall carpeting, behind radiators, along skirting and mouldings, in corners and other places that are difficult to clean. Remove clothing from storage closets and spray corners, baseboards, shelves and the ledges on which they rest, the ends of clothes rods, and cracks in the floors and walls. These sprays leave a killing residue. Do not apply them to clothing and blankets. Next treat your woollens.

CLOTHING AND BLANKETS can be mothproofed by spraying them with an oil-based insecticide, containing DDT. These can be bought in pressurized cans. Hang the blankets and clothing on a line if available, and spray them lightly but thoroughly until they are just moist. A white deposit will result when the articles have dried if too much spray is used. Usually this will brush off; if it does not, the clothing will have to be dry cleaned. Do not store sprayed clothing until it is thoroughly dry.

Mothproofing rinses seem to have disappeared from the market, but they are very effective. If you want to mix your own, use this formula. Mix together one ounce of sodium fluorosilicate (from your chemist) and about one-third the amount of a mild detergent. Add one gallon of lukewarm water and stir thoroughly. Immerse washed articles in this solution and let them soak for ten or fifteen minutes. Squeeze out excess water and allow to dry.

FURNITURE upholstered in wool or mohair, when threatened by moths, should be brushed or vacuumed thoroughly and sprayed with one of the insecticides recommended for clothing. If loose covered, be particularly alert. Let the upholstery dry before you use the furniture. If moths have invaded the stuffing of upholstered furniture, mattresses, or pillows, spraying will not help. You will have to discard the infested furnishings or have them fumigated by a professional. Select a firm that guarantees its work because this treatment is not always successful and a re-upholstering job may have to follow.

Frequently overlooked are the felts and hammers of pianos, which are often damaged severely by moths and carpet beetles. The chemicals recommended for clothing can be used to protect them, but let your piano tuner apply them lest other parts of the piano be damaged.

RUGS AND CARPETS threatened by moths can be mothproofed by a professional or you can spray them with a 5 per cent DDT oil-based surface spray. Pay special attention to areas beneath furniture and near radiators. Spray the pad beneath the rug also (on both sides) if it is vulnerable. If carpet beetles are the threat, use one of the sprays suggested for them earlier in this article.

STORED WOOLLENS (in boxes, chests, sealed closets) can be protected with paradichlorobenzene (para) crystals or naphthalene flakes or balls. Para crystals act faster than naphthalene, do not attract moisture and liquefy, and the odour disappears quickly. (But do not place clothes on a plastic hanger if you use it. It sometimes softens plastic hangers and buttons of the clear transparent type. If clothing sticks to the hanger some of the plastic may be absorbed, leaving a stiff, shiny stain. To remove it, see *Plastic*, page 153.)

You can use moth crystals by sprinkling them over woollens being stored; by placing them in a shallow container on a shelf, or suspended on a clothes rod or hook in a thin bag or perforated container; by blowing the fumes through them in your storage closet with a special vacuum cleaner attachment. The important thing is to use enough of the crystals and to store them sealed tight.

If you are using the vacuum cleaner method hang the clothes loosely on hangers so that the fumes may reach all parts. Place the vacuum, with the crystal container in place, inside the cupboard with the switch on. Close the door and seal it with newspaper wadding or with gummed tape (a special kind is made for fumigating). Plug in the vacuum and let it run. The instructions given by the manufacturer of your particular type of vacuum cleaner will tell you how much para to use and how to operate your machine. After removing the vacuum, reseal the cupboard.

If you use a container, let it be a shallow pan on the top shelf, a perforated plastic or metal box, or a little muslin bag suspended from a hook or rod. The reason for this is that the fumes work downward. Seal the cupboard tight and keep it sealed for two weeks for a complete kill. Allow one pound for each 100 cubic feet of closet space.

If you are storing woollens in boxes or trunks sprinkle each layer generously with crystals, using tissue paper between layers. Use one pound of crystals, flakes, or balls in a trunk-size container and seal with tape when filled. Felt hats should be brushed carefully, sprinkled with crystals and stored in sealed boxes for maximum protection. In handling blankets sprinkle one half the surface with crystals, and fold the other half over. Again sprinkle one half and again fold, until the blanket is of convenient size for storage. Wrap each blanket in paper and seal the flaps with gummed tape. Mothproof boxes and bags are useless if the clothing placed in them has not been cleaned and treated before being placed inside.

Cedar chests are effective mainly because they can be closed tightly. Play safe and mothproof articles stored in them.

Valuable rugs and furs are best stored professionally by a reliable firm that guarantees against moths, fire, etc. Less important rugs, if stored at home, may be sprinkled generously with crystals, rolled, wrapped in heavy paper and sealed with tape. If you store furs at home, use crystals, flakes, or balls in a tight container. Sprays are not recommended for furs.

NOTE: The MITIN moth-proofing process used by many manufacturers is durable for the life of the fabrics treated. It can be used on all woollen fabrics.

Moths – PANTRY: See *Pantry Pests*.

Pantry Pests If moths are flying around your pantry, a search for contaminated cereals, flour, dried peas, cornstarch, etc. is indicated. Flour moths, beetles, and weevils invade the home front via the packing house and grocery and multiply in the forgotten package on the pantry shelf. Look for lumpy masses in flour and corn meal and little webby threads adhering to the sides of cardboard containers. These indicate that the worms of flour moths are present. Holes in dried peas and beans have been made by beetles or weevils.

Your first step is to locate and destroy all contaminated packages Your second step is to remove all containers from the shelves and wash the shelves with hot suds, paying particular attention to the ledges on which the shelves rest. The third step is to spray all surfaces with household surface spray, recommended by your household store. Spray lightly but thoroughly. When the spray has dried, cover the shelves with clean paper or foil. Replace the packages.

Powder-Post Beetles These beetles tunnel through the frames and floors of houses and through furniture, weakening the wood. Their larvae feed on wood cellulose and increase the damage. Powder-post beetles, which include the old house borer, are of many kinds, varying from one-eighth of an inch to one inch in length. Some attack hardwoods, others softwoods, and still others prefer bamboo. Their presence is indicated by holes up to three-eighths of an inch in diameter in the wood, by little piles of borings near the holes or on the floor below ceiling beams, and by the presence of the beetles themselves.

If you think your house is infested with these pests, consult a reliable exterminator.

Rats When old barns or other buildings are torn down, rats which have infested them sometimes invade neighbouring homes in large numbers, in search of shelter and food. If you are ever confronted by such a situation, your best course will be to call in a professional exterminator.

For occasional invaders, use spring traps, poisoned baits, or both. Red squill and the anti-coagulants listed under *Mice* are relatively safe poisons. Red squill is a single-dose poison for Norway rats only – the ones that tunnel through the ground under floors and foundations. Anti-coagulants are multiple-dose poisons that kill all kinds. Sometimes it is a good idea to use both types. The use of anti-coagulants and effective baits for rodents are described under *Mice*.

Both types of poison can be bought in seed stores and chemists in ready-to-use form or as powders to be mixed with bait at home. Follow exactly the directions given for the rat killer you buy. Keep it out of reach of children and pets. Dispose of dead rats promptly and safely.

Red squill is usually mixed with

freshly ground meat or fish. Anti-coagulants are mixed with dry baits such as cornmeal or rolled oats. Other, more virulent, poisons are effective rodenticides but they should be used only by a professional exterminator.

Rats enter homes in search of food, shelter and water. Do not encourage them by allowing rubbish to accumulate. Keep garbage in tightly covered metal cans and do not leave food exposed. Close off all holes in the exterior walls of your home and check doors and screens for holes and rips. Leave no space more than three-quarters of an inch around windows, doors, and other openings.

Silverfish and Firebrats Silverfish are wingless, scaly insects, silvery grey in colour, with two long antennae in front and three long hairlike appendages behind. When fully grown they are from one-third to one-half an inch in length. They like damp cool places and flourish in basements. Firebrats are a mottled grey, very similar in appearance to silverfish. They like warm areas, the attic in summer and near the furnace in winter. Both insects are nocturnal and the damage they do is similar. The same insecticides will control them.

They attack foods and other materials that are high in protein, sugar and starch: flour, cereals, paper that is coated with glue or paste such as wallpaper and bookbindings, starched cotton and other fabrics, especially rayon.

Silverfish and firebrats can be controlled with household sprays or dusts. The results may not be immediate but, properly applied, the insecticide will leave a killing residue that should achieve control within two or three weeks. If not, repeat the treatment.

Select a household surface spray containing DDT, or malathion. Spray door and window casings, skirtings, closets and openings around pipes. Oil-based sprays should not be used near an open fire, electric motor, gas pilot flame, or other areas where they might ignite. In such places use a dust containing malathion. Blow it into cracks and onto the surfaces of areas suggested for spraying. See *Insecticides* for precautions.

Spiders Spiders destroy injurious household insects and most of those found in the British Isles are harmless.

All spiders can be controlled by spraying infested areas with a household surface spray; consult your Household Store. See *Insecticides* for precautions.

Termite If you have reason to suspect that your house or garage is infested with termites, call a reliable exterminator without delay. This is a job you cannot handle yourself. Termites, also called white ants, operate like an army, with battalions of soldiers and workers. The larvae (workers) and soldiers (pupae) are wingless. The adults have gauzy wings. Termites feed on wood and completely undermine it.

The presence of a termite colony may be indicated first by large numbers of reproductive (winged) termites, emerging or swarming from the soil or wood. Discarded wings on the floor beneath doors and windows, even when the insects themselves are not seen is another indication that a colony is nearby. While some termites leave small piles of wood dust, the subterranean termite leaves little or no indication of its presence. A telltale sign, however, is the shelter tube, an earthlike construction one-quarter to one-half inch or more in width, which these termites build from the soil to the wood where they are working.

Ticks Only brown dog ticks ever become a household pest in the British Isles. After feeding on a dog, such ticks drop off and hide in cracks and crevices, behind skirtings, and under carpets, rugs and furniture. They breed in these places and each succeeding generation finds the dog and repeats the cycle.

Control begins with the dog. Have your veterinary surgeon treat him in a bath containing a suitable insecticide, or bathe him yourself. Buy an emulsifiable concentrate containing 50 per cent of malathion. Mix one tablespoon of the concentrate in each gallon of water. Dip the dog into the water, being careful not to immerse its head. Sponge its ears. If the dog is too large to dip, prepare the mixture in a bucket and pour it slowly over its back so that it will soak through to the skin.

Next spray the areas in the house where ticks may be breeding, using a household surface spray containing malathion. Pay particular attention to cracks in the floor, skirtings, window casings, and places where the dog likes to sleep. A malathion spray can be applied to rugs, carpets and upholstered furniture – but be sure the label says that it will not stain. See *Insecticides* for precautions.

Wasps and Hornets Wasps and hornets are beneficial insects that destroy many garden pests. Only a few of the many varieties sting. However, they should be destroyed if they build their nests in the attic rafters, porch corners and near locations where children play. The nests may be circular combs of cells, large globular paper-like constructions, or little joined cells of mud. Some species nest in the ground.

DDT SPRAY: To one quart of water add six ounces of 25 per cent emulsifiable DDT concentrate or six level tablespoons of 50 per cent wettable DDT powder.

CHLORDANE SPRAY: To one quart of water add two ounces of 45 per cent emulsifiable chlordane concentrate or three level tablespoons of 40 per cent wettable chlordane powder.

DIELDRIN SPRAY: To one quart of water add one ounce of 15 per cent emulsifiable dieldrin concentrate.

See *Insecticides* for precautions.

Weevils See *Pantry Pests*.

Wood Worm Preparations are sold at Household Stores for dealing with this. For full-scale Wood Worm eradication it is best to employ a firm which specializes in it, e.g.: Woodworm Eradication Ltd., Chesterfield.

Cleaning agents and their uses

Abrasive Any material used to rub, or abrade, a spot or material falls into this classification. Examples are whiting, pumice, rottenstone powder and volcanic ash. Some of these materials are available in different degrees of finesse. All have specific household uses, described under various headings in this book. For more detailed information about each one, see *Whiting, Pumice* etc. These materials can be bought at Hardware Stores and sometimes at Chemists.

Commercially sold scouring powders for kitchen and bathroom use are abrasives, differing widely in their degree of harshness. Some contain strong alkalies such as washing soda and are too harsh for use on aluminium or porcelain enamel surfaces.

Absorbent An absorbent is a material useful in removing light or freshly made stains and grease stains by absorbing them. Examples are cornstarch, French chalk, talcum powder and fuller's earth. Absorbents are harmless to all fibres and are easy to apply. This is how they are used:

Lay the stained fabric flat on a clean cloth or towel. Spread a layer of absorbent on the stain and work it around gently. When the absorbent becomes caked or gummy shake or brush it off, or use a vacuum cleaner on rugs and carpets. Repeat this procedure until most of the stain is gone. Apply another layer and let it remain overnight or longer if necessary. Overnight treatment only will often remove a light stain.

When fruit juice, sauce or other undesirable liquid is spilt on a tablecloth during a meal a quick coating of salt before applying further treatment will remove the top layer.

To speed removal of a greasy stain put a layer of cloth or brown paper over the fabric upon which the absorbent has been spread and apply a warm iron for several minutes.

Absorbents are more effective on some stains when they are mixed to a paste with cleaning fluid. They are not recommended for dark unwashable materials because it is difficult to remove them completely. Soft cloths, cottonwool, paper napkins and face tissues are absorbent materials useful for soaking up quickly liquids spilled on rugs, upholstery, and other heavy fabrics that do not absorb them readily. Unless the fluid is greasy, still more of the stain can be removed by wetting and blotting the material.

Acetic Acid A colourless liquid, acid and pungent in odour and taste, useful in treating certain stains. In its pure state it is a clear colourless, strongly acid liquid, which crystallizes in cold temperatures. As a stain remover it is used in a dilution of 10 per cent. (White vinegar can be used as a substitute. It is five per cent acetic acid.)

Acetic acid can be used safely on silk and wool. It can also be used on linen and cotton. Do *not* use a strong solution of acetic acid on acetate.

On stains for which acetic acid or vinegar is recommended, follow this procedure. Moisten the stain with the acid, keeping it wet till the stain disappears. Rinse or sponge with water. If the dye changes colour, try moistening the fabric with ammonia. (See *Ammonia* for directions.) Section 2 on Stains will tell you when to use acetic acid.

Acetone A clear liquid, with an odour resembling peppermint, which can be bought at some chemists. Acetone is useful in removing stains caused by paint, varnish, lacquer and model plane cement (freely spread by youthful modellers). It is harmless to natural fibres and to all synthetics except acetate. Acetone affects some dyes, so test it before using on coloured materials. CAUTION: Acetone is flammable. It evaporates rapidly and its fumes are toxic. Use it in a well-ventilated place and be careful not to inhale it for any length of time. Store acetone tightly stopped in a cool place.

Acid A sour substance. In chemistry, acids have these common properties: they taste sour; they will dissolve in water and sometimes will restore colours that have been changed by an alkali (it's worth trying). Acids turn blue litmus paper red.

Mild acids like lemon, vinegar, and acetic acid perform a number of homely household chores, such as cutting soap film and bleaching stains, which are described in their proper alphabetic places. Other acids are violently poisonous and can cause severe burns, but few of these fall within our category. For treatment of stains caused by acid see *Stains*, page 138.

Aerosol Technically, an aerosol is a suspension of fine solid or liquid particles in air or gas, as smoke, fog or mist. Commercially, the word is used to describe any pressurized product which is self propelled through a valve, regardless of particle size, the type of propellant used, and the form in which the product is dispensed. While the term 'aerosol' is used for food and non-food foams as well as airborne and surface-deposited sprays of either liquids or powders, they are in pressurized products.

Alcohol Alcohol is a spirit distilled from fermented sugar and other materials. A powerful disinfectant, it can be used to sterilize thermometers and other instruments. As a solvent it is excellent for cleaning glass and for removing resinous stains from cloth.

Alcohol is inflammable; wood alcohol is poisonous.

Alkali In chemistry, an alkali is 'any one of various classes of substances having the following properties in common: solubility in water; the power of neutralizing acids and forming salts with them; the property of corroding animal and vegetable substances; the property of altering the tints of many colouring matters'. Thus, an alkali used in washing or for spot removal may change the colour of dyes in fabrics. It will turn red litmus paper blue.

Alkalis in household use include ammonia, lye and various soda compounds. They have important functions in the home but are harmful to certain materials, including silk, wool and aluminium. Their uses and limitations are described in this book under individual classifications as *Lye, Ammonia, Soda and Soda Compounds*. See also page 138.

Ammonia Ammonia is named from Ammon, the ram's-headed sun god of ancient Egypt, since it is supposed to have been prepared originally from camel's dung near the shrine of Jupiter Ammon.

Ammonia is an alkaline gas, dissolved in water. As sold for household use it varies from five to fifteen per cent in strength. For stain removal, obtain chemically pure ten per cent ammonia from a chemist or hardware store.

A small amount of household ammonia added to washing or rinsing water will help make windows and glassware sparkle and lighten numerous household tasks. This is because of its ability to cut grease. Remember that it tends to bleach slightly and to soften paint, so don't use too much.

For stain removal, use ammonia in the following way. On all fabrics except silk or wool and their blends, moisten the stain with ammonia and keep it wet until the stain has gone. Rinse with water. If colours seem changed by the ammonia try moistening the cloth with acetic acid or vinegar. Then rinse with water.

(Dilute the ammonia with an equal amount of water for use on silk or wool and add a small amount of vinegar to the last rinse. If colours are altered follow the directions given above.)

Ammonia is poisonous and should be well stoppered and stored with care in a cool place. It is caustic to the eyes and skin. If spilled on the skin, flood the area with water, then wash with vinegar or lemon juice.

WARNING: If you are using ammonia, do not add another cleansing agent. The combination could be lethal. Ammonia and chlorine bleach, for instance, react to release a deadly gas.

Amyl Acetate This chemical is a compound of acetic acid and amyl alcohol, useful in removing certain stains, such as nail polish and other lacquers. It is safe to use on fabrics damaged by acetone, but if the spilled lacquer contained acetone, damage may already have been done to the fabric. Amyl acetate can be bought at some chemists. For stain removal it should be *chemically pure*. It is inflammable and poisonous.

Benzene A hydrocarbon obtained commercially from coal tar. It is a clear, colourless fluid with a pleasant odour. Benzene is used as a solvent for gums, resins and fats. Though it is a valuable spot remover, it is highly flammable and should not be stored in large amounts in the home. Keep well stoppered in a cool safe place.

Benzine, Benzol A clear, colourless fluid, commonly called petroleum ether. It is obtained from a distillation of petroleum and contains a mixture of volatile hydrocarbons. It differs essentially from benzene by being such a mixture, benzene being a single hydrocarbon of constant composition. Benzine is used as a solvent for fats, resins and certain alkaloids. It is also highly flammable and should not be used in large amounts in the home or stored there. Friction alone can sometimes generate a spark, which in turn can cause combustion.

Biological Washing Powders See *Enzymes*.

Bleach (noun) Bleaches are chemical agents used to whiten any material, especially white fabrics, and to remove certain stains. They should always be used carefully because, if directions are not followed, they may weaken fabrics and fade colours, or have startling results, such as turning material bright yellow (and very fragile) when yellow is not required. Because metal may speed up their action, they should not be used in metal containers. For home laundry use there are two types of bleach – chlorine and peroxy. Chlorine bleaches are available as liquids, containing sodium hypochlorite, and in granular form, containing organic chlorine compounds. Peroxy bleaches are powders containing sodium perborate or potassium monopersulphate. In using either type, follow the directions on the container. Chlorine bleach is best for untreated cottons, linens and synthetics; peroxys are for fabrics which chlorine bleach damages.

Spreading wet fabrics in the sun, when available, is another way to bleach them, but some fibres are weakened by sunlight. If you use this method expose them briefly and infrequently. Other bleaches used in stain removal are hydrogen peroxide, sodium perborate and colour removers, sold at hardware stores and some chemists. For further information look up the specific bleach you are planning to use: *Chlorine Bleach, Sodium Perborate*, etc.

Blueing Blueing is not essential in the laundry, but even in these days of 'magic whiteners' many women like to use it. It is better to use too little than too much. Prepare blueing water according to the directions given by the manufacturer, just before it is to be used. If it stands too long the clothes may be streaked.

Soluble powder blueing is prepared by dissolving it in a small quantity of water. This liquid is then added a drop at a time to a bowl of cool clear water. Block blueing is put into a cotton or flannel bag and moved through the water until the proper tint is obtained. The tint can be tested on a small garment or scrap of material. All blueings are used in the final rinse water.

Stir blueing water during use and blue a few pieces at a time. The best method is to dip them in and out, one at a time. Never let them soak in the blueing water. Never draw off the blueing water, leaving the clothes in the bowl, because this causes streaks.

If cotton clothes are overblued, pour boiling water over them unless they have been treated for wrinkle resistance. Or rinse them in hot water in your washing machine. See also *Stains*, page 137.

The use of detergents containing fluorescent dyes makes blueing unnecessary.

Boracic Acid Boracic (boric) acid is a compound of chemical radical, boron, with oxygen and hydrogen ... just in case you were wondering. It has the properties of a weak acid and is an effective antiseptic. Boracic acid is bought at chemists as a fine white powder, which dissolves easily in water. A saturated solution made of sterile (boiled) water, plus as much of the powder as will dissolve in it, is often recommended as an eyewash. It is sometimes used to freshen nappies.

CAUTION: Boracic acid is toxic and should be stored, carefully labelled. On no account should it be left on a shelf with baby foods, where it might be confused with dextrose or milk sugar.

Borax A salt formed by a combination of boracic acid and soda. It is a white crystalline solid, slightly soluble in water. Borax is used in the manufacture of glass and enamel, as a flux for solder, as a cleanser and water softener for laundry, bath and shampoo and as an antiseptic. It cuts grease, loosens dirt and retards the growth of many moulds and bacteria which cause putrefaction. CAUTION: Borax is toxic.

Carbon Tetrachloride Carbon tetrachloride is an inflammable cleaning fluid. Like other such grease solvents it is sold under a variety of trade names. (E.g. 'Dab-it-off', 'Beaucaire'.) All such fluids are hazardous to use and directions given on their containers should be followed scrupulously. Once considered safe because it is non-flammable, carbon tetrachloride is now classified as one of the most dangerous of all cleaning fluids in this category.

Carborundum A carbon-silicon compound made by electric fusion. Its uses are similar to those of emery. See *'Emery'*.

Castor Oil Castor oil comes from the beans of the castor oil plant. It is not just a medicine, but also an excellent leather conditioner. It is specially suited to types of leather that are to be polished afterwards. Clean the leather first; apply a small amount of the oil with a pad of soft cloth or with your finger tips; rub it well in and remove the excess oil with a clean soft cloth. See *Leather Goods*, also *Books*.

Charcoal Charcoal is a form of carbon, a non-metallic chemical element. It is brother to the diamond and to graphite. You use it in outdoor grills, but it has household functions as well. It absorbs odours and a block of charcoal in a refrigerator will help keep the onions and fish from perfuming the butter. Heating the block in a frying pan will dispel the odours it has absorbed. Activated carbon, derived from coconut shell, is many times more efficient than ordinary charcoal for absorbing odours and gases. It is used in some of the air purifiers now on the market.

Chloride of Lime Chloride of lime is a combination of gas, chlorine, and lime. It is valuable as a disinfectant and deodorizer in damp basements and around drains, outdoor lavatories and dustbins.

Chloride of lime and sodium carbonate (washing soda) properly combined with water, make the bleaching solution known as 'household bleach' or chlorine bleach which is sold under many trade names.

Chlorine Bleach This is a bleach sold under such trade names as 'Parazone', 'Brobat', etc. It is easily recognized by its odour. It is useful in the home as a bleach for white cottons, linens and synthetics, as a disinfectant, and as a stain remover. It should not be used on silk, wool mohair, leather, spandex or on resin-treated cotton, linen or rayon. Resin is used in some drip dry finishes and creates both a yellow stain and weakening of the fabric if bleach is applied. Do not use chlorine bleach on fabrics that are already weak. On colourfast linens, cottons and synthetic materials, bleach can be used to remove stains, but only in a weak solution. The greatest caution must be observed to prevent the colours from fading. Always test a sample or inconspicuous place first. Chlorine bleach will weaken even cotton and linen fibres if it is allowed to remain in contact with them too long or if the material is not thoroughly rinsed afterwards.

To bleach untreated white cottons, linens or synthetics, use a cupful of bleach in a gallon or more of cold or lukewarm water. After mixing it around, immerse the articles to be bleached. (Do not add bleach to water containing clothing.) Allow the articles to remain in the water until the desired bleaching has been accomplished, but no longer than half-an-hour or the material will be weakened. Rinse articles thoroughly (at least three times) with plenty of water.

To remove stains from *washable* materials not likely to be damaged by chlorine bleach, use, for a *mild* treatment, a solution made by dissolving two tablespoons of liquid bleach or ¼ cup granular bleach in one quart of cool water. Apply this solution to the stain with a medicine dropper or glass rod, or soak the stained material in it for five to fifteen minutes.

Rinse thoroughly with water and repeat process if necessary.

For a *strong* treatment, use equal parts of liquid bleach and water. Apply this solution as described above but rinse with water immediately and thoroughly. Repeat if necessary and again rinse thoroughly.

For stains on *non-washable* materials (*mild* treatment), use a solution made by mixing one teaspoon of liquid bleach or one tablespoon granular bleach in one cup of cool water. Apply it to the stain with a medicine dropper and let it stand for five to fifteen minutes. Rinse and repeat process if necessary. Stronger treatment is hazardous, but if you want to try it on a bad stain, follow the instructions given for a strong treatment on washable materials.

Chlorine bleach will remove most stains from baths, sinks, enamelware, tiles and woodwork. After washing, wipe the stain with a solution containing about four tablespoons of bleach to a quart of water. If the stain does not disappear, keep it wet with this solution for five minutes. Repeat if necessary.

Some manufacturers recommend chlorine bleach as a lavatory bowl cleaner and disinfectant. If used for this purpose, no other compound should be added. Mixing chlorine bleach with lavatory bowl cleaners, ammonia, and other special preparations produces a chemical action which liberates toxic gases. If inhaled, these gases can cause prolonged illness or death.

'Chlorothene' 'Chlorothene' is the trade name of a chlorinated solvent for grease, oil, wax and allied stains. Chemically it is a special grade of *trichloroethane*. Having proved its value as a de-greasing agent for the metals and machinery of heavy industry, 'Chlorothene' has entered the home cleaning field as an almost ideal spot remover. 'Chlorothene' is non-flammable and of low toxity.

Citric Acid This is an acid obtained from many fruit juices, but especially lemons. It is sometimes called 'salts of lemon' and is useful as a bleach when treating certain stains. It can be bought at chemists in diluted or powder form.

Cleaning Fluids Cleaning fluids are effective for stains caused by grease, oil, adhesive tape and chewing gum. They are available at grocers and hardware stores under a variety of trade names. All should be used with great care.

The non-flammable fluids are carbon tetrachloride, methyl chloroform, perchlorothylene, trichloroethylene (not to be used on Kodel or Tricel) and trichloroethane, which is new in the retail field.

Non-flammable spot removers are toxic and their fumes should not be inhaled. Carbon tetrachloride is especially poisonous. If too much is inhaled, serious illness or even death may result. It is also injurious to the hands, which should never remain in contact with it more than a few moments. Trichloroethane (Chlorothene) is much less hazardous. Its fumes have one-twentieth the toxity of carbon tetrachloride.

Inflammable cleaning fluids are mainly petroleum naphthas. Those with a high 'flash point' (ask your dealer about this) are safest to use. The higher the 'flash point' the less likely a material is to ignite. Such fluids should never be used near an open flame (including pilot lights on gas equipment), near electric devices, or any source of static electricity. Their fumes are less poisonous but should not be extensively inhaled.

Many cleaning fluids combine two or more grease solvents, inflammable and non-flammable. Always read the label carefully and follow any directions given. If the contents of a non-flammable preparation are not stated on the container, assume that it contains carbon tetrachloride and use it with special care. On materials where cleaning fluids are likely to make rings, and on very delicate textiles, they are sometimes mixed with an absorbent and applied to the stain as a paste.

Some cleaning fluids are sold with little pads fixed to the lid of the bottles for easy application.

No cleaning fluids should ever be used in a washing machine, and clothing dampened with them should never be put in an automatic dryer. When using them it is best to work out of doors. If this is not possible, work in a room with windows open, in such a position that breeze or an electric fan are blowing the fumes away from you. Vapours from cleaning fluids are heavier than air and tend to accumulate near the floor.

Do not let small children play where they are being used.

Let a dry cleaner do your big jobs and confine your use of cleaning fluids to spot removal. Buy them in small amounts, use them sparingly – never in a bowl unless you can work out of doors. If you spill the fluid on your skin wash it off promptly. Store all such fluids in a cool safe place (with the lid or stopper firmly on) where children cannot reach them, even with the aid of a chair.

For technique in removing spots with cleaning fluids see *Sponge* (verb), page 186.

Colour Removers These are hydrosulphite chemicals, safe for all fibres, which are sold under various trade names e.g. 'Dygon'. Their primary use is to remove colour from cloth that is to be dyed. They should not be mixed in metal containers and they should always be tested on a sample or hidden portion of cloth before being used on coloured materials.

This is how colour removers are used to remove stains for which they are recommended in Section 2. For a *mild* treatment dissolve ¼ teaspoon in half a cup of cool water. Put a few drops on the stain and cover it with a pad of cotton dampened with the same solution. Let it remain from 1 to 15 minutes. Rinse thoroughly with water and repeat if necessary. For a *strong* treatment on fabrics that will stand it, use the same solution, but boiling hot water instead of cool water. Apply the solution with a medicine dropper and rinse immediately. Repeat if necessary. For large stains on white or colourfast materials follow the directions on the packet.

If use of colour remover alters

dyes, it is sometimes possible to restore the colour by prompt rinsing and drying in the open air. Colours that are faded cannot be restored.

Section 2 on *Stains* will tell you when to use this bleach.

Corundum Corundum is a native crystalline alumina. Pulverized, it is used for grinding and polishing gems, etc. Emery is impure corundum.

Deodorants Formerly, room deodorants often just covered unpleasant odours with others that were less objectionable, or temporarily dulled the sense of smell. Today there are deodorants that react chemically with odours to destroy them. These are especially useful when circumstances do not permit a room to be thoroughly aired.

The deodorant is distributed as an aerosol mist. One chemical in it combines with the nitrogenous and sulphur compounds in which most unpleasant odours originate, and another takes care of odours caused by stale tobacco, paint, alcohol, etc.

Detergent This is a word that came to the fore with the debut of soapless suds and other chemical cleaners. It means an agent used for cleaning, or purging, but is commonly applied to synthetic substitutes for soap.

See *Synthetic Detergents*.

Disinfectant Disinfectants containing quaternary ammonia compounds are non-toxic and effective for use with dishes, clothing and contaminated areas such as beds and clothes. These include 'Roccal', 'Cetavlon' and 'Savlon'. These may also be used in washing machines periodically and, provided they are safely used, liquid chlorine bleaches and pine-oil mixtures (e.g. 'Clean-o-Pine').

Quaternary and chlorine bleaches are effective disinfectants in hot, warm and cold water. Pine oil and phenolic disinfectants (e.g. 'Jeyes Fluid,' 'Lysol,' 'Dettol'), are effective in warm or hot water.

Liquid chlorine bleaches are used in the wash water. They are not safe for some fabrics. (See *Chlorine Bleach*.) Preferably, add the bleach to the water before putting in the clothes. Usually one cup is recommended for a top-loading machine (i.e. one teacup) and ½ cup for a front-loading machine.

Pine-oil disinfectants go into the water before the clothes are added. Use ¾ teacup for a top-loading machine and ½ cup for a front-loading machine.

To destroy bacteria living on the surface of the machine pour disinfectant into the empty machine and let it run for 15 minutes at a hot water setting.

Small articles not harmed by boiling can be washed and disinfected by boiling them for 10 minutes.

Emery A variety of the mineral corundum, which is finely granular in structure. In colour it is deep grey to bluish or blackish grey, sometimes even brownish.

Emery is used in polishing metals and hard stones, and sometimes, in reconditioning furniture. It may be had in varying degrees of fineness and the very finest only is used for furniture work.

Emery cloth and paper are prepared by dusting powdered emery on glue-covered cloth. Emery paper can be bought at hardware and household stores in handy packets graded from coarse to fine. Emery is also used to stuff some pin and needle cushions. It sharpens them.

Enzymes Enzymes are complex chemical compounds which are present in all living cells. There are various types and various uses. Their use in washing powders is fairly new and their efficacy a matter of debate. But, as they are not living organisms they do not, as some advertisements would seem to imply, actually eat the food, blood etc. which stain our clothes. However, many people claim that they do make such stains easier to deal with.

When using enzyme detergents the temperature of the water is important. The warmer the water the quicker the enzyme reaction. But if the water is too hot the enzyme loses its power to react with the protein molecules in the stain so it doesn't work. Chlorine also destroys enzymes.

The time necessary to remove protein stains depends mainly on water temperature. In cold water, overnight soaking is suggested – at least 16 hours. The highest temperatures at which enzymes will work are 140°F to 149°F (about 60°C). Above this the heat tends to 'set' the stains so making them more difficult to remove than before. If stains have set then repeated soaking and washing may be necessary.

It's important to remember that enzymes take some time to work and, for immediate laundering the cheaper, ordinary detergents are just as effective.

Some materials should never on any account be soaked. They are: 1. Non-colourfast materials. 2. Wool. 3. Silk. 4. Fabrics with flame resistant finishes. These may be quickly laundered in hand-hot enzyme detergent suds in which soaking is not necessarily recommended. (E.g. 'Ariel', 'Radiant'.)

Enzyme powders may be used in washing machines unless they are front-loading or suds-sensitive. For these pre-soak the clothes before laundering in a low-lather washing product.

Too much enzyme detergent is wasteful, but too little means the stains will probably not be completely removed. In twin-tub machines use about $1\frac{1}{2}$ – 2 cups in soft water; 2 – 3 cups in hard water. In a top-loading automatic use 2 – 3 cups in soft water; $2\frac{1}{2}$ – 4 cups in hard water. For hand washing one-third of a cup to a gallon of water – or a little more in hard water, a little less in soft water. Always dissolve the powder thoroughly before adding the clothes no matter how you are using it.

Enzyme soaking powders (e.g. 'Big S') can also be used for soaking burnt saucepans, saucepans in which scrambled eggs have been cooked, for cleaning blocked drains, for removing stains from teacups, milk bottles, vacuum flasks and flower vases. All require prolonged soaking in a moderate temperature.

Fabric Softeners Fabric softeners (e.g. 'Comfort', 'Stergene') make textiles soft and fluffy, minimize creasing and reduce static electricity. Follow the directions on the container. If too much is used, fabrics may be less absorbent. The effect of a softener is lost with the next washing.

French Chalk Soapstone, or steatite, a soft magnesium mineral. Tailors use it to mark cloth. Powdered, it is often used as an absorbent for removing fresh grease stains from fabrics. French chalk is harmless to all materials and leaves no ring. See also *Absorbent*.

Gum Tragacanth Another material

from plants, used instead of starch for finishing certain materials. See *Starch* and *Special Finishes*.

Hydrogen Peroxide Hydrogen peroxide is a good bleach, safe for all fibres, which is available at chemists. As sold, it is a dilute solution, about 3 per cent.

When used as a laundry bleach, peroxide is diluted with water, the concentration depending upon the amount of bleaching to be done. Add one pint to one gallon of water, or use one part of peroxide to eight parts of water. A teaspoon of sodium perborate or 'Borax' (or a few drops of ammonia) added to a gallon of this mixture makes the action stronger. These directions are for WHITE fabrics. Test colours before using hydrogen peroxide as a bleach or stain remover.

As a stain remover peroxide is applied with a medicine dropper or glass rod directly to the stain, a pad of clean cloth being placed under the fabric to absorb any excess. For a mild treatment, moisten the stain with a few drops of hydrogen peroxide and place it in the sun. Add more bleach, as needed, to keep the stain moist until it disappears. (This bleach acts slowly.) If the stain is not removed, add several drops of ammonia to about a tablespoon of hydrogen peroxide and moisten the stain immediately with this mixture. Then cover it with a pad of cotton dampened with the same solution. Keep the cotton damp until the stain is gone. (This may take several hours.) Rinse thoroughly.

For a stronger treatment, dampen a cloth with undiluted hydrogen peroxide, cover this with a dry cloth and press it with an iron as hot as the fabric will stand. Rinse with water afterwards.

Section 2 on *Stains* will tell you when to use hydrogen peroxide.

CAUTION: Once you have removed peroxide from the bottle, never put it back. Wash it down the drain instead. Peroxide is very allergic to impurities and strange things happen when it contacts some of them.

Hypochlorites See *Chlorine Bleach*.

Insecticides Insecticides recommended for home use contain such substances as DDT, and malathion. All are poisonous. Non-toxic preparations are based on formulations of pyrethrum (flowers of pyrethrum plants) and piperonyl butoxide. Ready mixed preparations in pressurized cans are the easiest to use. Insecticides should be bought thoughtfully, used carefully, and stored safely.

BUYING: Read the labels carefully when selecting an insecticide to see if it contains the ingredient recommended for the insect that is troubling you. It may not do so as commercial labels are very uncommunicative. The chemists of well-known firms – e.g. Boots and Timothy Whites will be able to help you – so, for that matter will your chemist-round-the-corner. And remember that there are two types of spray, surface and aerosol. If the label says 'surface spray' or 'residual spray', the insecticide is intended to be sprayed on surfaces to kill crawling insects. Sprayed surfaces retain their lethal power for weeks or even months. Such sprays are usually oil-based but sometimes they are emulsified water solutions.

Aerosols, which may be labelled 'air spray', or 'space spray', are for flying insects. They are excellent for clearing the air of flies, gnats, or mosquitoes. They do not leave a lasting residue and that is why

they can be used safely in the air.
USING: Always read (or re-read) the directions given on the container before using an insecticide; do not depend on your memory. Follow the instructions exactly. The following precautions apply to all insecticides:

Remove all pets, including fish in aquariums, from a room that is to be sprayed or dusted. Also remove their food and water dishes. Keep children away. If the label warns against inhaling pesticidal mists or dusts, leave the windows open while applying them. Remove food and utensils from shelves, drawers, and cabinets and scrub them thoroughly before applying sprays and dusts. When you finish the job, wash all exposed skin surfaces with soap and water, and change your clothes if the insecticide has come in contact with them.

Do not smoke while applying insecticides, even if they are not inflammable. Traces of insecticide can be carried from the hand to the mouth by a cigarette, and oil-based sprays could be ignited. Do not use oil-based sprays near any open flame (including a pilot light) or near an electric circuit.

Do not combine different insecticides.

STORING: Store insecticides with their labels intact in a place where children and pets cannot reach them. Those in pressurized cans should not be stored near any source of heat. Do not store an insecticide near food, under the sink, or in a medicine cabinet. If a container has lost its label, do not guess at its contents; get rid of it safely.

EMPTY CONTAINERS: Never re-use an empty insecticide container. Rinse it with water. Rinse the outside of pressurized cans. Wrap all empty containers with thick layers of newspaper, put them in the dustbin, and make sure the lid is on tight. Do not put pressurized cans in a fire or incinerator; they will explode. Do not burn cardboard containers or paper bags that have contained insecticides. Wrap them with newspapers too and put them in the dustbin.

HOUSEKEEPING PRECAUTIONS: For the use of oil-based insecticides include the following: Do not spray them on silk, rayon, or other fabrics that stain easily. Do not apply them to floors of asphalt tile: they dissolve asphalt. If treating cracks in a parquet floor apply the spray lightly; too much may soften the black cement under the wood and produce a stain. Oil sprays damage some linoleums and plastic materials. If you are in doubt about a surface, test it first in an inconspicuous place. Do not walk on carpets or rugs or sit in upholstered chairs that have been sprayed until they are completely dry, and avoid placing heavy objects on them. Weight or pressure on the damp pile will mat it and the disfigurement may last for several days.

EMERGENCY ACTION: If a pesticide is swallowed accidentally, or if someone becomes ill after using it, consult the label and call your doctor or a hospital immediately.

INSECT REPELLENT: When you go canoeing or on a picnic most in-

sects will find you repulsive if you apply an insect repellent to your skin. Sold as lotions and sprays under various trade names, insect repellents may contain such chemicals as ethylhexanediol, diethyl carbate, or diethyl toluamide. They are harmless to the skin and to most clothing, though some plasticize rayon and 'Dynel'. Read the directions on the label and follow them exactly.

Iodine A chemical element used as an antiseptic and to remove silver nitrate stains.

Iridium A metal allied to platinum and sometimes alloyed with it. Iridium enhances the value of platinum in an alloy, being a more expensive metal. See page 89.

Lanolin Lanolin is a substance obtained from the natural grease of wool. It is used in certain hair preparations, as a base for ointments and cosmetics, as a conditioner for leather and in many other products.

Latex Latex is the liquid exudation of rubber trees. The word is often used in the retail trade to indicate pure rubber, rather than synthetic.

Lemon Oil Lemon oil, used for polishing furniture, is paraffin (mineral) oil containing a little oil of lemon.

Linseed Oil Linseed oil used in the preparation of oil paints and varnishes and in many furniture polishes, comes from seeds of the common flax, or lint. It is the most valuable of the drying oils. The finest grade is called 'artist's oil'.

If you are following directions that call for *boiled* linseed oil, don't think you can cook up a bit of raw linseed oil in a saucepan. The process employed commercially is both complicated and tedious. The stuff is heated in a copper or iron boiler for two hours, then chemical 'dryers' are added and it is boiled

for several hours more. It is then left in the boiler, covered, for an additional 10 hours, after which it spends two or three weeks in settling tanks.

When you buy linseed oil at a paint or hardware store specify whether you want it 'raw' or 'boiled'. And remember that it is inflammable.

Lye Lye, a very strong alkali, is used in making soap and for various cleaning operations, notably the opening of stopped drains. If you use lye, follow the directions on the container with the utmost care because it is a dangerous, caustic agent and can cause severe external, as well as internal, poisoning. On no account must your skin come in contact with lye or lye water.

Lye will eat through cloth, enamelled surfaces, bristle brushes, rubber gloves, etc., and will damage severely certain metals, such as aluminium. It usually does a good job on a stopped drain but you are taking chances if you use it in a very greasy drain. Under certain conditions it can combine with the grease and form hard soap which blocks the pipe completely.

Trade-marked drain openers labelled sodium hydrate are lye.

When using lye, add no other cleaning agent.

Mineral Oil Mineral (paraffin) oil is a name used for crude petroleum and refined petroleum oil. When properly refined it is a clear, viscous fluid without odour or taste. Mineral oil is useful in the home in certain cleaning operations and is used as the base of some furniture polishes, such as 'lemon oil'. Do not use it on leather.

Muriatic Acid Muriatic acid is a solution of hydrochloric acid in water, used by professionals to clean down newly laid brick and tile work. Its function is to dissolve smears and splashes of mortar. As used, it is diluted with from eight to ten parts of water. The solution is brushed on with a scrubbing brush, then rinsed off with plain water. Muriatic acid is injurious to the skin, to woodwork and to fabrics. It should be applied by a competent worker who is familiar with its properties, not by an amateur.

Naphtha Naphtha is a member of the coal tar family. There are many grades, heavy to light. Naphtha is used for fuel and lighting in some areas, as a solvent for rubber and certain greasy stains and as an ingredient in some paints, varnishes and wax polishes. It is explosive and highly inflammable. Large amounts should not be used or stored in the home and it should be kept away from flames and sparks. If possible, work with naphtha should be performed out-of-doors. See *Cleaning Fluids*.

Neat's-Foot Oil An amber-coloured oil obtained from the feet of bovine cattle, such as cows. It is extremely valuable as a leather conditioner. You can buy neat's-foot oil at paint and hardware stores, at shoe shops and chemists. Neat's-foot oil does not clean leather; it protects it from deterioration due to drying. So use saddle soap or mild soap and water first, then rub the oil in with your finger tips or with a soft pad of cloth.

Neat's-foot oil is not suitable for articles on which a glossy shine is desired. It leaves a dull finish, difficult to polish.

Oxalic Acid The acid of sorrel, a family of plants. Its household use is as a bleach and stain remover, especially effective for ink and iron rust stains. Oxalic crystals may be bought in drugstores. They are very poisonous.

In removing stains from cloth with oxalic acid, follow these directions for a 'mild' treatment. Dissolve one tablespoon of crystals in one cup of warm water. Wet the stain with this solution and keep it wet until the stain is gone. Rinse thoroughly with water. For a 'Strong' treatment, make the water as hot as the fabric will stand or (except on nylon) sprinkle the crystals directly on the dampened stain, then dip it in very hot water.

Section 2 on *Stains* will tell you when to use oxalic acid.

Paint Cleaners Paint cleaners are sold commercially in liquid, powder and paste form. The liquid cleaners may be soap solutions, with or without water-softening agents, or non-soap solutions containing trisodium phosphate, washing soda or sodium silicate. The paste cleaners are similar to the liquids, using enough soap to form a paste. Some cleaners consist of wax emulsions, plus soap and an abrasive. The powders are the solid ingredients found in the liquid and paste types. If you are using a commercial paint cleaner, follow the directions on the container exactly and do not use more than advised. What we call 'paint cleaners', painters often laughingly call 'paint removers'.

A good cleaner for flat paint is trisodium phosphate, which you should be able to obtain at a paint store. Commercial paint cleaners often contain trisodium phosphate. If using trisodium phosphate, use one tablespoon to a gallon of warm water, rinse and wipe dry. Follow the directions in using packaged cleaners.

To clean glossy enamel paint and other paints with a glossy

finish in good condition use a cloth wrung out of plain hot water, or hot water containing one teaspoon of washing soda per gallon – more, if desirable. Rub gently. Soapless detergents also may be used. Trisodium phosphate and many of the commercial paint cleaners dull the finish of enamel paints and soap leaves a film. Scuffed paint calls for a fine abrasive, such as whiting.

Paraffin Oil Paraffin oil, also called mineral oil, is liquid paraffin. In a pure state it is colourless, odourless, translucent and tasteless. Paraffin oil is used in some furniture polishes, in cold creams and in hair preparations. Do not use it on leather.

Paraffin Wax Paraffin wax is a solid, waxy substance obtained from petroleum. Its uses include waterproofing, the prevention of decomposition, etc. The homemaker knows it best as a topping to preserve jellies from mould and a material to make her electric iron slick. For paraffin spilled on cloth see *Stains*, page 153.

Perchlorethylene See *Cleaning Fluids*.

Peroxide See *Hydrogen Peroxide*.

Peroxy Bleach Peroxy bleaches are not as strong as chlorine bleaches, but they are safe for all fabrics. Use them for textiles with durable-press finishes and for silk, wool, and spandex, which are damaged by chlorine. Such bleaches contain sodium perborate or potassium monopersulphate. See also *Bleach* and *Chlorine Bleach*.

Petrolatum See *Petroleum Jelly*.

Petroleum Ether This is the same as benzine. See *Benzine* and *Cleaning Fluids*.

Petroleum Jelly Petroleum jelly, better known by its trade name, 'Vaseline', is a soft greasy substance used as a soothing ointment and as a lubricant. It is one of many petroleum derivatives. In household use it is valuable for loosening heavy grease and tar stains to facilitate their removal with solvents, for conditioning leather and for preventing rust. For stains caused by this substance see *Stains, Vaseline*, page 156.

Petroleum Naphtha Most used of the inflammable grease solvents; sold under its own name and trade names. Use a type with a high flash point (less likely to ignite). See *Cleaning Fluids*.

Plaster of Paris A plaster made from calcined (dried out by heat) gypsum. When diluted with water to a thin paste it sets rapidly and, at the moment of setting, expands. Most types of earth shrink when they dry.

Plaster of Paris is valuable for filling cracks and cavities in plaster, for making surgical casts, ornaments, etc. 'Patching plasters' are Plaster of Paris containing retarders to keep it from setting too rapidly. Statues and other ornaments made of Plaster of Paris cannot be cleaned by any satisfactory home method. They can only be dusted.

Any material used to cover the plaster may change the colour and quality of the surface. However, if the piece is not valuable and it is awfully smudgy, try *a very thin spray* of the best covering flat white paint you can locate. Spraying paint requires considerable skill so undertake such a project with due forethought.

Pumice A spongy, porous stone tossed out by volcanoes. It is usually a form of obsidian, should you be curious, containing from 60 to 75 per cent silica. Pumice is a good scourer and polisher. It can be obtained in powdered form in varying degrees of fineness, at paint and hardware stores. Many commercial scouring powders contain pumice.

Rottenstone Decomposed siliceous limestone. Powdered rottenstone is used for all sorts of finer grinding and polishing in the arts. Mixed with linseed oil (see *Linseed Oil*) it will remove white spots and other light blemishes from furniture. The mixture is applied lightly with a soft cloth, following the grain of the wood. See *Furniture*.

Rouge Cleaning and polishing rouge is a red powder, consisting of peroxide of iron. It is used to polish gems, metal, glass, etc. Treated cloths, sold for polishing silver, are often impregnated with jeweller's rouge.

Silicones Silicones have been described as 'liquid glass' and as 'chemical cousins of glass'. Both are derived from the mineral element silica.

Silicones have countless industrial uses. They resist water, electricity, oxidation, weathering, chemicals, undesirable contacts, and are indifferent to high heat and bitter cold.

As invisible domestic helpers they now appear in furniture and floor waxes which are easier to apply and more durable; in metal polishes; on frying pans and baking tins that do not require greasing; in hand creams, baby lotions, hair dressings, lipsticks, suntan oils, hand creams, and increasingly on textiles. Silicone creams and cosmetics stay on when you go swimming and the lotions protect working hands. Silicone textile finishes give resistance to wear, water, weathering and stains.

There are no special instructions for silicone-treated cloth. It is unharmed by ordinary solvents. Pans with silicone linings should not be scrubbed with steel wool or abrasive powders. When the coating wears off, it can be replaced at the factory, or you can then use the pan like any other. Silicone dusters and polishing cloths lose some of the fluid with which they have been treated when washed, so deal with them gently. They are inexpensively replaced.

Silicone sprays are sold under various trade names for coating oven walls, lids of electric frypans, etc.

Silver Polish A fine grade of whiting on a damp cloth plus a little household ammonia or white spirit makes an excellent silver polisher. It keeps England's famous silver bright and shining.

Commercial polishes vary in composition but practically all contain fine abrasives like whiting, rouge or diatomaceous earth. Treated polishing cloths are handy for a quick job on lightly tarnished silver and to give added lustre to polished silver.

Avoid polishes that contain harsh abrasives, such as silica.

Soap Soap is usually made by heating, or emulsifying, fats or oils with lye. The quality of the soap depends upon the kind of fat that is used in making it, the manner in which it is prepared and the amount and character of foreign materials that are added to it to improve its cleansing action or give it special qualities. A soap is said to be 'neutral' when there is a correct balance between the fat and lye.

Soaps for general cleaning and laundry purposes are classified as 'built' and 'unbuilt'. Unbuilt soaps contain from 93 to 97 per cent pure soap, a little moisture and salt. The built soaps contain alkaline water softeners ... phosphates, 'Borax', washing soda, etc., which aid in removing soil, especially in hard-water areas.

Use the more expensive unbuilt mild soaps (e.g. 'Lux Flakes') for laundering fine fabrics. They are safer for colours and kinder to the hands. Use strong soaps for washing heavily soiled clothes.

Too much soap is as bad as too little in laundering clothes. Use just enough to maintain good suds.

See also 'Water and Water Softener'.

Soap Jelly Soap jelly, which has a number of uses in the home, can be made easily by dissolving about three tablespoons of white soap flakes in one cup of boiling water. This basic formula can be varied as desired. To increase its cleaning ability add a teaspoon of ammonia or two teaspoons of 'Borax'. To give it mild scouring properties add one quarter of a cup of whiting. This variation is good for flat paints.

Soda and Soda Compounds Let's take a look at the important chemical family of soda, or sodium, compounds that are often presented by manufacturers under various trade names as super cleansers. Behind the trade names there is less magic and less mystery than the advertising copy writers would have us believe. A few are very old household friends.

First and foremost, what is sodium? Actually, it is a silver-white metal, extremely unstable. It is the base of alkali soda and is an important agent in the production of such metals as aluminium and magnesium. It has a strong affinity for chlorine, in combination with which it is *sodium chloride*, and that, my friends, is common salt, abundantly available.

All soda compounds are derived from *sodium chloride*.

The four best known members of the sodium family are *sodium chloride*, or salt, *sodium bicarbonate*, *sodium carbonate* and *sodium hydrate*.

Sodium Bicarbonate is baking soda, or bicarbonate of soda. It will remove stains from china, clean your teeth, deodorize drains, clean your refrigerator, eliminate tummy aches due to gas, help make biscuits and cakes, and create bubbly drinks. It will also make jewellery sparkle; relieve the pain of bee stings, light burns and scalds; extinguish flash fires; clean glass, tile and porcelain, and kill odours.

Sodium Carbonate is washing soda, an effective cleaner. It also is referred to as sal soda and as washing crystals. Washing soda has many uses, enumerated in this book, among them the routine cleaning of drains and traps, washing certain types of floors, cleaning gas burners and greasy pots and pans. Probably its most notable use is as a water softener, for it is completely soluble. In hard-water areas it is invaluable in the laundry. Soda ash is partially purified sodium carbonate.

Sodium Hydrate is caustic soda, sold as lye. Sodium hydrate can give you a nasty burn and is not to be confused with its milder sisters. It is used to open sluggish drains. Follow the directions on the container exactly to avoid trouble.

While these are the four main sodas in household use, there are many others with which we should have, at least, a bowing acquaintance. This, as we have said, is a very important family.

Sodium Hydrosulphite for instance, is a dye-stripping agent, or colour remover, useful as a bleaching agent and for removing stains.

Sodium Hypochlorite is the chemist's Javelle water or Labarraque solution. It is our old friend, 'household bleach', or chlorine bleach. Washing soda and chloride of lime, with water, compose it. See *Chlorine Bleach*.

Sodium Perborate is a safe bleach for all types of fabrics. See *Sodium Perborate Bleach*.

Sodium Perborate Bleach Sodium perborate bleaches are safe for all fabrics but hot solutions should not be used on heat-sensitive fabrics such as those containing wool, or silk. In using laundry preparations sold at groceries for ordinary bleaching, follow the directions on the package.

For stain removal use pure sodium perborate crystals bought at a chemist. Do not use metal containers. Always test colours first.

For *stain removal* on *washable* materials dissolve one to two tablespoons of sodium perborate in a pint of hot water. (For silk, and wool, use lukewarm water.) Saturate the stain with this solution, or soak the stained article in it until the stain is removed. Since this bleach works slowly this may mean several hours or overnight. If silk or wool is yellowed by the solution, sponge it with 10 per cent acetic acid or white vinegar. Rinse. For a *strong* treatment on washable materials that will stand very hot water, sprinkle sodium perborate directly on the stain, then dip it into hot-to-boiling water. This should remove the stain in a few minutes. Rinse thoroughly and repeat if necessary.

On non-washable materials, for a mild treatment, sprinkle the stain with sodium perborate and cover it with a cotton pad dampened with water. Use lukewarm water on heat-sensitive materials, hot on others. Keep the pad damp until the stain is gone (several hours or more), then rinse. Or apply the solution described for washables with a medicine dropper and keep the stain damp until it disappears, then rinse. Sponge silk or wool with acetic acid or white vinegar if it has yellowed, then rinse with water. For a *strong* treatment place the stained material on an absorbent pad, dampen the stain with cool water, sprinkle it with sodium perborate, and saturate it with boiling water, using a medicine dropper or spoon. Rinse and repeat if necessary.

Section 2 on *Stains* will tell you when to use this bleach.

Sodium Thiosulphate is the 'hypo' solution used by photographers. It is purchasable, in crystal form, at drugstores and photo supply shops. Hypocrystals are useful in removing chlorine and iodine stains. They are safe for all fibres and harmless to colours. Directions for using these crystals are given in Section 2, on *Stains*, under *Iodine*.

Sodium pyrophosphate and sodium metaphosphate are desirable as water softeners because they combine with the minerals that make water hard, forming soluble compounds which are washed away. Some softeners, in combining with such minerals, form little grey lumps or flecks which adhere to the clothes and are difficult to remove. See *Water and Water Softeners*.

Trisodium Phosphate, an effective water softener and cleaner, is sold at paint stores as TSP, or as a 'paint cleaner' under trade names. One tablespoon dissolved in a gallon of water makes an excellent cleaner for flat paint, but removes the gloss from enamel paint. TSP is an excellent cleaner for glazed and unglazed tile, porcelain bathroom fixtures, etc. It has many other uses similar to those outlined for washing soda.

Softeners See *Fabric Softeners* and *Water and Water Softeners*.

Solvent A solvent is a substance, usually a liquid, which is used to dissolve another substance. First and foremost of the entire category is water, the safest and best. Try it first on all washable materials. Spot removers and cleaning fluids also are solvents; so are many of the chemicals recommended for various stains.

See also *Cleaning Fluids*.

Special Finishes Special finishes such as gelatine, gum arabic, and gum tragacanth (bought at chemists) are sometimes used to restore a crisp appearance to voile, organdie, batiste, silk and rayon. These finishes are transparent and thus especially fine for coloured fabrics. Follow the directions exactly; if too much is used, the material will be sticky.

GELATINE: Add one pint of cold water to one ounce of gelatine and until the gelatine has dissolved. To one part of this mixture add from eight to fifteen parts of hot water, depending upon the material and the amount of stiffness desired. Add a little 'Borax' if the mixture is to be saved. This is especially good for sheer cottons.

GUM ARABIC: Add one pint of cold water to one ounce of powdered gum arabic and heat until the gum has dissolved. To one part of this solution add from five to ten parts of hot water, depending upon the material and the stiffness desired. Use it when cooled. Add a little 'Borax' if the mixture is to be stored. This is especially good for silks and rayon.

GUM TRAGACANTH: Add one pint of cold water to one-sixth of an ounce of powdered gum tragacanth and heat until dissolved. To one part of this solution add from eight to twelve parts of hot water, according to the finish desired. Cool before using. Add a little 'Borax' if the mixture is to be saved.

Sponge (verb) When instructions say to sponge a stain with water or other solvent, your success in removing a stain will depend greatly upon your technique. This is how it should be done.

Place the stained material on a clean folded cloth so that the solvent can be applied, if possible, to the reverse side and the stain can be dissolved without having to go through the cloth. With a pad of cloth or cotton moistened with solvent, gently wipe the solvent into the stain, working from the centre toward the outer edge. Use the solvent sparingly and work it irregularly into the edge of the stain to avoid forming rings. Repeated applications of small amounts of solvent give the best results. Do not rub so hard that the fabric will be roughened, and move or change the pad underneath as the stain is absorbed. Dry the area quickly.

If a stain such as paint or tar has hardened, cover it with a pad moistened with solvent and let it remain until the stain has been softened. Apply fresh pads as they are needed. Then sponge the stain with solvent. On very delicate materials, dampen a pad or white blotter with solvent and place it on the stain. Do not rub. Replace the pad or blotter as required.

On materials that tend to form rings use solvents sparingly. The sponging pad should be scarcely damp. And take special care to sponge the edge of the stain irregularly so that no clear line will form as the material dries. Always dry the treated area as quickly as possible. Ring formation on some materials can be prevented by placing a fresh absorbent pad under the area treated and rubbing it gently with the palm of your hand. (Be sure the material is perfectly flat and unwrinkled.) Or place it on the palm of one hand and rub it gently with the other, following the threads of the material. Sometimes an absorbent powder is mixed with the solvent to make a crumbly paste which is applied to the stain and worked gently into it with the finger tips. Such a mixture should be sufficiently dry that the solvent does not seep out.

Let this mixture dry on the stain, then shake or brush it off. Repeat if necessary.

This method is not recommended for dark non-washable materials because final traces of powder are difficult to remove.

If rings have already formed you may have trouble eliminating them. On washable materials try dampening them with water and then working in a liquid detergent. On other materials try rubbing the cloth between your hands or scratching it lightly with your fingernail. Sometimes the application of the absorbent-solvent mixture already described will work.

Starch and Starch Finishes Manufacturers of laundry starch supply excellent directions for the use of their products and, since starches differ, these directions should be followed for best results.

Starch for finishing cloth can be obtained from many sources, but cornstarch is usually used. Substances such as beeswax and paraffin are added to it to increase the gloss and make starched textiles soft and pliable. Other treatments make possible starches that do not require boiling. Finishes other than starch include gelatine, gum arabic, and gum tragacanth.

Laundry starches come in various forms. There are dry starches which require cooking, starches that can be dissolved in hot water, and starches that are added to cold water. Also available are liquid starches in bottles and spray-on starches in pressurized containers. Study the labels, select the kind that best suits your need, and follow the directions on the container.

If a number of articles are to be starched, use your washing machine. It saves time and ensures even distribution of the starch if the fabrics are similar. Partially fill the washer with water, then add the starch solution required for the load. Agitate the washer for a few seconds to mix the starch and water. Add the clothes, damp from the previous final rinse and extraction, and agitate for about two minutes.

If you are using an automatic washer which provides a spray rinse during extraction, first turn the water off. Remove by spinning or wringing out enough of the starch solution to prevent dripping.

Starched articles can be put into a tumbler dryer, but do not include with them clothes that have not been starched. Remove starched articles from the dryer while they are still damp enough to be ironed, unless the directions for the starch you are using say they should be completely dry.

Instructions for removing traces of starch from the washer and dryer are given under *Washing Machine* and *Automatic Dryer*.

Statuary Dust Plaster of Paris and ceramic pieces, using a clean dry cloth or a soft brush. *No water.* Wash china ornaments with unbuilt synthetic detergent or mild soap and warm water, using a cloth or soft brush. Rinse with warm water and dry. Do not use ammonia on china ornaments that are decorated with silver or gilt. Lacquered bronze needs only dusting. See *Bronze, Marble.*

Steel Wool Steel wool consists of fine filaments of steel, often packed into pads and sold with or without an impregnation of soap. It is the best cleanser and polisher for aluminium and is good for removing stuck food from other metals and glass utensils. At hardware stores it is available in different degrees of fineness for abrasive purposes.

Stove Polish Graphite is the basic ingredient of most stove polishes. If finely powdered, it can be used without other substances. Just mix it with a little water. Other carbons such as bone black and lamp black are sometimes added to deepen the colour, but are of doubtful benefit since they are burned off much more easily than graphite. Stove polishes can be bought in powder, liquid, paste, cake or stick form. Avoid those containing inflammable liquids, such as turpentine.

Synthetic Detergents Synthetic detergents are made from petroleum and natural fats and oils by chemical processes more complicated than those involved in making soap. Because of the broader range of materials and methods used in producing them, they can be varied to suit many household tasks. They dissolve easily in either hot or cold water, are effective in hard water without the addition of softeners, do not create scum if enough is used, and do not leave a film on washed surfaces.

Their ingredients are varied to cope with specific problems and they are available in liquid, powder and tablet form – to wash clothes, shampoo hair, rugs and upholstery, and clean dishes, pans, floors, walls and woodwork. They have almost supplanted soap in the laundry.

Laundry detergents are of two types – light duty and heavy duty. Use light-duty, alkali-free detergents for laundering lightly soiled delicate fabrics, fabrics of doubtful colourfastness, silks and wools. Light detergents will not remove heavy dirt.

Heavy-duty detergents contain alkaline salts and other substances that increase their cleaning power. They are for clothing that is moderately or heavily soiled, and are safe for many fine fabrics. Some produce rich suds, others almost none. There is no real difference in the cleaning ability of the two types, but use a low-sudsing brand if the manufacturer of your washer suggests it. High

CLEANING AGENTS Water 189

suds interfere with the mechanical action of some washers, particularly front-loading (tumbler) models.

For lightly soiled synthetics and for clothes with durable-press finishes, which are best laundered in cold water, use a cold-water detergent. Consult your Hardware Store.

FOR STAIN REMOVAL liquid detergents are best. On *washable* materials, first dampen the stain, then rub in the detergent. Rinse the area thoroughly, or put the article in the wash. If the stain is embedded, rub the fabric between your hands, bending it so that all the fibres in the yarn are reached. Rinse thoroughly. On very heavy fabrics and rugs, work the detergent into the stain with the edge of a spoon.

For stains on *non-washable* materials, dilute the detergent with an equal amount of water and work it in, but use as little as possible. It is hard to rinse out the detergent without wetting a large part of the fabric, if too much is used. Rinse by sponging the spot with cool water or by forcing cool water through it with a medicine dropper or syringe. Alcohol is the best rinse for materials not damaged by it, and they dry more quickly.

Talc A soft mineral, consisting of hydrous silicate of magnesium. Talc is used for soothing skin powders and also as an absorbent for removing certain stains. See *Absorbent*.

Trichloroethane See *Chlorothene* and *Cleaning Fluids*.

Trichloroethylene See *Cleaning Fluids*.

Tripoli Tripoli is another name for rottenstone. See *Rottenstone*.

Trisodium Phosphate See *Soda and Soda Compounds*, page 185.

Turpentine Turpentine is a resinous juice obtained from pine and fir trees. It is used as a solvent in certain paints, varnishes and waxes and as an ingredient of furniture polishes and washes. Turpentine will remove wax from floors that need a complete rewaxing job. It will remove paint stains and grease. In treating furniture, turpentine is valuable because it has the ability to penetrate the finish and restore the original colour of the stain.

CAUTION: Turpentine is inflammable and poisonous.

Vaseline See *Petroleum Jelly*.

Vinegar Vinegar is often useful in cleaning because it cuts soap film. A little in a bowl of water will help remove cloudiness from furniture. It also is useful in stain removal to counteract alkalies and restore altered colours. Vinegar is about 5 per cent acetic acid. For stain removal select white vinegar.

Washing Soda is more properly known as sodium carbonate. It has been used as an effective cleaner for many purposes for a very long time. It is found in some mineral salt deposits in a natural condition, but most washing soda is manufactured. A process for making it from sodium chloride (common salt) was patented by the French chemist Nicolas Leblanc in 1791. The Leblanc process was used throughout the world until superseded by the more efficient Solvay process and by electrolysis of brine. See *Sodium carbonate*.

Water and Water Softeners Water is said to be 'hard' when it contains an excessive mineral content (usually calcium, magnesium or iron), which counteracts the action of soap and makes successful laundering difficult. More soap is needed in hard water, and a scum is deposited on the clothes.

The problem can be solved by

using synthetic detergents instead of soap or by adding a softener to the water. Water softeners are of two types: precipitating – those that combine with the hard-water minerals and form an insoluble compound (precipitate), and those that do not form a precipitate but keep the minerals in solution.

Precipitating softeners such as soda, should always be dissolved in the wash water before soap is added because once soap scum is formed they cannot dissolve it. Non-precipitating softeners, among them Calgon, prevent scum from forming and dissolve scum left on clothes by previous washing. (Add softener to the first rinse too.)

Water hardness varies and it is important to use the right amount of softener. Too little will not correct the trouble and too much may make the water alkaline. A simple test will determine the proper amount of softener to use.

To one gallon of hot water (140°F) add ½ teaspoon of the softener you intend to use; stir to dissolve. Put two cups of this solution in a quart jar and add ½ teaspoon of the soap you have selected. Shake the jar vigorously for ten seconds. If good suds result and they hold for five minutes, the water has been softened. Repeat the experiment, using less softener, to see if a smaller amount will do the job.

If ½ teaspoon of softener fails to produce good suds, repeat the experiment with fresh hot water, using one teaspoon of softener in one gallon of water. Continue experimenting until you have determined the proper amount of softener. You save on soap (and detergent) if the water you use is soft.

Home owners in hard-water areas can solve the problem once and for all by installing a water-softening system. Such systems are available from manufacturers specializing in this field. They make use of complex soda compounds in a form that resembles clay. These compounds are called zeolites.

For the care of water-softening systems see *Zeolites*.

Wax Two basic types of wax are made for floors: *polishing waxes*, which require buffing, and *self-polishing waxes*, which dry to a glossy finish without buffing.

Polishing waxes may be either liquid or paste. The ingredients of these are the same, but the liquid wax contains more solvent. Polishing waxes provide a beautiful and lasting finish and, if properly applied and maintained, do not ever need to be removed. Paste wax is highly concentrated, very durable, and economical to use. Liquid polishing waxes are excellent for cleaning floors. The naphtha in them dissolves surface grime so that it can be wiped away, while the wax in the mixture remains on the floor to be buffed. Polishing waxes can be used on many types of floor and are the best kind for wood. They can be identified by their pungent odour.

Self-polishing waxes use water as a carrier for microscopically small particles of solid wax. The water keeps the particles separated, and when it evaporates, a shiny film of wax remains on the floor. These waxes have practically no odour and do not require buffing. They are not as durable as polishing waxes but are easier to apply and not difficult to remove with standard floor cleaning mixtures. Such waxes are most often used on types of flooring not harmed by

water, which require frequent cleaning.

Similar in use are polyethylene emulsions which provide a tough spot-resistant finish that will last through numerous damp moppings. Such finishes may be applied, when the floor is clean and thoroughly dry, to linoleum, asphalt, rubber, vinyl and cork tiles, plastic sheet flooring and terrazzo.

In buying paste wax for floors or furniture, remember that you can get light and dark shades. Use light shades for blond woods, dark for mahogany, walnut, etc.

Many different kinds of wax are used in making the prepared waxes we know, and the hardest of these is carnauba, obtained from the Brazilian wax palm tree known botanically as *Copernicia cerifera*. Carnauba is valuable because it makes possible self-polishing and high-gloss wax polishes.

Wax Applicator Long-handled applicators eliminate knee action in waxing floors. Some have hollow handles so that liquid or self-polishing waxes can be poured in and dispensed evenly by pressing a lever. For cleaning operations with liquid wax there are steel wool pads that slip over the base to scrub the floor gently as the wax goes on. Push a cloth across the floor and the grime is taken up.

Nylon and chenille pads, washable and replaceable, make light work of the chore of applying self-polishing waxes. Always wash applicators promptly before the wax hardens.

Waxer Weighted buffers are to be had for polishing wax floors but an electric model makes things easier. These can sometimes be rented. See *Electric Polisher*.

Whiting Whiting is a very fine preparation of chalk. It is used in cleaning powders, polishes, in making putty and oilcloth. It can be bought by the pound at paint stores.

In preparing whiting, the chalk from the chalk cliffs of Dover, is dried in the air or in a kiln and then ground. After that it is levigated (floated off on the surface of water) and again ground. Fine whiting, moistened with ammonia, is used to polish silver. There are many other household uses for whiting, noted in this book.

Whiting is known, in trade, by different names, depending on the amount of labour that has been expended to make it fine and free from grit. The grades are: ordinary, or commercial whiting, Spanish white, gilders' whiting and Paris white, the best grade. Gilders' whiting is suitable for polishing silver.

If you have trouble finding whiting in ordinary hardware stores, go to a paint store of the type patronized by professional painters.

See also *Silver Polish*.

Zeolites Zeolites are complex soda compounds in a form resembling clay. They are used extensively in commercial laundries and in private homes in connection with water-softening systems. Hard water is filtered through a thick layer of zeolites and, by chemical action, the calcium and magnesium which make water hard are absorbed by the material, while soda compounds pass from the zeolites into the water. These soda compounds soften the water before it reaches the taps.

Zeolites lose their strength as they work and when this happens a strong solution of salt is passed through them and the chemical action is reversed. The calcium and magnesium compounds which have collected in the zeolites are thrown into the water. This water is discarded and the system is again ready to do its water-softening job.

In the older zeolite systems solutions of salt are added to the tank manually every week or two. In the newer models the flushing is done automatically from a brine tank, to which salt is occasionally added. If you buy or rent a house that has a water-softening system, make a point of finding out what care it requires.

The installation of zeolite tanks involves considerable expense, but in areas where the water is extremely hard, such a system is worth considering. Zeolites usually can be purchased only in connection with commercial installations.

See also *Water and Water Softeners*.